THE CAMBRIDGE COMPANION TO CREATIVE WRITING

Creative writing has become a highly professionalised academic discipline, with popular courses and prestigious degree programmes worldwide. This book is a must for all students and teachers of creative writing, indeed for anyone who aspires to be a published writer. It engages with a complex art in an accessible manner, addressing concepts important to the rapidly growing field of creative writing, while maintaining a strong craft emphasis, analysing exemplary models of writing and providing related writing exercises. Written by professional writers and teachers of writing, the chapters deal with specific genres or forms – ranging from the novel to new media – or with significant topics that explore the cutting-edge state of creative writing internationally (including creative writing and science, contemporary publishing and new workshop approaches).

DAVID MORLEY is Professor of Creative Writing at the University of Warwick.

PHILIP NEILSEN is Professor of Creative Writing at the Queensland University of Technology.

A complete list of books in the series is available at the back of this book.

THE CAMBRIDGE
COMPANION TO

CREATIVE WRITING

EDITED BY
DAVID MORLEY
and
PHILIP NEILSEN

CAMBRIDGE UNIVERSITY PRESS
Cambridge, New York, Melbourne, Madrid, Cape Town,
Singapore, São Paulo, Mexico City

Cambridge University Press
The Edinburgh Building, Cambridge CB2 8RU, UK

Published in the United States of America by Cambridge University Press, New York

www.cambridge.org
Information on this title: www.cambridge.org/9780521145367

First published 2012
Reprinted 2012

Printed and bound by MPG Books Group, UK

A catalogue record for this publication is available from the British Library

Library of Congress Cataloging in Publication data
The Cambridge companion to creative writing / edited by David Morley, Philip Neilsen.
p. cm.
ISBN 978-0-521-76849-8 (hdbk.) – ISBN 978-0-521-14536-7 (pbk.)
1. Creative writing. 2. Authorship.
I. Morley, David, 1964– II. Neilsen, Philip, 1949– III. Title.
PN189.C29 2012
808'.02–dc23
2011025694

ISBN 978-0-521-76849-8 Hardback
ISBN 978-0-521-14536-7 Paperback

CONTENTS

ILLUSTRATIONS

NOTES ON CONTRIBUTORS

JONATHAN BATE, born in 1958, was educated at Sevenoaks School and St Catharine's College, Cambridge, where he read English Literature. After completing his doctorate, he was a Fellow of Trinity Hall, Cambridge. He was appointed King Alfred Professor of English Literature at the University of Liverpool in 1990. Since 2003, he has been Professor of Shakespeare and Renaissance Literature at the University of Warwick. Well known as a critic, biographer and broadcaster, Jonathan Bate has held visiting posts at Harvard, Yale and UCLA. Among his books are a biography of Shakespeare, *Soul of the Age*, and a history of his fame, *The Genius of Shakespeare*. He is on the Board of the Royal Shakespeare Company and was chief editor of the RSC edition of Shakespeare's Complete Works. His biography of the poet John Clare won Britain's two oldest literary awards, the Hawthornden Prize and the James Tait Black Prize; and his *The Song of the Earth* is one of the founding texts of ecopoetics. His one-man play for Simon Callow, *The Man from Stratford*, went on national tour. A Fellow of both the British Academy and the Royal Society of Literature, he was made CBE in the Queen's 80th Birthday Honours. He is publishing a biography of Ted Hughes and is now Provost of Worcester College, Oxford.

RICHARD BEARD'S eighth book, *Lazarus is Dead*, was published in 2011. From 2003 to 2006 he was Visiting Professor at the University of Tokyo. In 2009/2010 he was Senior Lecturer in Creative Writing at Birmingham City University and is now Director of the National Academy of Writing. His chapter expands further on an article 'Answers, Answers' that first appeared in *Writing in Education*, 42 (Winter 2007), and which was itself a response to Andrew Cowan's 'Questions, Questions: Can the Creative Survive in Proximity to the Critical?', *Writing in Education*, 41 (Spring 2007). Richard Beard is indebted to the insights of Andrew Cowan both here and in 'The Anxiety of Influence', *Wordplay: The Magazine of the English Subject Centre* (April 2010).

RON CARLSON is the author of ten books of fiction, most recently the novel *The Signal*. His novel *Five Skies* was selected as one of the best books of 2007 by the *Los Angeles Times* and as the One Book Rhode Island for 2009. His stories are collected in *A Kind of Flying*, and he has been called 'a master of the short story'. His short fiction has appeared in *Esquire*, *Harpers*, *The New Yorker*, *Gentlemen's Quarterly*, *Epoch*, *The Oxford American* and other journals, as well as *The Best American Short Stories*, *The O'Henry Prize Series*, *The Pushcart Prize Anthology*, *The Norton Anthology of Short Fiction* and dozens of other anthologies. His book on the process of writing, *Ron Carlson Writes a Story*, was published in 2007. Among his awards are a National Endowment for the Arts Fellowship in Fiction, and the Cohen Prize at *Ploughshares*, the McGinnis Award at the *Iowa Review* and the Aspen Foundation Literary Award. He is Director of the Graduate Programs in Writing at the University of California, Irvine.

MAUREEN FREELY was born in the US but grew up in Turkey, where her family still lives. She was educated at Radcliffe College (Harvard University) and has made her home in England since 1984. She is the author of six novels – *Mother's Helper*, *The Life of the Party*, *The Stork Club*, *Under the Vulcania*, *The Other Rebecca* and *Enlightenment* as well as three works of nonfiction – *Pandora's Clock*, *What About Us? An Open Letter to the Mothers Feminism Forgot* and *The Parent Trap*. She has been a regular contributor to *The Guardian*, *The Observer*, *The Independent* and *The Sunday Times* for two decades, writing on feminism, family and social policy, Turkish culture and politics, and contemporary writing. Now a Professor at the University of Warwick, she is perhaps best known for her translations of *Snow*, *The Black Book*, *Istanbul: Memories of a City*, *Other Colours and The Museum of Innocence*, all by the Turkish novelist and Nobel laureate Orhan Pamuk, and for her campaigning journalism after Pamuk and an estimated eighty other writers were prosecuted (and in the case of Hrant Dink, assassinated) for insulting Turkishness, state institutions, or the memory of Atatürk.

KÁRI GÍSLASON lectures in Creative Writing at Queensland University of Technology (QUT). After graduating in English and Law he wrote his doctoral thesis on conceptions of authorship in medieval Iceland, and has since published numerous scholarly articles dealing mainly with the family sagas. He has an enduring interest in travel writing and has published travel articles and essays in literary journals and in the mainstream press. He is a judge for the Steele Rudd Australian Short Story Collection. His book *The Promise of Iceland* is a memoir about going back to the country of his birth and the complexities that accompany that process of return. He has also taught at the University of Iceland and University of Queensland and in 2010 received a Dean's Award for Excellence in Teaching at QUT. As part of his teaching approach he maintains a blog about travel writing. He is currently writing a book based on the travels and personal reflections of former UN Secretary-General Dag Hammarskjöld.

CHRIS HAMILTON-EMERY is Publishing Director of Salt Publishing, an independent literary press based in Cambridge, England, which won the 2008 Nielsen Innovation of the Year award in the Independent Publishing Awards. He was formerly Press Production Director at Cambridge University Press. He was awarded an American Book Award in 2006 for his services to American literature. He has sat on the Board of the Independent Publishers Guild and Planet Poetry, and has worked widely as a consultant in the publishing industry in the United Kingdom. He is the author of two volumes of poetry, *Dr Mephisto* and *Radio Nostalgia*, and a writer's guide, *101 Ways to Make Poems Sell*, and editor of *Poets in View: A Visual Anthology of 50 Classic Poems* as well as selections of Emily Brontë, John Keats and Christina Rossetti; in addition he writes the annual poetry section for *The Writer's Handbook*, was recently anthologised in *Identity Parade: New British & Irish Poets* and is a contributor to *The Insiders' Guide to Independent Publishing*.

A. L. KENNEDY is the author of five novels including *Everything You Need* and *Paradise*, and five collections of short stories including *Indelible Acts* and *What Becomes*. The most recent of her nonfiction books is *Luwak Care and Breeding*. She won the Costa Book of the Year prize for her novel *Day* and has twice been listed among the *Granta* Best of Young British Novelists. Other awards include the *Mail on Sunday* / John Llewellyn Rhys Prize, a Scottish Arts Council Book Award and the Encore Award. She has been a judge for both the Booker Prize for Fiction and the *Guardian* First Book Award, and was made a Fellow of the Royal Society of Arts in 2000. She wrote the screenplay to the BFI/Channel 4 film *Stella Does Tricks*, and edited *New Writing 9* with John Fowles. A. L. Kennedy lives and works in Glasgow. She has taught creative writing at the University of St Andrews and currently works with writers on the Warwick University Creative Writing Programme as an associate professor.

BRONWYN LEA holds a BA in Literature from the University of California San Diego and an MA and PhD in Creative Writing from the University of Queensland. She is the author of *Flight Animals*, winner of the 2001 Wesley Michel Wright Prize and the 2002 Fellowship of Australian Writers Anne Elder Award; it was also shortlisted for the 2002 NSW Premier's Kenneth Slessor Poetry Prize; the Judith Wright Calanthe Poetry Prize; the South Australian Premier's John Bray Poetry Prize and Colin Roderick Award. Her most recent collection of poems, *The Other Way Out*, won the 2008 Western Australia Premier's Book Award for Poetry and the 2010 South Australian Premier's John Bray Poetry Prize, and was shortlisted for the Victorian and Queensland Premier's Prizes. She was Poetry Editor at the University of Queensland Press from 2003 to 2009 and founder and series editor, with Martin Duwell, of *The Best Australian Poetry* anthology. In 2009 she was awarded a residency at the B. R. Whiting Library in Rome from the Australia Council. She is a Senior Lecturer in the School of English, Media Studies, and Art History at the University of Queensland where she teaches Poetics and Contemporary Literature. In 2011 she was appointed the inaugural editor of *Australian Poetry Journal*.

DAVID MORLEY is an ecologist and naturalist by background. His poetry has won fourteen writing awards and prizes including the Templar Poetry Prize, the Poetry

Business Competition, an Arts Council of England Writer's Award, an Eric Gregory Award, the Raymond Williams Prize and a Hawthornden Fellowship. A recent collection *The Invisible Kings* was a Poetry Book Society Recommendation and a new collection *Enchantment* explores the world of the magical short story in verse. He is also known for his pioneering ecological poetry installations within natural landscapes and the creation of 'slow poetry' sculptures and I-Cast poetry films. His 'writing challenges' podcasts are among the most popular literature downloads on iTunes worldwide: two episodes are now preloaded on to all demo Macs used in Apple Stores across the globe. He writes essays, criticism and reviews for *The Guardian* and *Poetry Review*. A leading international advocate of creative writing both inside and outside the academy, he wrote *The Cambridge Introduction to Creative Writing* (2007) which has been translated into many languages. He currently teaches at the University of Warwick where he is Professor of Writing.

PHILIP NEILSEN has published five collections of poetry, including *Without an Alibi* (2008) and been anthologised most recently in *The Making of a Sonnet: A Norton Anthology*, *The Penguin Anthology of Australian Poetry* and *Australian Poetry Since 1788*. He has published five books of fiction for young adults and children, his adult short stories have appeared widely, and he has edited major anthologies including *The Penguin Book of Australian Satirical Verse*. His life writing has been published in print and digital formats and he currently researches the therapeutic effect of life writing for those with serious mental illness. He has won an Australian Notable Book award and an Australia Council Writer's Fellowship. His work has been translated into a number of languages including Chinese, German and Korean. He has been a member of the Literature Board of the Australia Council and after teaching English at the University of Queensland founded the writing programme at the Queensland University of Technology, where he is Professor of Creative Writing.

JEWELL PARKER RHODES is the author of six novels, *Voodoo Dreams*, *Magic City*, *Douglass' Women*, *Voodoo Season*, *Yellow Moon* and *Hurricane Levee Blues*, a children's novel, *Ninth Ward*, and a memoir, *Porch Stories: A Grandmother's Guide to Happiness*. She has also authored two writing guides, *Free Within Ourselves: Fiction Lessons for Black Authors* and *The African American Guide to Writing and Publishing Non-Fiction*. Her literary awards include a Yaddo Creative Writing Fellowship, the American Book Award, the National Endowment of the Arts Award in Fiction, the Black Caucus of the American Library Award for Literary Excellence, the PEN Oakland/Josephine Miles Award for Outstanding Writing, two Arizona Book Awards and a finalist citation for the Hurston-Wright Legacy Award. She has been a featured speaker at the Runnymede International Literary Festival (Royal Holloway, University of London), Santa Barbara Writers Conference, Creative Nonfiction Writers Conference and Warwick University, among others. She is the Artistic Director for Global Engagement and the Piper

Endowed Chair of the Virginia G. Piper Center for Creative Writing at Arizona State University.

FIONA SAMPSON studied at the Universities of Oxford, where she won the Newdigate Prize, and Nijmegen, where she received a PhD in the philosophy of language. This research arose from her pioneering residencies in health care. She has published nineteen books, including *Rough Music* (shortlisted for the Forward Prize and T. S. Eliot Prize), *Poetry Writing* (2009) and *A Century of Poetry Review* (PBS Special Commendation, 2009). Her eleven books in translation include *Patuvachki Dnevnik*, awarded the Zlaten Prsten (Macedonia). Previously shortlisted for the T. S. Eliot and Forward single-poem prizes, she has also received Writer's Awards from the Arts Councils of England and Wales and the Society of Authors, the US *Literary Review*'s Charles Angoff Award, and was AHRC Research Fellow at Oxford Brookes University 2002–5 and CAPITAL Fellow in Creativity at the University of Warwick 2007–8. In 2009, she received a Cholmondeley Award and became a Fellow of the Royal Society of Literature; she now serves on the RSL Council. She is Distinguished Writer at the University of Kingston, and her most recent books are *Music Lessons: The Newcastle Poetry Lectures* and *Percy Bysshe Shelley* (both 2011) in the Faber poet-to-poet series, PBS Online Book Club Choice.

HAZEL SMITH is a research professor in the Writing and Society Research Group at the University of Western Sydney. She is author of *The Writing Experiment: Strategies for Innovative Creative Writing* (2005) and *Hyperscapes in the Poetry of Frank O'Hara: Difference, Homosexuality, Topography* (2000). She is co-author of *Improvisation, Hypermedia and the Arts Since 1945* (1997) and co-editor with Roger Dean of *Practice-led Research in the Creative Arts* (2009). Hazel Smith is also a poet, performer and new media artist, and has published three poetry volumes, three CDs of performance works, and numerous multimedia collaborations. Her latest volume, with CD Rom, is *The Erotics of Geography: Poetry, Performance Texts, New Media Works* (2008). She is a member of austraLYSIS, the sound and intermedia arts group, and has performed her work extensively internationally. She has been co-recipient of numerous grants for austraLYSIS from the Australia Council, and has had many large-scale commissions from the Australian Broadcasting Corporation. She is co-editor with Roger Dean of *soundsRite*, a journal of new media writing and sound, based at the University of Western Sydney.

MICHELENE WANDOR is a playwright, poet and fiction writer. She was the first woman playwright to have a play on one of the National Theatre's main stages – *The Wandering Jew* – in 1987, when she also won an International Emmy for Thames TV with her adaptation of *The Belle of Amherst*. Her prolific radio drama over more than three decades includes *Tulips in Winter* (Radio 3, 2008, about Spinoza) and a dramatisation of *Lady Chatterley's Lover*, complete with 'language' (Radio 4, 2006). Forthcoming are *Mrs Dalloway* (after Virginia Woolf) and *Isabella and Lucrezia* (Radio 3), both in 2012. Her poetry collection, *Musica Transalpina*, was a Poetry Book Society Recommendation for 2006. *The Music of the Prophets*, a narrative poem about the resettlement of the Jews in England, was supported by an award from the European Association for Jewish Culture. Her nonfiction includes *Postwar British Drama: Looking Back in Gender* (2001), and *The Author Is Not Dead, Merely Somewhere Else: Creative Writing Reconceived* and *The Art of Writing Drama* (both 2008). She has taught creative writing for two decades, currently as tutor for the MA at Lancaster University. She has been a Royal Literary Fund Fellow since 2004.

KIM WILKINS was born in London and grew up in Brisbane, Australia. She completed Honours in English literature at the University of Queensland in 1998 and was awarded the University Medal for academic achievement. She subsequently earned a Master's and a PhD in creative writing, and teaches at the University of Queensland and in the community. She is a designer and teacher in the Queensland Writer's Centre's 'Year of the Writer' workshop series, and was co-designer of their 'Year of the Novel Online' course. She is the author of twenty-one novels, including a fantasy series for children, and three contemporary women's popular fiction novels under the pseudonym Kimberley Freeman, for which she has won the Romance Writers of Australia 'RuBY' award. She is best known, however, as an award-winning author of speculative fiction for adults, including *Rosa and the Veil of Gold*, *Angel of Ruin* (*Fallen Angel* in the UK) and *Giants of the Frost*. Her books are published in Australia, the UK, the USA, Denmark, France, Germany, Italy and Russia. She is currently working on an epic medieval fantasy series, and researching in the field of popular medievalism. She writes widely on creative writing pedagogy.

ACKNOWLEDGEMENTS

We thank our contributors for their stylish and generous contributions; Ray Ryan at Cambridge University Press for editorial support; and Maartje Scheltens for seeing the book through press. David Morley wishes to thank his wife Siobhan Keenan who provided wonderful help and criticism; the University of Warwick for research leave to work on the book; and the Higher Education Academy for a National Teaching Fellowship part of which was spent researching this project. Philip Neilsen wishes to thank his wife Mhairead MacLeod for her generous support and criticism; and Professor Robert King and Ellen Thompson at Queensland University of Technology for their collegial assistance.

FOREWORD: ON CRITICISM AND CREATIVITY

Creative writing has been the subject of university-level study in American universities and colleges far longer than it has been within British higher education. The common pattern in the American system has traditionally set the 'writing program' apart from the critical, historical and theoretical work of the 'literature' department. Typically, the *writers* will be employed for the drudgery of instructing students from almost every discipline in 'freshman composition' (how to structure an argument, a paragraph, even – remedially – a sentence) and then be rewarded with some small-group teaching in which, at a more advanced level, they assist the aspirant writers of the future in the improvement of their novels, stories, scripts and poems. The *academics*, meanwhile, will teach a freshman survey course of the kind that used to be known in the trade as 'from Beowulf to Virginia Woolf' but that is now more likely to be a guided tour of competing theoretical approaches to the subject and to include a high proportion of contemporary, often international, literature; they will then teach other, more advanced courses in their specialism, which could be anything from Shakespeare to the Victorian novel to some aspect of literary theory to postcolonial women's poetry. In terms of their ambitions for publication, the 'writer' will be working on, say, her latest novel and the 'academic' on a learned conference paper that will later be worked into a critical book for a university press. It is not unknown for the writers and the academics to neglect each other's work and even to view their counterparts down the departmental corridor with a degree of suspicion.

There is no inherent reason why there should be such a division between criticism and creativity in English studies. Consider the higher-level teaching of music and art, the disciplines of writing's sister arts. University degrees in music do not confine themselves to questions of form, history and cultural context, as English degrees often do. They have an emphasis on technique and on practice that is rarely encountered within a traditional English degree. The serious student of music will be expected to read music, to play an instrument, to hear a shift from major to minor key. Similarly, the serious student of art will be expected to know about perspective, to discover the different properties of different materials, and (one hopes) to draw in a life-class. It is not usually demanded of literature students that they should be skilled in the literary equivalents of such techniques as playing a scale, composing a variation, sketching a nude: they are not habitually asked to scan a line of verse, compose a sonnet or sketch a fictional *mise en scène*. An education in the art of writing is often regarded as marginal to an education in the art of critical reading (as the agenda of most English departments used to be) or the art of cultural poetics (as the agenda of most English departments has become). But it is precisely this gap – an education in the *craft* of putting together words, analogous to the craft of putting together musical notes – that creative writing programmes can fill. A healthy dialogue is one in which critics are interested in writerly skills – rhetoric, narrative construction, pacing – and students of creative writing are unafraid of critical judgement.

Historically, the origins of English literary criticism belong within the realm of creativity, not that of academic analysis. John Dryden was long known as the father of English criticism. In the second half of the seventeenth century, he established the terms of debate that dominated critical discourse for a century: what were the relative merits of the ancients and the moderns, of native and continental models, of blank verse and rhyme? What was the correct balance between 'art' and 'nature', the best means to achieve verisimilitude? What ultimately constitutes good writing? As he put it in his preface to *The State of Innocence* (1677), his dramatisation of Milton's *Paradise Lost*, 'By criticism, as it was first instituted by Aristotle, was meant a standard of judging well; the chiefest part of which is, to observe those excellencies which should delight a reasonable reader.' But, and this is the key point, Dryden developed his critical art not in an 'academic' context but in a creative one, that of the prefaces to, and essays about, his own plays and poems, in which he had self-consciously set about modernising and classicising English writing during the Restoration era.

In the early eighteenth-century *Spectator* essays mainly by Joseph Addison and *The Tatler* mainly by Richard Steele, questions of literary style were closely linked to debates about national identity and gentlemanly behaviour. The figure who dominated literary debate in the public sphere in the second half of the eighteenth century was Dr Samuel Johnson, a journalist and all-round writer, not a university teacher. So too with the Romantic and Victorian eras: the major critical opinion formers were themselves either poets (most notably Samuel Taylor Coleridge and Matthew Arnold) or journalists, lecturers and what we now call 'public intellectuals' (William Hazlitt, John Ruskin). T. S. Eliot was not only the most admired poet but also the most influential critic of the modernist period of the first half of the twentieth century. It was only from the 1930s onwards that what might be called 'pure' or 'academic' criticism became the norm.

Furthermore, criticism was often forged *through* creativity. Alexander Pope's *Essay on Criticism* was a poem and there was a symbiotic relationship between the creation of his mock-epic masterpiece *The Dunciad* and his dispute with rival textual editor Lewis Theobald over the highly technical critical matter of the emendation of Shakespeare's texts. Coleridge's lectures on Shakespeare were partly shaped by, and help to explain, the search for inner unity that he also undertook in his poetry. John Keats offered a 'reading' of *King Lear* not only by way of marginal annotations in his copy of Shakespeare, but also through writing a sonnet. T. S. Eliot's essays on the rich complexity of the metaphysical poets and the Jacobean dramatists were intimately bound to the difficulty and originality of his own verse.

The ascent of literary theory in the late twentieth century took the divide between criticism and creativity to an extreme. Writers became notoriously wary of theory: they found its jargon repellent and its reports of 'the death of the author' unacceptable. Theorists, in turn, were more interested in patterns and deep structures, ideological formations and hidden abysses, than writerly craft and the judgement of 'literary' qualities. In the early twenty-first century, the symbiosis between criticism and creativity has to some degree been restored. At school level, it is now quite common for a 'critical' essay to take the form of a 'creative' response: instead of writing a formal essay about the motivation of Lady Macbeth, students are invited to write her imaginary diary. At a higher level, the *fin-de-siècle* age of anxiety in English studies is well and truly over. Academics have learned to stop worrying and to live with a diversity of critical practices. And it is practice as opposed to theory that is making the running.

Late twentieth-century theory was dominated by a hierarchical model, a pyramid-like corporate structure with gurus at the top (Derrida, Foucault, Lacan, Said), high-profile publishing and conference-going disseminators just below, then the foot-soldiers of the profession (the overworked, undervalued lecturers and assistant professors) and finally the students. Orders went out from the top, prescribing the latest theoretical *diktat*. Early twenty-first-century practice, by contrast, is more like the modern 'flat' corporation, in which different approaches are respected and students are empowered. More than lip-service is paid to the rhetoric of 'transferable skills' and student preparedness for the workplace. Old taboos have been stripped away: styles of critical discourse are more colloquial, less mandarin; personal testimony and the articulation of feeling are no longer outlawed; attention to the texture of authors' lives is once again allowed. The latter interest signals a radical departure from the old 'new criticism', in which the text was king, and from deconstruction, in which the author was dead, and from 'new historicism', in which texts were generated less by individual agency than the circulation of social energy.

Critical approaches are now judged more by the criterion of their usefulness – for students and, more utopianly, for society and the world. The author has returned, biography is newly respectable within the academy and there has been a growth of metabiography and 'cultural influence' studies that have placed literary works within a wider context than that of their purely critical or academic reputation. And criticism has itself become more creative, with fiction, memoir and the personal essay beginning to be regarded as acceptable forms of critical practice – though if this sort of thing is to be done, it has to be done well, self-critically and not self-indulgently.

In the work of the teachers and students in writing programmes, we witness ample, and highly diverse, examples of the dialogue between criticism and creativity, with a focus above all on the practical application of writerly techniques. The essays in *The Cambridge Companion to Creative Writing* demonstrate how the personal, creative and critical combine to create a fresh and important debate about the discipline of creative writing, its relation to literary studies and to other forms of knowledge including science, and to understanding how it might evolve in the future in the academy and the wider world. Here, the writers and the academics are genuinely companions, not rivals – in fact, the distinction dissolves.

Jonathan Bate

1

DAVID MORLEY AND PHILIP NEILSEN

Introduction

In recent years, the development of creative writing as a discipline in higher education has changed the shape of literature departments in universities across the globe. It has also changed the development of literary studies through creative reading ('reading as a writer') and through practice-led teaching. As Jonathan Bate explains, many of our best critics were creative writers. Creative writing is a rearrival at a balance in which the practice of writing is placed on an equal platform to its study. An act of criticism can also be an act of creativity, and vice versa. It is a falsification of how our minds work to suggest it could be otherwise.

Creative writing as a discipline has also begun to find its way beyond literature and humanities departments. Creative writing is not some add-on to literary studies, nor are its students schooled solely in the study of novels, plays and poems. Creative writing can be an education in the craft of writing in a larger sense. Writers, at their best, are *creative* writers whether they are writing journalism, plays, philosophy, novels, history, poetry or scientific nonfiction. These creative writers are found not only among the teachers of these subjects but also among their students; and not only in the academy but in the world at large. Whatever its setting, the act of writing is almost always an uncertain process. As one cultural commentator has argued, creative writing is best suited to people who have a high toleration of uncertainty. It should be no surprise that the teaching of creative writing embraces uncertainty, experiment and even purposelessness in order to arrive at recommendations and ideas that will only need to be reviewed again in a few years. In this way, creative writing as a discipline is not unlike science – or any open and evolving knowledge system for that matter. But it is a discipline.

It is essential to recognise that creative writing has always had and always will have a potent existence outside universities. Schools, libraries, reading and writing groups, internet writing communities, and residential writing centres such as the Arvon Foundation in the UK – all these aspects of the University of Life do not require the freemasonry of literary theory for a serious engagement with creative writing and reading. In our experience, and that of thousands of writers of our acquaintance, aspirant writers are as varied and rich in experience whether they are from a background in bookbinding, biology or business; or were brought up in environments that fettered the desire to shape and make a writer's voice.

New writers are drawn to creative writing not only because they wish to make their truths, although that's part of the discovery, but because they understand intuitively that beyond education, origin or power, it is language that most shows a person. Language is who we are to the world and to ourselves. And beyond the necessary specialisation of knowledge, our ability to write – to write with panache, clarity and joy – *to tell our story* – can make the difference between being heard and being ignored or silenced. It is why one of the informing values of *The Cambridge Companion to Creative Writing* is that all writing, at its best, is creative writing. This value also opens the door to the notion that creative writing as a discipline can create a synthesis between work in universities and non-academic professions for which good writing is essential. This book describes and explores the worlds of creative writing both inside and outside the academy without making the false assumption that one of those worlds is more or less real than the other.

We also value the often-underrated or understated fact that creative writing as an art form brings immense pleasure to the lives of many people. As humans we warm to things that are well made; that bring unexpected insight into our lives; that provide epiphanies above and beyond the need for us to make a living, important though that is. Creative writing makes us wake up to the world around us; helps us understand the natures of the people we meet or will never know by name; and alerts us to the intense interplay of language, ideas and feeling. Many other art forms depend on the writer to shape narratives through the apparent magic of what is a practical and teachable craft – a craft that is also a vocation. Above all, creative writing allows us to tell the story of our species.

The making and shaping of creative language and story is as natural as speech. It is part of our experience of being human. As the neuroscientist Mark Turner has argued, the literary mind is the fundamental mind while metaphor is an everyday ingenuity for how we read and express the world around us and in us. We are all born writers in the sense that we are all born storytellers, whether of ourselves or of what we come to know as our knowledge. How fluent we are at recreating language depends on our neural flexibility – and that takes training. The basic pedagogy for creative writing – reading, practice and playful experiment – remakes and reshapes the hardwiring of our minds. Think about reading and then writing a story or poem: the complexity and simplicity of an imaginative creation. At even a very basic level, your mind will interact with itself, with memory and your senses for sound and music: hearing language, seeing language, speaking or even singing language and making verbs. In terms of neurology there are timezone-like distances between the places in our brains where these actions occur. Hearing language might as well reside in the brain's equivalent of a hamlet in Warwickshire; seeing language runs through the ravines of Tasmania; speaking language shouts (or even sings) between Micronesian islands; and our mind's verbal explosions trigger avalanches in the mountains of Spitzbergen.

Why does creative writing need a friend in a high place, a *Companion* from Cambridge University? An academy provides a haven and structure in which writers can play, develop and deepen in craft (for a short while at least; the world is always waiting). It is important therefore that universities review and incorporate the very best practice in the teaching and research programmes for creative writing, and do not settle for structures, ideas and values that fudge or fake the reality of a writer in the world. There has been much debate over the past decade about whether a creative writing course can teach the unteachable; whether the creative writing MFA fosters a homogenised literary style; and whether creative writing has become its own industry.

The Cambridge Companion to Creative Writing opens an exchange of ideas between acclaimed creative writers, all of whom are also creative readers, all of whom publish their work in the world outside the academy, and all of whom are teachers or publishers who subscribe to the idea that the discipline of creative writing has come of age. Yet our writers are not signing up for some pledge: their critical intelligences inform their creative contributions. Independence invites a responsibility to reflect, review and then to act. We believe that creative writing has achieved a measure of independence as a discipline at many levels of education, including universities. The creative work of its teachers – their novels, poems and plays – is now accepted as a valid form of research, although our chief aims as writers should always be to bring pleasure and purpose to the lives of our readers rather than publish for tenure.

We'd argue that our discipline has, over the past fifteen years, grown global in its reach where before it was the preserve, by and large, of the United States. Our international faculty of contributors is testament to the spreading of those wings. We suggest that all the current debates about creative writing show that the subject is still evolving as a discipline, working across academic fields and knowledge systems while, at the same time, it continues to flourish in the world outside the academy. We think that what people call the 'creative writing industry' requires a steady assessment, one that looks critically as to where the discipline might be going; and how we can further improve and enhance our practice as teachers, writers, students, publishers, editors and experimenters.

The titles and styles of many of the chapters in *The Cambridge Companion to Creative Writing* are themselves acts of creative writing. Some are written as personal essays in the manner that Jonathan Bate describes as acceptable forms of critical practice and, in this book, they display adventurous variety, wisdom and play. They also demonstrate significant scholarship, vocation and practical experience. The book is divided into explorations of specific genres and discussions of more general topics.

Beginning with fiction, Ron Carlson takes us on a personally guided tour as step by step we develop a scenario into an effective short story by balancing our writer's mind with our editor's mind. He shows us the rich potential of short narrative, its key elements, and answers the vital question 'How much of writing is about control and how much is about letting go?' Maureen Freely proposes a new approach to teaching long fiction. Though accepting the value of more traditional workshops and one-on-one consultation, she argues for also developing a space that allows a 'community of writers' and explains the 'open house' and '*tertulia*' teaching methods. These assist students to overcome preconceived ideas, find new ways of working and imagining, find their voice, be bolder and more precise. Kim Wilkins draws on her experience of having published twenty-one genre novels to explain how writing well in popular genres requires a skilled ability to balance which generic elements are replayed, and which are set '*in* play', to make possibilities and pleasures. She uses speculative fiction as a focus, and offers fresh perspectives on the treatment and deployment of genre elements in the fantastic and unfamiliar, leading us through the key building blocks of the novel.

Many books about creative writing sidestep or ignore the process of writing drama. In our book Michelene Wandor 'reconstitutes' drama writing as a discrete literary process by separating it from its fusion with performance and its alliance with fiction and poetry, so as to focus upon it as a writerly practice with its 'own formal characteristics'. She deconstructs and challenges common assumptions about drama writing (collaboration, performance, the visual) and restores its autonomy as a conscious fictional genre, which through dialogue shapes the imagination to produce form on the page. Wandor carefully exemplifies this by explaining how she teaches drama writing in the classroom.

Bronwyn Lea gives us a clear and practical account of the forms and techniques that organise and enable the writing of poetry, demystifying this form of creative writing that many students, at least initially, find somewhat daunting. She impresses upon us that poetry is transcendent – capable of transporting us into an alternate awareness – but that it is also, as W. H. Auden argues, 'a verbal artefact that must be as skilfully and solidly constructed as a table or a motorcycle'. She engagingly provides a reflective account of writing one of her own poems.

Kári Gíslason is both craft-based in his suggestions about *how* to go about writing up your travels, and analytical and literary-historical in his close reading of influential texts in the genre. In this way, the chapter reflects the broadening of creative writing as a discipline to include both practitioner-led and reader-oriented approaches. He presents structures and modes in different subgenres of travel writing, thereby allowing for the wide variety of aims among writers: the chapter does not seek to prescribe the single right way of approaching travel writing, but rather to give options; the task is to improve what a writer is already doing, not limit individual aims.

Hazel Smith's chapter highlights the new possibilities for contemporary writing which are emerging through the dynamic interaction of humans and computers, and argues that they are changing both the activity of writing and our concept of authorship. New media writing, which is screen rather than page-based, extends opportunities for innovation and artistic complexity by means of verbal kineticism, increased reader interactivity, split screens, computerised text generation, textual variability, and the multimedia blending of text, sound and image.

Is literary translation also an act of creative writing? Fiona Sampson captures the creative essence of translation, and its many benefits: 'Seeing what other ways of writing do is a way of seeing what your own practice leaves out. It helps focus creative choices, especially those to do with register and form.' She explains how translation must work hard 'to convey *both* the meaning and the innate character of a text', but dismisses as limiting the claim that texts should only be read in their original tongue. Translation also proves that a work is never finished. Sampson leads us through the process of a translation she made herself – a valuable and instructive insight into this intricate form of creative writing.

By viewing life writing as storytelling that utilises fictional techniques – including a narrative arc, through-lines and characterisation – Philip Neilsen explores the way life writing tackles concepts of memory and identity while constructing a 'self' in order to make meaning of a life. He analyses in detail several successful examples of memoir and biography to show how life writing defines us – by means of psychological complexity, openness, and conscious selectivity and subjectivity – while also maintaining a 'contract with the reader' to attempt a representation of 'truth'. He concludes with the case for life writing having therapeutic benefits for individuals, through building a coherent self-narrative.

The book moves on to explore significant topics that shape the past, present and future of creative writing in the academy and the wider world. David Morley explores two questions. Can studying science make you a more inventive creative writer? Even more radically, can the study and practice of creative writing make you a better scientist? Morley explores these questions with reference first to literary and scientific history and case studies of the practice and thinking of Wordsworth, Humphrey Davy, Blake, Keats, Osip Mandelstam, Barry Lopez, Marianne Moore, Les Murray and Miroslav Holub; and second to the practice-led teaching of creative writing, contemporary environmental writing and ecology. The author, who is both a poet and trained ecologist, draws on twenty years of experience and research in this field and suggests fresh ways in which to teach writing inside and outside the academy, as well as in schools and the community.

Any book of this nature needs to be constructively provocative, exploring topics that cannot be quietly ignored. Richard Beard argues that a freelance approach to teaching creative writing courses does little to assuage a writer's anxiety. The same tensions apply as with freelance writing – the hunt, the gather, the begin again. Increasingly, the salaried comfort of a full or part-time university post seems ever more attractive. But is teaching creative writing in an institution compatible with simply writing? Beard explores the topic of divided loyalties. For the writer there are advantages and disadvantages to working within the academy, and decisions must often be made about when to be a writer and when a teacher. Is this schizophrenia sustainable? It depends on the course, and the university. His chapter argues that some university courses are increasingly hostile to the act of writing. At which point creative writing as a discipline stands in danger of becoming the territory of qualified academics and not practising writers. The chapter offers some suggestions for greater flexibility, while concluding that flexibility may also be found outside the academy. If writers are to stay involved in the teaching of creative writing, writers and not academics need to lead from the front.

Reaching into his considerable experience as a cutting-edge publisher, poet and editor, Christopher Hamilton-Emery explains the dynamics of the tasks and aims of all who work within a publishing house and also makes a convincing and timely prediction of the likely shape of the future of publishing – one that will be a time of pivotal change and of which contemporary writers and editors need to be aware now.

Jewell Parker Rhodes provides valuable suggestions directly from her position as an experienced novelist: how trans-global and trans-cultural narratives rely on the primacy of the imagination, no matter how rooted they are in social experience; how to avoid the solipsism of the seductive

'I' point of view; how to create characters in action; and how to go beyond the comfort zone of writing 'what you know'.

In her groundbreaking chapter on workshops, vital to the evolving teaching of creative writing, A. L. Kennedy persuades us that workshops should respond as much as possible to the participants in any group, be as flexible as possible and rooted in the practicalities of human nature, the nature of writing and the realities of being self-employed, rather than what is easiest for the tutor, an academic or institutional agenda, or a pattern of established habit. Everyone involved should be aiming to grow as a writer – workshops affect who we all are as people – and vice versa. She recommends that teachers and students should aim high and accept failure as part of the development process. In class we are always working with other writers – just how we do this tells us much about our own appreciation of our work and roles and writing.

Creative writing is often taught using practice-led teaching. Such procedures have become popular and successful – the 'serious play' of a workshop allows students to grow into skills through a combination of pleasure, practice and exaction. Other subject areas are borrowing the pedagogies of creative writing, including business and science. As in David Morley's *The Cambridge Introduction to Creative Writing*, there are practical writing exercises in this book. Contributors have recreated these from their own best practice. The writing exercises can be used by readers and students for their own writing. They can also be used by teachers of writing, by writers and by you.

PART I

Genres and types

2

RON CARLSON

A writing lesson: the three flat tyres and the outer story

This is not an essay for readers, but rather a lesson for writers. I want to speak to the artist first and the reader second by having us write a short short story as an exercise in examining the way writing can lead the discovery process. Our model is not going to be: knowing the story first and then writing it, but rather: writing to find the story. Along the way, we will write four additional brief practice exercises which illuminate various elements of a story. I know this is a brisk introduction, but we can talk later. Let's get started.

Get into the room alone and open a blank page.

Do it now.

Rather than studying the big book of swimming, we will swim.

Here is the exercise: *The Flat Tyre.*

> We will write a short story of three to five pages (about 600 to 1,000 words) typed, double spaced.
>
> Two people are in an automobile driving along a country road. (They can be any relationship: a married couple, brother and sister, father daughter, mother son, co-workers, strangers, etc.) In the first paragraph, first sentence if possible, they should become aware that they have a flat tyre. In the story, they will do their best to change the tyre. The story should be the process of them changing or trying to change the tyre.
>
> The challenge being issued to us is to use the physical process and world of the outer story (plot/motor) to discover the inner story (character/freight). We don't know the characters, we only know we have a flat tyre and we will use that problem to find our way towards what we do not know. (There are three examples included below.)

One quick word. This activity is strange in that I'm asking you to step off in the dark, embark without a map. You might say: I don't know where I'm going! That is true, and that is the truth of the lesson. We will find where we're going by writing our way there. Write a sentence; it will lead you. Please know that in my examples (all three) I did not – when I wrote the first sentence or even the first paragraph – know where I was going. I did not have a plan beyond creating a credible moment. In a moment this is what you are going to do; I'll signal when to start.

Our rule in writing this exercise is *to include*. Our sentences are going to take us out into an imagined scene and things are going to volunteer to be in our story and we are going to include them: a hair colour, a tattoo, a cologne, a blister, a brand of cigarettes, an old grey cat, a striped sweater dropped on the sidewalk, a neon sign with the letter G missing, a shiny new pocketknife, a twitch, a torn pocket, a red golf tee. We have put the editor's blue pencil in the kitchen in the freezer, along with the editor; we won't be using them today. We are going to open our hearts and our minds; we are going to open whatever it takes to seize permission to include whatever occurs before us as we type along. We are going to be concrete and we are going to be specific. The rule again is: include. There is no such thing as a digression because we are not sure of the main path.

Very well, *so write the first paragraph*. It will end up being between 25 and 150 words. We are not going to edit as we write, we are going to write. Do not outline or make a list of events or character traits or any such thing; we are going to start and then find out. So much of this exercise depends on doing things out of the conventional order. Some of what we'll do will seem counter-intuitive, but in fact it is exactly intuitive. It depends on your real intuition, not your conventional understanding of what a story is. Don't think: write. Do it now.

What I've done in this lesson of the Flat Tyre is that I have written the exercise three times and offer each of the three short stories below with guided commentary. Don't read them now. Read them as we go and write along with me on this first example: 'Martin and Dana'.

Flat Tyre example 1: Martin and Dana

> Martin studied Dana's face as she pulled the old blue Ford Taurus onto the shoulder of the rural highway. He could hear the gravel shifting under the tyres as she stopped the car. Her expression was serious and it was focused on something not in the car; she looked as if she were listening for the smallest noise, both of her hands tight on the top of the steering wheel. 'Oh yeah,' she said finally. 'It's flat.'

Now that you've written your paragraph and you are committed, let's talk for a moment – and just a moment – about some general features of the short story.

In a short story something happens in time which matters to someone. That is a fairly broad definition. Something happens. Sometimes the event is very small such as someone dropping a tray of food in a crowded cafeteria and sometimes it is the eruption of a volcano and the subsequent hurried evacuation of the families nearby, but regardless of its magnitude, the event of any story has the same responsibility. It needs to be compelling. It catches the reader by the sleeve and draws the reader closer for the story. Even in the most internal of stories, there are small things that occur. The dramatic moments of the current story, the scenes, are the outer story. Our outer story is that two people are confronted with a flat tyre on a country road.

The responsibility of the outer story in all fiction is the same: to be involving. We could say that it must be convincing and many times this is the case. The outer story creates a credible vicarious experience for the reader with concrete and vivid imagery, whether it is a man carrying a wriggling box of white mice as he boards an overcrowded and overheated underground carriage at Leicester Square or a woman with a loose tooth entering the icy blue meditation cell in her pod on the remote prison planet Eighty-eight. The outer story is the motor of fiction. It drives the story forward. It is also the element of the story which is going to help us – the writers – find our way forward into the dark and make the discoveries we need to make. It is the event of the story.

We have an exercise before us which was not of our own making. Some of us have had flat tyres in the past and some of us have repaired them. Some of us have not. Where will it lead? The only way to find out is to write our way forward. We are going to include everything that suggests itself to us, and for the purposes of this exercise we are going to overdo it.

Okay, back to our Flat Tyre exercise. You've established the flat tyre, the two characters and the car coming to a stop on the country road. Now what? I'm going to recommend that you do the hardest thing writers are asked to do: *stay in the room and keep writing*. I've got Martin and Dana in the car and I understand one of the tyres is flat. I see also that Dana is driving. I didn't mean anything by this when I put her in the driver's seat, but it is a signal that it is her car, and I have an inkling, a shadow of a suspicion for some reason that Martin is not her husband. I don't even know this yet. Seriously. I only know that I have Dana and Martin in a car. Who are they?

Let your characters talk, if they so desire. One of them may be a talker. There is more in your head than you know and by writing, you can access it. Things will emerge from your memory, from events earlier in the day, from your imagination, from your youth, your victories and troubles, from song and story; we shall see.

There is a compelling premise operating in this exercise (an ancient story-telling premise actually) and we've all applied it. *We have started in the middle*. Our characters have just come from somewhere and they are going somewhere. We open our short story with the flat tyre (beat number two) and then we find out who they are and where they've come from (beat number one) and then back in the outer story we advance (beat number three). This is a pattern: 2–1–3. Middle, Beginning, End. We can see from here that the ending is going to be informed and amplified by the brief history of these characters. Who these people are gives their story resonance.

In fiction, a compelling outer story is necessary; as I noted: it is the motor. But it is not the freight. It is not what is being delivered. The characters and the light and shadows in their hearts are being delivered. Plot (event/outer story) is what we use to reveal character. It is the viable test by which our characters become one-of-a-kind creatures, complicated and nuanced as humans can be.

So, now in the next part of the story, we will take our time and watch and listen to these two people. We will not hurry. We will sit in each seat and try to imagine what each person is thinking.

Among the things a creative writing teacher cannot teach are attention and empathy. Attention is the act of bringing all of your focus to the current scene and inventing it from the ground up, carefully, not leaning on any of the thousands of scenes we've seen in film and television for aeons. Empathy requires a writer to sit in the chair with a character and imagine what he or she is experiencing. What is on her mind? What does he want? What does she fear? Attention and empathy, more than diction, syntax, vocabulary, help us avoid the generic and stereotyped scenes we so often see in 'good enough' fiction.

Right here, stop reading and turn back to your Flat Tyre exercise and write the next section. Let's try for half a page or a page as they confront their problem. Do it now.

Here is my second offering, continuing the saga of Dana and Martin:

> He waited until she turned her incredulous face to his to say, 'Perfect.'
>
> 'Right,' she said. 'We got what we hoped for.' She slid across the seat into his arms, turning her body against his with the kiss.
>
> 'I was hoping for a metaphoric flat tyre, something for a story I was going to tell when we got back.' He ran his hand up along her leg under her black skirt. 'I needed this half hour for something else, not a genuine flat tyre.'
>
> She whispered: 'How long could it take, a tyre? Hurry. We're still OK.'

I see that I had decided somewhere between the first sentence and his ironic 'Perfect' that these two are lovers hoping to steal half an hour for a tryst. This flat tyre has changed their plans. Maybe.

Now the thing I didn't see when I first assigned this exercise was that because they are in a car, there is a terrific opportunity for inventory. By inventory I simply mean the things in your story. The things in a car help anchor the characters in our credibility. You can't put a baby seat in the back seat of a car without amplifying character. A box of monogrammed towels. A bloody knife. A French dictionary. A shoebox full of macaroni painted golden. An Etch-a-Sketch. Seven glass doorknobs. A photograph of a famous Sumo wrestler. One woman's red slipper. A menu from The Anvil Arms, a pub in Glasgow.

The key to writing is not to wait, not to let today slip away in the evanescent hope that tomorrow somehow we will have the knowledge, the real plan and the confidence to commence our story with vivid élan and muscular gusto. Don't wait. In my travels everyone I meet is a writer: the students and the housewives and the doctors and businessmen. Everyone. They are going to write their book, their story, they say, very soon. We'll do them right here one better: we will write this little story. Now.

There are two minds we bring to the writing table. One is the reader/editor who is highly evolved as an evaluator and critic. This mind reacts to story, reads it, edits it, measures it and stands in judgment. The other mind is the writer. This mind wants to create something, something that hasn't existed before. This mind wants to play, and not necessarily play by the rules. The editor wants to make something good; the writer wants to make something. How much of writing is about control and how much is about letting go? When adults come to the writing table, the dominant mind they bring is the editorial mind. It is informed by all they have read and their understanding of form and craft. But, for a writer, this editor often overwhelms, cautions, and limits the work. For the duration of our exercise we are going to leave the editor at the door and let the writer go into the room to the writing table.

This is not easy. This works so powerfully against the instincts of many adult writers that they cannot do it. They want to know where they are going when they start out. They want to know if their idea is any good and if their writing is any good, checking all the way that things are good, so that they might continue. We are not going to work this way; we are going to write without overt caution. It would be nice if we could plan a short story, chapter and verse, and then execute it perfectly, threading the silver needle with the golden thread on the first try. But. For the purposes of our work together on this one brief exercise, let us only commit to making a mess.

Now we are ready to continue writing our Flat Tyre story. I have my two impatient lovers hurry around to the back of the car:

> Dana pulled the trunk release and Martin went around to the back of the car. There were three large cardboard boxes filling the trunk cavity.

What? Three boxes? I don't know. The writer does not know. Let's find out. Meanwhile, my character seems to speak for me:

> 'What is this stuff?' he said hoisting the first box out and setting it on the shoulder. The large white address box on each had an ornate border of loopy flowers and the return address was Lantern Ministries of Mercy. He lifted the second and third box onto the ground. 'Is this Wilson's stuff?'

So now I'm confronted with this inventory, three odd boxes with a religious label, and I find out as I type it that Dana's husband's name is Wilson.

'Yeah,' Dana said. She had lifted the trunk floor and revealed the spare tyre. It appeared to be new. 'Shall we?'

Martin stood a moment over the three cartons. 'Wow,' he said. 'My buddy starts a church.'

'He does,' Dana said, backing to give him room to swing the tyre out and around the car. 'While his wife has a flat tyre on her way home from her mother's on old route 141 with a strange man.'

After typing this line, I echo it (repeat 'strange' below) because I'm taking my time, listening, watching Martin. You can see in the following paragraph that I slow down, add a little setting. *Since I don't know where I'm going why would I hurry?* I've created a kind of charged scene, that is: two lovers, flat tyre, religious boxes. If you look at what I have so far, you can actually begin to see the contour of where I might go.

'I'm strange, all right,' Martin said, popping the tyre iron with his palm to loosen the lug nuts. They were quiet as he worked, and behind them in the stubble field, they could hear the hundreds of sand hill cranes settling at the edge of the lowland. 'Is this field part of Huber's place?'

'Don't let Wilson's pamphlets bother you,' Dana said. She was sitting on one of the boxes, and when Martin pulled the flat tyre off the hub and laid it in the gravel, he saw her there.

'Get off of that,' he said.

'Oh, don't,' she said. 'I knew you'd go off if you saw these boxes.'

So, listening and proceeding very slowly, I've uncovered the agendas. The boxes of religious pamphlets bother Martin; they've put him off his romantic rendezvous; his conscience has struck. She is much more pragmatic. This is something I've learned in the hour since I started typing the story. Below, you can see it play out against more of the simple outer story, changing the tyre.

'Get off,' he repeated. 'Really.' He worked the flat tyre free of the hub and laid it in the gravel. She didn't move. When he looked again after setting the spare on and finger tightening all the lug nuts, she folded her arms and recrossed her legs. His actions now changed tenor; he was no longer hurrying. He cross-tightened the tyre and let down the jack. Pulling the jack from under the frame, he went back to the trunk and wiped all the tools with a towel he found there and put everything in its place.

He lifted the first carton back into the trunk. 'I'm going to put the flat in the backseat so Wilson can get at it tomorrow.' Dana had still not moved when Martin moved the second box from beside her. When he turned for it, she sat arms-folded and looked at him. He stood and waited. There had been no traffic and there would be no traffic on 141 tonight.

If I'm sitting in both chairs, or rather, if I'm sitting with her on her box of pamphlets, I come to understand that she is angry at Martin's response. They had a chance to be together that he has now rejected. She tells him off.

> 'Fine,' she said at last, standing up. 'You better put your good buddy's stupid flyers in the trunk.'

What I'm going to do now is simple: return to the outer story. You can see how the process of changing the tyre knitted the story together and offered the hot element (the boxes) which revealed both Martin's and Dana's character for this episode. In the paragraph below I step from the physical beats in the outer story to Dana's last pointed remark.

> He finished loading the trunk and closed it carefully so the lock registered. Dana was already in the driver's seat. He stood for a minute behind the car to give her a chance to drive away without him, if she wanted. When he got in the car, she said to him, 'Well you've surprised me, Mr Suddenly Quite Holy.' Martin saw her face soften. 'Thanks for the repair work.'

And now the final paragraph. The work of my story is complete and I am going to end on a neutral note so that Dana's last remarks can still resonate. Martin's comment below seems to be thanking fate for what has happened (or not happened):

> She pulled the blue Taurus onto the roadway and accelerated. In the dark the fence posts rose and flashed by. 'I think it's unusual to get a flat on this old road,' Martin said. 'Some nail finds your tyre out here, that's a stroke of luck, good or bad.'

So in my first example, a flat tyre changes the plans of the two lovers and the inventory of the trunk changes the man's mind further. It is, like all three examples, a little episode with credible details which reveals something about the characters. I am not going to annotate the next two examples as closely, but simply make some further notes about the power of the outer story and the reason for some of my choices.

Flat Tyre example 2: Janice and the Reverend

In this first paragraph I quickly establish that Janice is with her father on the small road, and I employ a valuable character tool: the 180 degree rule. Read that first paragraph and then let's do an exercise.

> Even before Janice had pulled onto the gravel shoulder of the two-lane, her father had taken the owner's manual out of the Lincoln's glove compartment. 'This is going to be good,' he said, meaning it. 'I've been waiting to find the jack in this thing.' He'd had the car two years.

The 180 degree rule simply suggests that we look at all of the character's possible reactions to the current problem and we choose the one as far from the expected choice as possible. In my paragraph, when they become aware that they have a flat, Janice's father looks for the car manual and says, 'This is going to be good.' And he means it. What a strange reaction to an event which would simply cause most people to swear! Where will it lead me? We'll see in a minute.

Continuing my story, I am going to create some exposition. I suddenly knew I was going to use a community meeting I'd been to one Sunday at a local church years before, though I would exaggerate it a touch:

> His daughter smiled at him in the dash light. They had just come from the colloquium the Reverend had moderated in the church social room on the topic of gun control, the best-attended monthly meeting he'd ever conducted. But it had been rough. The forum had careened wildly from extreme to extreme, and though he had handled the one or two hard cases on the extreme edges of the issue with the kind of grace his congregation adored him for, there had still been hard feelings. One man had stood near the end and said to the entire panel that they were exactly the same kind of left-wing fools he'd expected to meet, and then to the Reverend himself that he would continue to be part of the problem and not part of the solution until he truly opened his heart to the truth of the issue, the way he urged others to. The Reverend heard everyone out, including his four panelists, and then he asked everyone an indulgence: that they shake hands at the door and say goodnight. Janice had been proud of him there, a peacemaker.
>
> But now, it was late and Janice knew they would not get home before Doug called. He called once a week from his drilling platform in the Gulf; they were all but engaged. It was an important call. She had known the tyre was low as soon as they'd left the church, feeling it just a touch when they left town, and then every mile it had pulled harder. Someone had done this with his little knife.

I added Janice's agenda: she wants to get home to get Doug's call. This doesn't add much to the story except the small pressure of a ticking clock. Many times stories take some of their coherence from time pressure. (For example: I wanted to leave the party before Jason arrived; or I needed to get home before my parents.) And I also added Janice's knowing little observation that she feels the tyre has been sabotaged, cut on purpose by someone at the meeting.

Now, I turn to the outer story to find my way forward with my clergyman, who remains a stubborn optimist to the very end. I added the rain because I wanted to increase the obstacles and see if the Reverend would also relish it – he does. But key in reading the end of this story is simply noting how much of it is outer story: the world, the tyre, the rain, the process.

> 'Oh boy,' he said pushing the trunk release and getting out of the car. 'It's under the spare.'
>
> Janice left the parking lights on though there was rarely a car on 141. It was the passenger front tyre, and while the Reverend was positioning the jack behind the tyre on the frame, the rain began, the scattered fat drops cutting through the charged air and rapping in a desultory pattern on the surfaces of the big grey car.
>
> 'Dad,' Janice said to him where he lay in the dirt, his shoulder under the car.
>
> 'There's a slot for this baby,' he said. He'd taken his jacket off and it was folded across the front seat, but he was flat on his back, knees up in his dress clothes as the

rain began to make its decision. 'Can you hand me the handle right there,' his hand pointed to her feet and she picked up the light metal rod and put it in his palm. He quickly pulled himself up and over onto his knees and began to turn the jack. It took a minute before the car nodded and rose an inch.

Janice stood beside him letting the periodic rain drops pelt her. 'Dad,' she said now. 'It's raining.'

He stood and put his hands on the dirty knees of his trousers. His back was dirty, the rain opening spots of mud. Then he straightened and put his hands on his lower back and looked out over Huber's fields. 'Are the cranes here still?'

'I can't hear them,' she said.

'Is it going to rain?' he said. 'This is going to take ten minutes, tops.' The big drops stepped around and over them.

'We need the rain,' Janice said. She knew she couldn't get back in the car now.

The Reverend knelt again and turned the jack, slower this time as the weight was realised. The car came up two and then three inches. He located the tyre iron on the lug nuts and began to struggle them off.

He was a Reverend never so pleased as when he was dirty in his church clothes. She knew that. He'd go off on a home visit after Sunday dinner and not come home until dark, his suit ruined with grease and something else that had come out of a plugged sink at somebody's house, his shoes wet with what he'd been standing in when he'd solved this plumbing problem. 'These suits,' he'd say. 'They're better for sopping something up in a person's home than for standing at the pulpit.'

Before setting the spare onto the waiting hub, the Reverend leaned it there because the wind had gusted, a skirl of dust and weed ends riding in the edge of the storm, and he stood up, his chin high. 'Oh this fine weather,' he said. 'Blow, wind.' He turned to Janice and smiled. 'You're a sport. We'll be home in twenty minutes.'

The spare was a little low, but not enough to matter, and she sat in the car while he finished putting everything away and shutting the trunk. Now the rain was all business, a thick steady delivery running down the windshield in sheets. The Reverend was soaked when he got in, smelling the sooty smell of tyres in his smudged now transparent shirt. His short grey hair was matted against his forehead and there was a crescent of grease across the bridge of his nose. Janice started the car and turned on the lights and the wipers. She pulled onto the dark roadway.

'A tyre's flat,' her father said, 'you fix it.' He was lit like a football player after a game. 'It actually rained. I'm sorry we missed Doug's call. Let's try to reach him when we get home.'

'OK,' she said. 'That's good.'

Hearing her tone, he added, 'I'll check that flat tyre tomorrow, Janice. You know it's probably just a nail. They're putting a roof on Meyer's.'

'They are not putting a roof on Meyer's, you optimist.'

'Well,' her father said. 'They're putting a roof on somewhere.'

Upon finishing this second example, I knew it was a better story than the first, simply for finding this surprising man, the Reverend, who leans forward into the flat tyre, the conflict at the church discussion, the rain.

And below is the third example for the exercise with very little commentary. I smiled as I went into the story seeing that each of my three examples had some kind of religious note: pamphlets, the Reverend, this crucifix; and they each had the birds off in the dark field. I made Boyd a guy easily alarmed who speaks in exclamation points, and I learned right away that they had stolen the car. In this little story, they don't quite change the tyre. I'll offer it without commentary.

Flat Tyre example 3: Jodi and Boyd

The car was making a real noise suddenly, and Boyd said, 'Oh now, that's not right! That's not right! What is that? What is that right now!' The rhythm then grew louder and they both could feel something trying to get up under the car as it was pulled off the narrow two-lane. Jodi tried to hold the wheel as she braked and left the brand new Camaro cocked off the pavement. 'What?' Boyd said. 'We have got a problem now!'

Jodi's necklaces were tangled outside her thin peach camisole top. She looked at him, and shrugged.

The tyre was blasted, shreds and layers, protruding as if from some unfinished thing. Boyd put his hands on his hips. He wore old denim bell bottoms and a faded black tee-shirt under a Levi vest.

'Can you change it?' Jodi said. She'd come up beside him in the dark and fallen against him on the uneven ground.

'Middle of nowhere,' Boyd said. 'That's the good news and the bad news.' He kicked at the tyre softly.

'Is it the kind you can drive on even when it's flat?'

'No, Jodi. It's just flat.'

'Can you change it?'

'Look at how big it is. That thing weighs a ton.'

'What are we going to do?'

'I'll try to change it. If I can't, we'll get your backpack and head that way.' Boyd turned and pointed into the dark of the field behind them. There was a high overcast and no stars were visible. The still air smelled of dust and mesquite. 'The meeting at the church doesn't get out for half an hour. We got half an hour.'

The trunk was full of brown bags of landscaping bark. 'That's not right,' Boyd said. 'Where's the spare?'

'I don't want to sleep out there,' Jodi said. 'I don't want to sleep on the ground again.'

Boyd began lifting the big bags out of the trunk and throwing them behind the car where they spilled open and bark scattered. He'd thrown the last one and was examining the bare trunk floor when Jodi cried out.

She was in the front seat on her knees looking into the back seat. 'What is it?' she said. 'I was just getting my backpack. What is this? What have we done here?'

'Easy,' he said, his hand on her shoulder easing her out of the vehicle. He looked in. A large gold crucifix lay across the back seat, three feet tall, with Jesus there, his eyes blue and the blood painted red.

'Whose car is this? Whose car did we take?'

'It must be the decoration guy. That's a tricky looking thing for sure.' The crucifix had Boyd's attention. 'You said, "The Camaro. Let's get the Camaro."'

'And what's that noise,' Jodi said, pointing into the dark field. She was jumpy now.

'Oh god, no more noises,' Boyd said, standing up to listen. Jodi stood behind him and he closed the car door so it was dark and there was a sound, but he couldn't be sure, some rustling, some whispering.

She followed him to the back of the car, too closely, saying, 'Do you think we've committed a sin?' He was into the trunk trying to reach around the spare. This was all getting to him. Unsure of where she was when he lifted up the heavy tyre, he swung it to the right and heard her gasp and felt the bump. He dropped the tyre and went to get her where she'd fallen. As he pulled her up, she was crying, but another sound stilled them. They heard the tyre crash through the weeds in the ditch.

'What?' Jodi said.

'Come on,' he told her. 'Get your backpack.'

'Will you get it, Boyd? It's in the back seat with that guy.'

When Boyd had the backpack, he took her hand and led her down through the ditch to the two-strand barb wire fence. The tyre lay there in the grass. Somehow they could see the silhouette of the dark Camaro against the dark sky. Miles away, far enough that people were still up, there were lights on in some village, and it was against that light they could see this car.

'There it is again,' Jodi said.

Boyd turned and faced the whispering noise in the vast space across the fence.

'I don't know what that is,' Boyd said. 'It sounds like a million birds. But we have got to go. This tyre doesn't want changing tonight.' He held the top strand of the fence for her and she ducked under. They couldn't see very far, but in their months together that had been the way.

Finish up your draft, using the outer story process and the inventory to find out who your characters are. Check the imagery – all the sensory writing in your outer story – to ward off clichés and make the world real. Of course, you are bringing your intuition, expectations, history and all of your attention to the writing. It's what we want: a fresh look at an old problem so that new features of your characters are revealed.

Congratulations. You now have the successful writer's problem: you have to turn and go again into the dark. Consult your notebook, that list of story ideas. The key is to choose something that matters to you. Take a deep breath and be specific as you start, staying in the physical world, the outer story of your characters, whenever possible.

Good luck.

Do it now.

Practice 1. Seeing outer story

Think of three of your favourite stories and determine what happens. Don't consider the theme of the story or the meaning of what happens or what it leads to, but simply: what happens. This is the current outer story.

Practice 2. Story ideas

Let's take a side trip right now onto another page and write down ten 'story ideas'. I'm using the word 'idea' with a tilt, because for our purposes, I want you to write down ten 'events' which you know of (drawn from your life or not) which might supply the initial event or germ of an outer story for your next fiction. Write each event down in one or two lines, don't just put a shorthand phrase. For example, instead of writing: 'couch at San Diego', write down: 'The afternoon that Lorrie and I found that old ruined red sofa washed up in the surf and we dragged it back to where David was reading his students' papers under the umbrella. It took an hour and those two boys helped us. It weighed a ton.'

Possible prompts:

1. an event at the ocean
2. an event (good or bad) involving money
3. an event as far north (or south) in the world as you've been
4. an event about an injury
5. an event late at night in autumn
6. an event involving someone's collection
7. an event involving a first kiss
8. an event at an amusement park
9. an event involving food
10. an event involving an athletic event
11. an event involving a dog

Writers, of course, have notebooks, a repository, for all of their story ideas and notations, and they carry the notebooks with them all the livelong day and usually add to their notebooks every day. When making notations, make them as complete as possible – take a minute; it will be a help later. (From my own notebook, I see I pinched the names Martin and Dana; I wanted simple convincing names.)

Practice 3. Character inventory

Let's go sideways again and open a blank page for an exercise on character via inventory. We'll do this to loosen up for upcoming opportunities in our Flat Tyre story. In the three paragraphs you will write for this exercise, select things not because they have trenchant and powerful 'meaning' or melodrama, but because they are original and concrete and specific.

(a) A woman goes home with a man for the first time and sits at his kitchen table while he pours her a glass of wine. She sees three things in his kitchen: one on the wall, one in the sink, and one on the fridge. What are they? Write this as a short 60–150-word paragraph.
(b) A man sits down next to a woman at a funeral as she drops her purse and three things fall from the bag. He helps her pick them up or does he? What are they? Write as a short 50–150-word paragraph.
(c) A boy borrows his step-father's car and has a flat tyre. He goes around and opens the trunk. What three things does he see? Write as a short 50–150-word paragraph.

Practice 4. The 180 degree rule

Let's write one short (half page to one page) scene in which either:

(a) outside a grocery market a man is knocked down by a shopping cart pushed by a hurrying teenage boy; he offers an unexpected response; or
(b) a young woman is pulled over by a policeman for speeding; her reaction is surprising.

3

MAUREEN FREELY

In conversation: a new approach to teaching long fiction

Long fiction and the traditional writing programme

Novelists write novels to evoke the world as they see it, or to move beyond received ideas to understand that world more deeply. They may draw from life, using words, voices and narratives that come with long histories attached, but (if they have literary aspirations) the trajectory they take will be theirs and theirs alone. How to teach such a difficult and fragile art? How to encourage students to go their own way without forcing them down the paths forged by other writers or (even worse) imposed by other cultures?

Creative writing programmes first began in the United States; it is not surprising, therefore, that they reflect American cultural attitudes. The traditional fiction workshop, which continues to sit at the heart of most writing programmes, requires that all students submit work to be scrutinised on a rota basis by the entire class. The expectation is that a monthly dose of group criticism will toughen them up, fostering a pioneering independence of mind. But it can be a brutalising experience, even in the United States. In cultures where discourse traditionally proceeds along less combative lines, it can be entirely inappropriate. If students must defend unfinished work before a committee of peers, they may opt for safe writing, concealing all that makes their imaginations unique, and stunting any idea that might cause consternation. This can foster what one might call the 'cabinet-maker's' approach to creative writing, in which novel writing is not a way of thinking, but a craft requiring a predetermined toolkit. Students learn to write a certain sort of novel in a certain sort of way. The ideas they wish to explore are less important than the modes of narration.

Most novelist-tutors of my acquaintance will admit (at least in private) that they would like to dispense with the classic fiction workshop altogether. But we all understand why they look so good on paper. They sit comfortably inside institutions that want clear, cost-effective structures, and they are easy to sell to students, many of whom will enter creative writing programmes looking for a toolkit and quick results. Of course, this adds another layer of difficulty for tutors: those wishing to draw students into the art of fiction must first divest them of the illusions that brought them into the workshop in the first place.

Most of this hard work is done in the one-to-one tutorials that run in parallel with most fiction workshops. In most writing programmes, the real teaching happens behind closed doors. So it is tempting to imagine a writing programme that dispenses with workshops altogether and offers only one-to-one tutorials to students working on long fiction. But a programme offering such students only one-to-one tutorials would give them no opportunity to know each other, converse with each other, learn from each other. It would fail in what I think should be a writing programme's first aspiration, which is to create the space for a community of writers.

I view such spaces as being of particular significance for writers of long fiction, as we spend most of our lives working in isolation. We do not need someone breathing over our shoulders, telling us what to write, and we have perhaps chosen long fiction because we really prefer to be alone most of the time. But I really do think it is important for us to get out of our heads sometimes and spend time with other writers, new and experienced, young and old, and it is never more important than at a time like this, when the publishing industry is imploding. We can no longer depend on it to offer more than a few literary writers a living wage. It is up to today's novelists to bring along the next generation, just as it is up to us to find ways to keep the literary tradition alive.

Good fiction programmes already do a great deal to support that tradition. They run ambitious events series. They encourage students to engage with contemporary fiction in all its variety. They forge links between their students and the publishing industry: even more important, they influence the way in which the publishing industry sees literary fiction. So they are not just teaching new writers how to write: they are creating communities of writers that are active in shaping the future of literary fiction.

It is in the much maligned fiction workshop that these communities begin to take shape. And perhaps this is the moment to admit that the workshop does have its virtues: it offers students an escape from the lonely garret, a space in which their work will be read and discussed and taken seriously. So long as the emphasis is on constructive, not destructive, criticism, workshops can bring students into a lively conversation with their first readers. If a workshop is run well, student writing can and does improve over time. Students will learn not just from the tutor but from each other.

At the end of this chapter, I shall offer advice to those who are obliged, as I am, to teach fiction by the workshop method and who wish to make the most of its virtues. I shall also say a few words about the one-to-one tutorial and its application to the teaching of long fiction. But I would like to begin by describing two other strands in our work with students of long fiction at Warwick University. The first we call the open house. The second we call the *tertulia*. Both strands operate outside our formal taught programme. Our original idea was to use these separate spaces to enhance the more traditional work we do in our writing workshops and one-to-one tutorials. Over time, we have come to think that these new approaches to the teaching of long fiction are central to our work. In my conclusion I shall suggest ways in which our ideas might be adapted in other universities and other parts of the world.

New approaches to teaching long fiction

The open house

I designed our first open house for undergraduates working on extended writing projects in their final year. They were bright, talented, and terrifyingly good at writing short pieces at a moment's notice. They were sophisticated in their understanding of technique; if they produced a story that did not 'work', they knew how to go about redrafting it. They read contemporary fiction like writers, by which I mean they were interested not just in what a particular author had to say but also in determining 'how they got there'. In other words, they were able to see how the decisions that a particular novelist made about tone, voice, style and narrative mode opened up possibilities at the same time as they shut others down.

The one thing these bright young sparks did not quite understand at this point was how to go about writing long fiction. They assumed, for example, that the best way forward was to write the same sort of proposal they might write for a dissertation, complete with detailed plot synopses highlighting their novel's intended literary features. Some even proposed strict schedules, committing themselves to *x* hundred words of quality prose a week, with a view to completing a solid first draft by the end of our first teaching term and a polished Booker-level final draft by the end of the second. It did not occur to most of them that their understanding of their fictive worlds might not be complete yet, or that they might, once they understood them better, wish to depart from their original plan.

I, for my part, did not want to over-direct them. My ambition was to create a space for them to think their own way out of their received ideas and into ways of working and imagining that were entirely theirs. I wanted to push each and every student towards a long story or a novel that only he or she could have written. I conceived the open house almost as a delaying tactic, obliging the students to think before they wrote.

So I told them we would have no formal classes. Instead I would hold an open house in my office on Thursday afternoons. I encouraged them to drop by even if they had done no work that week, and especially if they had written themselves into a corner. They were free to bring in passages for us to look at, but during the first teaching term, I asked them to keep these short. I did not take attendance (a requirement in most undergraduate modules): if they failed to turn up, I would perhaps write a note to ask how things were, but I would not make a big effort to chase them down. They were writers now, and as writers they needed to take responsibility for their own work. It was up to them to decide how much they wanted to put into it.

The first open house of the year was generally a crowded and earnest gathering at which students described their plans in the round and I offered general advice. Though our extended writing project is only 10,000 words, most students were keen to use this opportunity to start work on their first novels. Having already attempted first chapters, they were astonished to find out how hard it was to find the right voice and to turn a plan for a story into a story that lived and breathed. They were surprised to hear that many or most novelists had similar difficulties when embarking on new work. So I told them a few true stories. I spoke from my own experience, too. I suggested books that spoke in some way to their ideas. I located a few relevant passages and read them out. I sent each student off with a few ideas as to how they might proceed. In some cases, I advised trying several different ways into the story. In others, I advised a reframing of the idea itself. There were always some students who seemed to know exactly what they wanted to do and were already churning out impressive pages; I told these paragons to keep writing and let us know each week how things were going. It was always understood that students who felt shy or unusually downhearted or were working with sensitive material could speak to me privately as and when they thought it necessary, but these students, too, seemed to enjoy taking part in the general discussions.

The second open house of the year would be just as crowded as the first, with a lot of shuffling in and out and at least eight students in my office at any given time, but the atmosphere would be more relaxed. Some students would have attempted new beginnings or even several possible new beginnings; after they had read them out, the others in the room would offer comments and suggestions. But instead of reining every discussion in to produce a teaching point, I let the conversation meander, just as it might in a gathering of working novelists. If a student was writing a novel inspired by a mathematical concept, we would talk about mathematics. If another was writing about Iran, we would talk about politics, too. But along the way we might also talk about the Beats, the Frankfurt Book Fair, the Spanish Civil War, the problems of publishing in a globalised world, and Borges's long shadow. Not one of these conversations was instrumental. Each began as a departure and spiralled off into unintended directions. There was, I fear, a lot of laughter. This would lead to colleagues approaching me grimly in the corridor afterwards. 'I walked by your office,' they would say. 'What were you doing in there – throwing a party?'

I would keep the atmosphere as relaxed as I could, while also keeping track of each student's progress, encouraging them to keep writing, and keep writing at their outer limits. I was fascinated by the different ways in which different students tapped into their imaginations. Over time, students came to appreciate these distinctions, too. They came to understand that no two people write their books in the same way, that the imaginative process is messy, with many false dawns and cul-de-sacs. They learned that just about everyone engaged in fiction will endure periods of despair and confusion, and that this was often a good thing, because it was when they were confused and despairing that writers find the need to break new ground. They learned that while writing is mostly a solitary enterprise, it helps to be in touch with others who are similarly engaged. And they learned that the best and ultimately most helpful conversations are the ones that involve others who share their interests, and that appear at the outset to have no purpose, or no immediate application. But the great reward comes at the end of the teaching year, when we read the work that our students have submitted for assessment. Almost without exception, that work is far more ambitious and original than anything they have done previously.

The tertulia

The *tertulia* is an Iberian and Latin American convention, whereby writers gather on a regular basis to discuss ideas, share work and enjoy literary conversation. It is, in effect, a literary salon, though Plato might have been minded to call it a symposium. For as long as there has been literature, there have been gatherings of this order. But this might be a good time to remember that natural scientists, social scientists, artists and philosophers also understand the importance of creating social spaces where they can meet with their peers and converse across disciplines, and that from the time of the Greeks, these have been spaces that have allowed for the elaboration of new ideas. The way in which such groups organise themselves will depend in large part on their cultural and intellectual preferences: what is constant is the conviction that advances in the arts and sciences depend not just on solitary endeavour but on the intellectual companionship of like-minded friends.

I have never had occasion to offer a full-blown *tertulia*, which would call for a chef, a wine cellar and a moonlit veranda. Working as I do within the realm of the possible, I have (at least for now) confined myself to classrooms during daylight hours. As is the case with most of my experiments, the spur was a passing frustration. It was snowing. The classroom was cold. Our students were looking glum and writing listlessly. I was talking too much in class, and they were talking too little. Each time I was presented with a new piece of student writing, I felt under pressure to examine its existing parts in detail and offer advice on line-editing, when what I really wanted to do was to inspire that student to use that story as a launch pad for something bigger and bolder, something that only he or she could have written.

So I decided to try another sort of gathering. For our first *tertulia*, I booked a two-hour slot in a smallish classroom and told our students to come with a short list of things they might like to discuss. They were halfway through our one-year course by then, and we spend a great deal of time acquainting them with the realities of the literary marketplace, so it is perhaps not surprising that what they most wanted to talk about was dashed expectations and fear of failure. Some had lost their confidence because of criticism from tutors or fellow students. For others, there was the recognition that they were far, far away from achieving the impossible goals they had set themselves at the start of the academic year. They had by then heard many grim dispatches from the many editors, publicists, novelists, agents and literary journalists who had visited the programme. Some students were feeling so discouraged that they could no longer find the will to write. Some were convinced that they were simply looking at a weeding process – that while most writer-aspirants could expect to fail and disappear, writers who went on to be published must certainly have escaped the curse of failure altogether. I was able to offer many examples to the contrary, drawing first from my own life and moving on to authors our students had (until then) assumed to lead lives free of humiliation, disappointment and self-doubt. And slowly, very slowly, they came around to the idea that such horrors were the lot of all writers, and that writers often produce their best work when struggling to rise out of their failures. At no point did we discuss the stories the students were working on at that time, but when I next read their work, I saw that it was indeed bolder and more imaginative than the fiction they had conceived while fearing failure, craving safety and courting the approval of the group.

A *tertulia* (as we define it) can be anything you want it to be, so long as it brings together writers who know and trust each other and understand the value of purposelessness. It offers an opportunity for students to meet and converse outside the formal structures of the course. Good writing can and almost certainly will come out of it, but its main purpose is to create an opportunity for students and tutors to meet off *piste*. Tutors running a *tertulia* on the Warwick Masters Programme in Writing will generally set aside a certain time of the week or the month when they and their students can meet under relatively informal circumstances. The conversations will be general and discursive. Students and/or tutors can suggest a topic in advance, or they can each bring along an assortment of ideas and let the conversation take its own course. Though much of this conversation can be about work in progress, there is frequent reference to contemporary writers and literary culture. Novels, poems and essays are described and quoted and discussed and dissected. Every answer leads to a new question. Over time, this spirited, wide-ranging exchange encourages students to question their received ideas about fiction and the way in which they have until then assumed that fiction should be written; this in turn prompts them to become bolder and more imaginative in their writing. Questions of technique remain important, but the focus is on their reasons for wanting to write a novel in the first place – on their thinking about the world, and on their ideas.

A *tertulia*'s form depends entirely on the interests and preferences of those attending. One colleague likes to offer sessions that equip students with skills or strategies that they may not even know they need yet: how to live with damning reviews, how to give a reading if there is a man at the back glowering, how to project your voice, how to stay sane when still a new published writer, how to hold your own with editors and agents, and even how to avoid back pain. My own *tertulias* continue to be free-form and open-ended, although each finds its own level. I have particularly fond memories of a *tertulia* in which we discussed sociological as well as literary challenges to dominant narratives of illness, a second *tertulia* at which we spoke mostly about the City and neoliberalism, and a third *tertulia* which began with a student asking 'how one constructs a metaphor'. My answer challenged the idea that metaphors were consciously constructed. It just so happened that a number of other students had brought in poems, essays and interviews that also addressed the mystery of metaphors. These allowed us to discuss how it is one thing to examine a finished, polished metaphor in a finished, polished piece of work, and quite another to be writing a piece of work in which certain things or certain patterns seem to suggest more than one originally intended.

From this we moved on to a discussion of that elusive virtue, precision. I was always telling them to be more precise, the students reminded me. But what I had just described to them sounded a lot like writing in a fog. To this I said that writing an early draft of a novel was often just like moving through fog – precision was not a given but an aspiration. If you were driving on a motorway afflicted with patchy fog, it was, after all, pointless to expect to see things clearly, but that made it all the more important to keep all your faculties sharp, to watch out for those strange shapes looming just ahead. My own metaphor reminded yet another student of the poem she had brought with her, and on we went. At no point did we feel obliged to get back to the point, as we might have done, had we been conversing in a fiction workshop.

A world without workshops

If I were given a pot of money and a blank slate, and was told to create a writing programme that aimed to give today's new fiction writers the best possible start, I would cut out fiction workshops altogether. Instead I would offer a weekly meeting that ran along the lines of an open house. Once the group had gelled, I would offer a second strand of *tertulias*. I would offer a third strand of one-to-one tutorials tailored to the needs of each individual student. Some of our taught modules would explore the finer aspects of technique; others would introduce them to all manner of contemporary poetry, fiction, literary nonfiction and drama. There would also be modules to acquaint them with the complex workings of the literary marketplace, the ethical questions raised by any writing that draws from life, and the basics of literary entrepreneurship. I would create hybrid modules with colleagues from other parts of the university, so that students had the chance to draw from disciplines outside their normal fields of action. It would be in the *tertulia* that we would bring all these strands together.

Or so the dream goes. In the real world, I may never have the opportunity to design a programme that puts intense and passionate open-ended conversation at its centre. I may never be able to convince the bureaucrats that the best and most serious thinking starts in conversation, when there is a shared sense of play, when people are having *fun*. But the best thing about such conversations is that you don't have to wait for the moon to turn blue. All you need for an open house is a room with ten chairs in it. All you need for a *tertulia* is a group of students who are passionate about writing and know each other well enough to converse comfortably. So long as the conversation is generous in spirit, and so long as it prizes purposelessness, it will give writers of long fiction the best possible start.

Practical suggestions for the real world

The good-enough fiction workshop

A good-enough fiction workshop (as I define it) runs along pretty standard lines, with three-hour sessions and students submitting work for discussion on a rota basis. It is designed for students with a good grasp of fiction technique. It aims to offer the things that the traditional workshop has always done well (bringing students together at a set time once a week and so helping them to cohere as a group, giving each an equal voice and equal time, modelling ways of discussing and redrafting work in progress). At the same time, it should steer away from confrontation, instead encouraging students to act as constructively critical readers: the emphasis is not on tearing a student's work to pieces but on looking for ways to make it tighter, stronger, bolder. Such conversations do not benefit only the student whose work is under inspection. Almost always, those giving advice will later discover that they could apply it to their own writing.

Students will generally meet their tutor for a one-to-one a week or so after they have been workshopped. It is during this meeting that they decide what they make of the class's response to their work and how they intend to move forward. It is wise to avoid over-direction: better to describe an array of possibilities and their likely consequences. The tutorial also offers a chance to identify blind spots, and to suggest new approaches.

Because there is a limit to what students and tutors can read in a given week, workshops work best for short fiction. But confident and advanced students who arrive with novels in progress can use the workshop to try out their opening chapters. This generally proves helpful, as the workshop format allows them to see the problems in the overall conception and try out new approaches.

If the group is small, it is usually possible to find time to break out of the rota to address topics that the students are interested in discussing in greater depth. If, for example, more than a few students are struggling with voice or dialogue or having a hard time maintaining point of view, a short general talk on the subject can move them along much faster than yet another text-based critique.

The one-to-one tutorial

Tutorials offer a novice writer a chance to work closely with an experienced novelist. No two tutorials are alike. That is their greatest virtue. But like most offerings on most writing programmes, they are subject to structures and regulations that limit their effectiveness. Often universities will cap the number of words a student can submit for assessment. If a dissertation for an academic Masters degree is 20,000 words, students doing a Masters in Writing will generally be required to work within the same limits, even if they are working on novels. This results in students leaving the programme with only a few finished chapters. Even if they do manage to finish novels before they leave, tutors will not be able to assess more than the first 20,000 words. If they are kind-hearted, tutors may well read to the end, but the bureaucrats will see this as unnecessary work, to be done in the tutor's own time.

So my advice is simple: a tutorial strand for writers of long fiction should be designed to see students through to the end. While tutors can offer their students invaluable advice at the outset and keep them from flagging during the novel's middle stages, it is only when a tutor has read to the end of a finished draft that he or she has a clear sense of the whole, and a clear understanding of the work still to be done. If a programme does not offer a structure that sees its fledgling novelists through to the end, it is doing them a serious disservice as they will go out into the world with novels that are not yet fit for publication.

The open house

The open house works best for students who are well versed in fiction technique and have already written a fair amount of short fiction. It also helps if the tutor already knows the students well: this makes it easy to keep the sessions informal. Or rather, it helps to make them *seem* informal, as the tutor must still lead the conversation. Her first task is to ensure that everyone gets a chance to speak. If a student has brought in the first page of his first draft, and if he can be persuaded to read it out, it is always a good idea to ask for the views of the other students in the room before jumping in with your own. Students writing about a sensitive subject will sometimes want to meet in private. In my experience this does not stop them from enjoying and benefiting from the open house proper.

During the first half of the teaching year, I put most of my energies into getting my students to think around their ideas, and to experiment with different structures, points of view, and voices. Towards the middle of the year I begin to read drafts. I let the students know that they must send me their drafts a few days before our open house, so that I can have read them in advance. I can never predict when a particular student will have a breakthrough. But I am always amazed to see how many make the great leap only weeks from the end . . .

The tertulia

The *tertulia* works best with students who have already been working together in other settings. They must have reached the point where they can speak together comfortably – and without an agreed purpose. I generally confine them to two-hour slots: it is always better to end while the conversation is still lively. A *tertulia* strand will always find its own level, but until it does, it is a good idea to suggest topics in advance and bring in more ideas and books than you will need. The most important thing is to talk about things you feel passionate about.

Getting started

Before you schedule your first *tertulia*, you might consider doing a mental inventory. What are the students' main areas of interest? What are yours? What would you like the students to know more about?

If, for example, you wanted them to know more about the problems one encounters when 'writing from life', you might ask students to bring in examples from their own writing as well as from their reading. You might want to tell them about defamation, libel and privacy law. You might want to mention a few famous cases, quoting from novelists who have written from life controversially and defended themselves well. You might want to lead the conversation to questions of ethics. Your aim would be to leave the students with new questions that will, with luck, lead to new conversations and deeper reading, and more interesting work.

Or you might want to move on to look at the problems thrown up by historical fiction. You might ask students to come prepared to talk about novels that draw from history in unusual or troubling ways. You could quote from interviews and essays in which historical novelists have justified or explained their particular approaches.

You might want to give your students a chance to define their literary terrain. You could ask them to come prepared to speak about the novels in which they see their lives reflected in a new and surprising way. You could then ask them what areas of their lives they see reflected nowhere. You could ask them why such gaps exist. You could invite them to think about how one goes about closing them.

If some of your students are writing books that necessitate research that takes them beyond the 'literary', you could invite them to come prepared to talk about the problems they have encountered, not just during the research stage but also when attempting to make that research clear to a general reader. You could move on to the question of authority. Do we live in a time when only experts have the authority to discuss biology, medicine, philosophy, law, politics, string theory and the Big Bang, rarely conducting such discussions with those they do not regard as peers? If novels and novelists can exist only outside the domain of expert knowledge, how can they address the great questions of our day? A discussion of this order could lead on to a second *tertulia* in which you invite students to bring in books or essays that bring expert knowledge into the public domain without dumbing it down.

You could decide to introduce the students to a particular strand of writing. You might want to talk about the Oulipo School, or prison memoirs, or new writing coming out of Eastern Europe/China/Latin America, or graphic novels that touch on political, philosophical and historical subjects in an unusual way. Or you could spread the joy by inviting students to come prepared to talk about a book or strand of writing that they find particularly illuminating or inspiring.

You could set a topic and ask each student to do a bit of research in advance. If, for example, your topic was 'the world after copyright' – you could ask students to come prepared to speak about various aspects of the new dawn. Some could look at the problems posed by information technology. Others could look at possible solutions currently like collective licensing and the creative commons.

The symposium, the salon and the *tertulia*

How I wish, said Socrates, taking his place as he was desired, that wisdom could be infused by touch, out of the fuller to the emptier man, as water runs through wool out of a fuller cup into an emptier one; if that were so, how greatly should I value the privilege of reclining at your side![1]

These words from Plato give us a sense of the distance between a symposium in ancient Athens, where wise, well-watered men would wax philosophical on love while reclining at the side of hetaerae and beautiful boys, and a no-frills *tertulia* offered without refreshments in a stark twenty-first-century classroom. But both derive from the same idea – that interesting things happen when like-minded people come together to share their ideas, and that the most interesting things happen when they are also able to relax, and that they take the conversation in unusual directions when they are actually having fun.

Such conversations seem to yield most when they bring together people in contact with others they would not have had a chance to meet socially. The symposia of ancient Greece made a point of cutting through social divisions to create spaces where poets, historians, philosophers and musicians could converse as equals. The salons of Renaissance Florence brought the innovators of the age together with those who were excited by their ideas, while the salons of pre-revolutionary Paris helped to bring people from diverse backgrounds in contact with the ideas that would go on to inform the Enlightenment. Wherever you find new thinking – artistic or scientific, political or social – you will almost always find that it has first been aired and refined and enriched in a social space that allows for a free, easy and *aimless* exchange amongst equals.

Borges and the myth of the lonely garret

We like to think that artistic genius, at least, feeds on solitude. It is not uncommon for new writers to worry that they will become less distinct, less original, if they spend too much time sharing ideas with their peers. But consider the case of Jorge Luis Borges. When he went to Europe as a young aspiring poet, he found his feet (and an education) in the *tertulias* of Madrid. Returning to his native city of Buenos Aires, he continued the habit. The almost nightly conversations he had with Adolfo Bioy Casares and other writers fed directly into his writing, and into theirs. If Latin American literature then went off in a direction not yet possible in Europe and North America, it is largely thanks to this unruly group of literary hybrids, who drew as much inspiration from Edgar Allan Poe and G.K. Chesterton as they did from Shakespeare and Verlaine. They gave each other the courage to break conventions, question received ideas, and imagine the unimaginable.

NOTE

1. http://classics.mit.edu//Plato/symposium.html, accessed 24 October 2010.

4

KIM WILKINS

Genre and speculative fiction

The pleasures and possibilities of genre

This chapter is all about writing genre fiction. In that statement lies our first problem: genres are often defined by what is common, reused or similar; creative writing is often defined as the pursuit of originality, especially when being conceived, theorised and taught in tertiary institutions. Generic expectations are often viewed as 'a constraint on textual energy'[1] and this perspective can act as a disincentive to write in genres. I argue here for a recognition of the pleasures and possibilities of genre and offer you some ways to approach the creation and composition of texts within one of the most widely read genres: speculative fiction.

When creative writers choose to write genre fiction – fantasy, historical, crime and so on – they have to grapple with unique complexities regarding how their work is positioned in a literary community that still delineates between writing for art's sake and writing for a market. The term 'genre fiction' is often used interchangeably with 'popular fiction'. The reason the two terms are considered synonymous is because the marketplace is presumed to be a significant influence over both popularity (in the form of sales) and genre (in the form of marketing categories). Pierre Bourdieu writes of two principles that position literature in the field of cultural production: the 'heteronomous', which is concerned with 'the economic field' and measured 'by indices such as book sales'; and the 'autonomous', which is concerned with 'artistic prestige' and freedom from 'the laws of the market'.[2] Popular and genre fiction are aligned with the heteronomous principle and therefore sectioned off from, even viewed as antagonistic to, the autonomous principle: it cannot be 'Literature' because art and the marketplace are held to be mutually exclusive. This division between autonomous and heteronomous texts is easily problematised. Feted writers such as Annie Proulx or Ian McEwan are also bestsellers; and the occasional genre novel garners critical acclaim (e.g. vampire novels such as John Ajvide Lindqvist's *Let the Right One In* and Justin Cronin's *The Passage*) or wins a big literary award (e.g. Philip Pullman's fantasy novel *The Amber Spyglass* won the Whitbread Prize in 2002 in the UK and Peter Temple's crime novel *Truth* won the Miles Franklin in 2010 in Australia).

Criticism of genre fiction usually revolves around taxonomy: identifying elements that are commonly used and suggesting that they are deployed cynically to fulfil the requirements of genre, rather than to achieve new self-expression: not 'new richness' but 'the exact same thing'.[3] Perhaps the genre that attracts the most scorn in this regard is romance fiction. Common wisdom holds that there is a 'formula' for romance fiction, which can be obtained from Harlequin Mills & Boon. This 'formula' is held as evidence that there is no art to romance fiction's composition. However, the 'author guidelines' provided by Harlequin Mills & Boon could be read as evidence against this perspective. There are eighteen varieties of romance published by HM&B (which, it should be noted, is only one publisher in the vast field of romance fiction) and they differ widely. The Desire imprint, for example, calls for the stereotypical 'alpha male with a sense of arrogance and entitlement', while the Superromance imprint is 'open to innovation' and wants authors to 'break free of stereotypes, clichés and worn plot devices'. The Blaze imprint encourages authors to 'push the boundaries in terms of [sexual] explicitness', while the Steeple Hill imprint only accepts 'euphemisms for the more intimate body parts'. The Sweet imprint is 'highly focussed on the relationship', while the Luna imprint features romance only as 'subplots that enhance the main story but don't become the focus of the novel'. The suggested upper length of the texts ranges from 50,000 words to 150,000 words. The website is keen to point out that there is 'no formula' and that the guidelines cannot be 'a substitute for extensive reading' across the many imprints, foregrounding a point I will make below about reading as a part of the process of genre formation.[4] Yes, these guidelines are prescriptive but, importantly, there are eighteen different prescriptions. While it would seem to be an easy task to decide what generic elements belong in a romance novel – two people meeting and falling in love – these elements are mobilised via a variety of approaches. In fact, all we can say with certainty about romance fiction is that it contains romance; just as all we can say with certainty about crime fiction is that it contains crime; historical fiction is about history and so on through other genres (including: literary fiction is marked by its literariness). This core element may be the very thing that attracts writers and readers in the first place: it is one of the chief pleasures. But, beyond the core of a genre, the rest of the elements are under constant negotiation and renegotiation.

Genre emerges, Jason Mittell writes, 'out of specific cultural relations, rather than abstract textual ideals'. Because those cultural relations are specific, that means that genres are 'wide-ranging, ever-changing cluster[s] of discourses', not 'uniform transhistorical essence[s]'.[5] These cultural relations are the relations between authors and readers, as I have already suggested, but also institutions. In most cases readers will have developed 'literary competence' in their favourite genres, indicating that texts 'have structure and meaning because [they] are read in a particular way'.[6] The meaning of a genre is not inherent to specific texts, then, rather it is 'derived from a system of conventions which the reader has assimilated'.[7] This competence means that readers come to a text in any genre with a 'horizon of expectations', some of which will be met and some of which will remain unmet or will even be changed by the individual text.[8] Those expectations are formed in the public sphere and therefore are not free of institutional influence; rather genres are processes that involve the interactions of authors *and* readers *and* institutions in more or less equal measure. The HM&B guidelines are right: in such a shifting and contingent system, there can be 'no formula'. Genre texts always have the potential to be 'transformative instantiations' of a particular genre,[9] rather than being the result of 'words poured into a mould'.[10] That is, generic conventions are 'always *in* play rather than simply being *re*played'.[11] Between these two principles – the pleasure of the genre as it stands (replay) and the possibilities of doing something fresh or unexpected with the genre (in play) – there are many potentially rewarding opportunities for creative writers.

What is speculative fiction?

Speculative fiction, one might argue, provides almost infinite scope for putting elements in play because it deals openly with that which is fantastic and unfamiliar. Speculative fiction, as its name suggests, speculates in a fictional way on things that are not true. I am sometimes told that all fiction speculates and that is correct. But speculative fiction is distinguished by the use of the fantastic mode. Ruth Rendell creates a not-true person in Inspector Wexford and then goes on to speculate about how he may act in certain situations. But in these situations he never reaches for a sonic screwdriver, does battle with a dragon, nor banishes ghosts from a haunted hotel: Ruth Rendell's crime fiction uses the mode of realism. Futuristic technology, magical beasts and spirits of the dead are generally held to be not of the real world, but of the fantastic imagination (in the case of technology, of course, what is true is constantly changing; and many people believe in spirits, though dragons, unfortunately, do not really get a look-in).

Speculative fiction is usually broken down into three distinct subgenres: fantasy fiction, science fiction and horror, though this breakdown is inadequate to anyone familiar with the genre. Hybrids abound (my own work has mixed fantasy and horror); short fiction may use different forms (high fantasy, for instance, is very rare in short fiction); subgenres proliferate (within science fiction we find cyberpunk, steampunk, space opera, alternative history and others); new subgenres form, grow popular, then subside (for example, the 'new weird'); while other subgenres arguably do not fit under the umbrella term at all (for example, slasher horror, which may not turn to the fantastic mode and, in fact, may be more usefully conceived as a subgenre of crime).

Of course this inability to define the limits of the genre is in keeping with what I have written above. And yet speculative fiction is a coherent genre for the devoted and active fan community that surrounds it. Readers in the genre, like readers in any genre, know it when they see it. It interpolates its readers effectively even as it excludes the non-readers ('those wizard books' as a reader of realist literary fiction once said to me). It is inadvisable to approach writing in this genre without having read in it widely, understood fully the depth and breadth of it and developed due reverence for the fantastic mode: how it is created and what pleasures it provides the reader. The rest of this chapter offers a place to start writing, but below are a few suggestions of where to start reading.

Classic: *Beowulf* (anonymous), *Sir Gawain and the Green Knight* (anonymous), *Macbeth* (William Shakespeare), *The Monk* (Matthew Lewis), *Frankenstein* (Mary Shelley), *Dracula* (Bram Stoker).

Contemporary: *Consider Phlebas* (Iain M. Banks), *American Gods* (Neil Gaiman), *Assassin's Apprentice* (Robin Hobb), *Brown Girl in the Ring* (Nalo Hopkinson), *Duncton Wood* (William Horwood), *Ethan of Athos* (Lois McMaster Bujold), *Perdido Street Station* (China Miéville), *The Earthsea Quartet* (Ursula Le Guin), *Moonheart* (Charles de Lint), *The Baker's Boy* (J. V. Jones), *Bold as Love* (Gwyneth Jones), *The Lord of the Rings* (J. R. R. Tolkien), *City of Saints and Madmen* (Jeff Vandermeer), *The Crooked Letter* (Sean Williams), *The Doomsday Book* (Connie Willis).

Contemporary short-story writers of note: Octavia Butler, Ted Chiang, Greg Egan, Jeff Ford, Margo Lanagan, Kelly Link, Robert Shearman, Lucius Shepherd, Angela Slatter, Michael Swanwick, Zoran Zivkovic.

Approaches

Realism

One of the chief pleasures of a speculative fiction narrative is the use of fantastic elements, for example magic, futuristic technology or paranormal occurrences. The paradox remains that those fantastic elements must be represented in a realistic way if they are to be effective. Henry James remarked that '[a] good ghost-story must be connected at a hundred points with the common objects of life'.[12] The more realistically the fantastic elements are represented, the greater the feeling of immersion in the fantastic systems and logic of the story.

Some subgenres, in fact, derive much of their energy from the clash between realism and the fantastic. Urban fantasy relishes the careful building of realistic detail – usually, as the name suggests, within an industrialised urban setting – as a foil for ideas and effects that are radically pre-industrial. Neil Gaiman's *American Gods*, for example, reimagines figures from mythology into an American road novel. In the quotations below, Shadow, the protagonist, follows the mysterious Mr Wednesday (the Norse god Odin) into a roadside attraction that has supernatural wonders hidden in its centre.

> The place seemed to be a geometrically reconfigured 1960s bachelor pad, with open stone work, pile carpeting and magnificently ugly mushroom-shaped stained-glass lampshades ... they walked past it into the pizzeria-cafeteria, empty but for an elderly black man, wearing a bright check suit and canary-yellow gloves ... A black cigarillo was burning in the ashtray in front of him.[13]

> ... and then the red and white lights of the carousel stretched and shivered and went out and he was falling through an ocean of stars, while the mechanical waltz was replaced by a pounding rhythmic roll and crash, as of cymbals or the breakers on the shores of a far ocean.[14]

Gaiman concentrates in the first quotation on details that are close and particular, layering the images one on top of another or relying on startling ideas or colours to create a strong and realistic picture in the reader's mind. He secures the reader in a present that is familiar and shared ('magnificently ugly' is associated with 1960s decor, for example, in a way that suggests a nudge-wink mutual sense of taste between author and reader). The details here are very much 'real-world' details – he writes of carpet and cafeterias and ashtrays – to anchor the reader in a world that they know. Once this sense of realism is established, Gaiman then turns to the fantastic, whipping the security of reality out from under the reader, so to speak, thereby enacting for the reader the sense of 'falling' through the fantastic setting. Proximity telescopes into distance. The feeling is one of defamiliarisation, a key pleasure in the speculative fiction genre.

Writing exercise

Write a descriptive scene of an urban setting, including as much realistic detail as possible. Now introduce into this setting a fantastic creature from mythology (e.g. a fairy, a basilisk, a figure from folklore). What patterns of contrast and comparison can you draw out? What do you think would happen next?

Not every speculative fiction novel has a real-world counterpart for contrast against fantastic events and images. A great deal of work in this genre creates new worlds entirely. Once again, realism plays its part in making a fantastic secondary world convincing. I want to concentrate in this section on the idea of emotional realism. My contention is that the best way to describe fantastic ideas is through the viewpoint of characters who have realistic and familiar reactions to the world around them, even if that world is unfamiliar. In fact, it is arguably more important for the characters in fantastic secondary worlds to have realistic reactions, to keep the fantastic elements anchored to lived experience.

In fact, one of the most powerful tools in the toolbox of writers in any genre is the ability to make viewpoint work. Your viewpoint characters are the characters whose thoughts and feelings you will represent in narrative, whose heads the reader will have access to and who experience the story for the reader. Viewpoint is a limited word because your characters offer more than view (sight); they offer access to a full physical and mental response. They experience the fantastic story in their minds and bodies, just as real people experience real lives in their minds and bodies.

You should aim in every scene to be tracking your viewpoint character's experience of the story. By this I mean their emotions and introspections, but also the *material effect* the story has on their body. Perhaps your character is an alien child who loses his mother in quadrant four of the Jupiter colony: if you describe that child's panic in ways that are familiar to your readers, you create a sympathetic connection between character and reader that deepens the reader's experience of the story because it has the ring of emotional truth about it.

Writing exercise

Remember last time you experienced fear. Now write down how that fear felt in every part of your body: feet, knees, stomach, hands, heart, scalp, ears, eyes and anything else you can think about. The idea is to map in detail the material impact of fear on the body. Now, place yourself as a character in a secondary fantasy world scenario, for example, entering a dragon's den. Write a short scene, transferring across those material details of fear to make the fantastic scene seem as emotionally real as possible.

The fantastic

Writing in the fantastic mode creates some wonderful opportunities for the creative imagination, but comes with its own set of concerns. Writing about unfamiliar objects and settings can be challenging and putting in enough information without overwhelming the reader is tricky. Likewise, maintaining the logic of a created world is no small feat.

By far the commonest challenge writers of speculative fiction face is integrating the information necessary for readers to understand the fantastic systems and logic of the story. The 'info dump' has become a much-scorned technique, where the author crams as much information into a paragraph or page as possible, abstracting it from the characters in order to provide the information needed quickly. Of course, not just speculative fiction writers have to deal with integration of unfamiliar detail. Historical fiction writers, or any writers who use exotic settings and ideas will, at some stage, have to grapple with integrating those ideas so that they are understood.

This temptation to info dump can happen both at small or 'line' level and at large or 'structural' level. Often, writers of speculative fiction need to introduce objects or creatures beyond common experience. The writer could explain plainly what the object or creature is, but not only is that explanation abstracted out of the story, it can break the 'fourth wall' if it seems too much as though the author is addressing the reader directly. Jeff Vandermeer, in *City of Saints and Madmen*, accomplishes the task much more smoothly:

> Eventually, he emerged from the alleyway onto a larger street, strewn with rubbish. A few babarusa pigs, all grunts and curved tusks, fought ... for the offal.[15]

The exotic creatures here, 'babarusa pigs', are defined immediately in terms of their appearance (curved tusks) and behaviour (grunting and fighting for offal). Moreover, they are framed through the character's experience as it is he who sees them for the reader. (Babarusa pigs, it should be noted, are not fantastical creatures but a type of pig native to the eastern Indonesian islands; but the example still holds.)

At a structural level, info dumping most often occurs when filling out contextual detail, for example, history, lore or setting. The author becomes anxious that the reader comprehends enough about the context to follow the story, but this anxiety is usually misplaced. It is actually far more difficult to comprehend a huge amount of abstracted information delivered in one blow than it is to gradually learn the context through carefully integrated details. The best way to integrate information is to mete out small amounts consistently over a long period.

Robin Hobb's *Assassin's Apprentice*, an epic high-fantasy novel, features pre-industrial seaside settings. Hobb does not spend a page or two unfurling the backdrop, so to speak, so that she may put characters to work in the foreground. That kind of separation of background and foreground leads to a stagey feel: there is an uncomfortable constructedness about it. Instead, she weaves small details, images and ideas into the story over the first few chapters. We see a little history about raiders from the sea,[16] we learn of the lore of magic names that are '[p]assed through fire and plunged through salt water and offered to the winds of the air'.[17] A historian writes with 'sea-spawned ink'.[18] A character notes 'the unfamiliar warmth of the sea breeze'[19] and 'the brackish iodine smell of the immense water'.[20] Then a more extended introspection about the smell of the sea is introduced: 'The smell of the bay was stronger as if the day-smells of men and horses and cooking were temporary things that had to surrender each night to the ocean's power.'[21] The main character, Fitz, notes that he has learned 'a smattering of trades': 'fish-buying, net-mending, boat-building'.[22] All of this adds up, over an extended period, to a strong sense of context, particularly setting, without an info dump in sight.

Writing exercise

Take a common object from everyday life (e.g. a paintbrush, a bicycle, a bookshelf). Now try to explain what it is to somebody who has never seen one, without describing it directly. If it helps, give the object a defamiliarised name.

The other side of this coin is that many writers give us too little description, especially when setting action in an exotic or unusual setting. It creates a problem known as 'white space': action and dialogue are happening, but they seem detached from the surroundings. The reader can't visualise the scene and so it loses its impact and invites skimming. Two useful words here are *orient* and *anchor*. In each scene, you should aim to orient the reader quickly, then anchor the setting securely in their imagination.

Within the first two paragraphs of a scene, earlier if possible, you should orient the reader. Where are we? Is it day or night? Inside or outside? Are there crowds of people around, or nobody? And, of course, whose head are we in? Then, within one double-spaced page, earlier if possible, you should aim to put in a set of anchor points using specific images: towering bookshelves, furniture under dust covers, boarded-over windows. It is fine to cluster them tightly together, but do it with a light touch. These anchor points begin to map the white space for your reader: already they are starting to see and feel the setting. The next step is to start evoking the other senses in little beats: the faint smell of mould, the creak of a floorboard, the itch of dust on the lips. These beats are spread throughout the action, are part of the narrative rather than standing outside it – a little here, a little there – and as much as possible they are attached to a viewpoint character. You are recording the effect of the setting on somebody's senses and somebody's thoughts:

> The room smelled of food, of beer and men's sweat, of wet wool garments and the smoke of the wood and drip of grease into flames ... My stomach clutched my ribs suddenly against the smell.[23]

The specific sensory impressions here are evocative, but they gather their full weight and meaning when we apprehend them through the material reaction of a viewpoint character.

In fantastic fiction, it is important to emphasise the fantastic elements of setting and to spend time on fantastic detail to create the sense of wonder that readers expect from the genre. Describing these unfamiliar things through familiar comparisons can evoke a feeling of strangeness or the exotic without being too heavy-handed. For example, say you have a fantasy world with two suns. Instead of resorting to the abstracted (and clichéd) 'he watched as the two suns set', describe instead something familiar (perhaps, sun shining on long waving grass) with the fantasy twist (where are the shadows? are there two? does it create a rolling effect, like waves?). These concrete, familiar descriptions are more engaging and help to build that crucial sense that this fantastic world of the imagination has depth and breadth.

Writing exercise

Come up with a well-worn fantastic setting (e.g. a castle, a spaceship, a haunted house) and a well-worn plot idea to match it (e.g. the wizard dispensing mentorship, a laser gun battle, a young couple sheltering from a storm). Now, applying the rules of orient and anchor, can you make the setting come alive? If the setting feels detailed and deep, can it actually lift the action out of cliché?

One of the key challenges facing writers of the fantastic is how to build an entire secondary fantastic world. This skill, known as 'world building', is far more difficult than popular opinion might have it. There is no 'just making it up'. J. R. R. Tolkien writes of how the 'story-maker' creates 'a Secondary World which your mind can enter. Inside it, what he relates is "true": it accords with the laws of that world. You therefore believe it, while you are, as it were, inside.'[24] A secondary fantasy world must cohere logically and convincingly, must be fully mapped in time and space and must be integrated at all levels with the lives of the characters who people it. This daunting task is best broken down into three processes: reading, living and writing.

Reading refers to the process of taking in information that can inspire ideas for how the secondary world operates. By this, I certainly do not mean merely reading inside the genre to discover and adapt what other writers have done. What I do mean is research. A fantasy novel set in a faux-medieval world written after researching the actual medieval period is likely to be more sophisticated in scope than a copy-of-a-copy, where the genre elements have worn so smooth they no longer have the power to engage. Likewise, approaching science fiction via an open-minded reading of scientific research rather than a brief review of the *Star Wars* movies will provide for the author much more scope for building a convincing world. That is not to say that fantasy fiction is only worthy if it is historically accurate, or science fiction is only worthy if it is 'hard' science fiction. Consider Lois McMaster Bujold's *Ethan of Athos*, part of her *Vorkosigan* science fiction series: the plot revolves around a missing item, in this case, ovarian tissues. The premise is that a male-only colony reproduces with uterine replication technology and the tissues are needed because the existing stock is ageing. Clearly, reading and research have gone into the science behind the world building, allowing for a sophisticated and interesting context.

Living refers to remembering that there must always be a balance between the 'big picture' of world building and the lived experience of the characters in that world. World building does not have to be approached from the outside in: that is, starting with geography, history, religion, etc. It can usefully be approached from the inside out: that is, starting with a character and tracking that character through a typical day of life as it is lived, to discover which aspects of the world are most important to develop for the story's purposes. This task involves taking a notebook with you for the day and writing down everything you do. From this list, you begin to map lived experience so that you can adapt it. 'I had breakfast' translates into a series of questions about common foods, their source, how they are grown or transported, how they are received culturally and so on. This appeals to me particularly because it means that at the heart of fantastic creation is, once again, ordinary realism. I have known many budding fantasy writers who fill notebooks with details about the facts of their secondary worlds, but until those facts are mobilised in relation to characters, they remain abstract. The danger also exists that, because the writer has taken the time to develop the ideas, they must appear somewhere in the story even if they don't naturally fit. Writers of speculative fiction, like all writers, must learn to serve the story before they serve themselves.

Finally, writing refers to the process of making journeys into secondary worlds before they are properly 'finished'. The rationale here is that until you actually start writing about your characters in your world, you won't know what details you might need: so writing becomes something like a reconnaissance operation. When you hit a white space, it is time to go back to the world building. In the meantime, you are getting to know your character better and testing out the boundaries. Your secondary world is provisional right up until it goes into print: the process of reading, living and writing is iterative.

You cycle through and repeat through first and second drafts and beyond. Eventually, you will know that secondary world as well as you know your own.

Writing exercise

Look around you right now. What aspects of your real, lived existence would have to be reconfigured and reimagined if you were building a world for an epic high-fantasy novel. Choose an aspect of your world (e.g. study practices, food culture, transport) and derive from it a list of questions to be answered about your secondary world.

Structure

Genre fiction is often assumed to be more bound by structure than literary fiction, which is expected to be more experimental. While it is probably nominally true that literary fiction is more concerned with style than structure, really no story can dispense with good structure altogether.

My chief contention in this section is that stories should have a beginning, middle and end and that managing the proportions of those parts of the narrative structure is crucial for pleasing and persuasive pace, especially in longer forms. A recent emphasis on three-part narrative structure in the pedagogy of commercial scriptwriting has meant a perception that Hollywood 'invented' the structure for its purposes. That is not the case. As long as there have been novels they have had front covers, back covers and pages in between. A story has a rhythm: a set-up, a development, a resolution. This rhythm is in line with the expectations of the reader about narrative structure. There is much enjoyment to be gained from the three-part structure.

To understand the rhythm of story, we can loosely adapt the Freudian ideas of the pleasure principle and the death drive. That is, story can be seen as an interplay between the desire to stay forever in pleasure and the desire to return to an inert state. Or, if you prefer the classics, narrative structure grows from an interplay between *eros* (desire) and *thanatos* (death). We all know the intense gratification of being in the midst of a huge novel, wanting to stay lost in the story forever and yet at the same time finding ourselves unable to stop turning the pages and racing towards the resolution. While most good storytelling uses this structure, speculative fiction thrives on it because so much of the pleasure of the reading experience is taken where the world building unfolds (*the pleasure principle/eros*).

The three parts – beginning, middle, end – have different functions (introducing, developing and resolving) and should represent different proportions of the story. This is not, and can never be, an exact science. But a beginning that takes up more than 25 to 30 per cent of the word count can drag, making the reader wonder when the story will start to develop. If the middle takes up roughly half of the word count, leaving an ending equal to or a little shorter than the beginning, there is a feeling of substantial development and economical resolution. Readers can enjoy the set-up, take their pleasure stuck in the middle for a long time and then be pulled through on the tide of the end. (Short fiction often has a longer middle and a shorter end, but I am using the novel as the main example of form in this section, because narrative structure is so important to the success of the novel.)

These ideas rely on there being relatively clear transition points, at least for the writer, between the beginning and middle and the middle and end. These transition points are like gear changes in the narrative structure: if you listen closely enough, you will nearly always hear them in good storytelling. Certainly, they are evident in the work of Shakespeare. *Macbeth*, a speculative fiction story about witches and ghosts, has very clearly marked transition points. The beginning of the story introduces us to Macbeth and his wife, to the prophecy of the witches and the plan for murder. Macbeth kills Duncan one-fifth of the way into the story (at the end of act I), signalling the end of the beginning. Here is the first gear change: the story has kicked off and moves into the next gear. The first transition point is an indicator that the beginning is over and the middle is upon us.

The second transition point is a more slippery customer than the first. The escalating sense of conflict throughout the middle should generate a number of scenes that 'up the ante', so to speak (see my section on episodic narrative below). But only one changes gears and propels us into the ending. Broadly speaking, the second transition point is an indicator that matters have become so intense as to force an ending either way. A Rubicon is crossed, a die is cast, a watershed moment is reached: the amount of clichés available to me here demonstrates just how entrenched the idea of a 'point of no return' is in narrative. When Macbeth returns to the witches and consciously aligns himself with evil, we hear the gear change clearly: the ending is rushing upon us now. With the transition points in place, you have the spine of the story. Writing it is as simple (and as horribly complex) as negotiating the distance between them with scenes.

Writing exercise

Think about a story you may be working on in terms of the parts and their transition points and build a 'plot skeleton'. Does it help you to conceptualise the story from outside?

Fantasy fiction, particularly epic high fantasy, is one of the genres that can fall too easily into an episodic structure. Other genres, such as the women's romance saga or the historical novel, are also at risk. The narrative can start to look like a long string of events of equal interest, which are nominally connected but lack coherence. Tension is concentrated only in each event, rather than building slowly over the course of the story. It is what Kate Forsyth, borrowing from Elbert Hubbard, calls 'just one damned thing after another'.[25]

The episodic feel is usually concentrated in the middle of the narrative. Take, for example, the classic quest narrative. After the character hears the call to adventure and gathers resources for heading out on the quest, the narrative becomes a chain of events – travel to location, something happens, repeat – rather than a story with a sense of overarching development and slowly rising tension. It can help here to divide up the middle into three parts. They are all still performing the function of the middle, that is, developing the promise of the beginning towards the pay-off of the ending, but they differ from each other slightly. The first part pays more attention to the *eros* principle: this is the place for world building, for indulging the reader, engaging their senses while still gently tugging on the narrative so they are drawn forward. The second part balances the two principles, shading slowly from *eros* to *thanatos*. The third part pays more attention to the *thanatos* principle: scenes grow shorter, feature more action and drama, the stakes get higher. Using these ideas as a guide, it quickly becomes clear when a scene can be there simply to develop the world and when it needs to be pulling its weight in terms of moving the plot forward.

The second book of J. R. R. Tolkien's *The Lord of the Rings* trilogy, *The Two Towers*, is characterised by an episodic structure. While it is inadvisable either to criticise Tolkien (without whom the fantasy genre may not exist), or to judge by contemporary taste a novel written many decades ago, comparing the written version of *The Two Towers* with Peter Jackson's film version demonstrates very well the point I am trying to make here. Jackson reworks the battle at Helm's Deep, just one equal episode in the written version, as a narrative crisis point. All the events that come before it refer to it or point towards it in some way. The Frodo and Sam plot, once a completely separate section in the written version, is interleaved between the stories of the rest of the Fellowship, gaining extra narrative purpose. The tension around whether or not Gollum can be trusted now builds to a climactic moment (when Frodo betrays Gollum to Faramir), which screens close to the Helm's Deep crisis point and is therefore revealed as a crisis point itself.

Writing exercise

Jot down the random events of your day. Now see how you can reshape them towards a notional narrative crisis point, say, eating your dinner. What images, introspections, subtle shifts of meaning would you have to add to those ordinary events to make them seem to signal towards the crisis of dinner time?

I have been writing in the speculative fiction genre for fifteen years and have never felt constrained by it nor felt frustrated by any sense of limitation. I am still a heavy reader in the genre too. What initially attracted me to speculative fiction is the precise same thing that continues to attract me: the use of the fantastic. But while the core of the genre has held, the range of texts that I have read (and, indeed, written) and enjoyed is vast. I have enjoyed texts that play with the genre and push at its boundaries, such as the strange and defamiliarising short stories of Zoran Zivkovic or the mind-bending world building of Jeff Vandermeer. I have enjoyed, too, perfectly generic epic high fantasy, space opera and vampire novels. And I have enjoyed the send-ups of speculative fiction provided by authors such as Terry Pratchett and Diana Wynne-Jones: pleasure is still available to 'serious' speculative-fiction readers in parodic and ironic texts. In no way do I feel I have exhausted the possibilities available to me in this genre and I am confident, too, that I never will. Once we move past the idea that genre is somehow a brake on the writer's imagination, the pleasures and possibilities will be there for all to see.

NOTES

1. John Frow, 'Reproducibles, Rubrics, and Everything You Need: Genre Theory Today', *PMLA: Publications of the Modern Language Association of America*, 122 (5) (2007), pp. 1626–34, p. 1626.
2. Pierre Bourdieu, *The Field of Cultural Production: Essays on Art and Literature* ed. Randal Johnson (Cambridge: Polity Press, 1993), p. 38.
3. Nancy J. Holland, 'Genre Fiction and "the Origin of the Work of Art"', *Philosophy and Literature*, 26 (2002), pp. 216–23, pp. 218–19.
4. Harlequin Enterprises, *Mills & Boon™: Author Guidelines*, available online at www.millsandboon.com.au/authorguidelines.asp, accessed 1 June 2010.
5. Jason Mittell, *Genre and Television: From Cop Shows to Cartoons in American Culture* (New York: Routledge, 2004), p. 23.
6. Jonathan Culler, *Structuralist Poetics: Structuralism, Linguistics and the Study of Literature* (London: Routledge & Kegan Paul, 1975), p. 113.
7. Ibid., p. 116.
8. Hans Robert Jauss, 'Literary History as a Challenge to Literary Theory', *New Literary History*, 2 (1) (1970), pp. 7–37, p. 8.
9. Frow, 'Reproducibles, Rubrics, and Everything You Need', p. 1633.

10. Judy Wilson, 'Wooden Bowls', *Eureka Studies In Teaching*, 4 (1) (2003), pp. 87–8, p. 87.
11. Steve Neale, 'Questions of Genre ', in Barry Keith Grant (ed.), *Film Genre Reader II* (Austin: University of Texas Press, 1995), pp. 159–83, pp. 170–1.
12. In T. J. Lustig, *Henry James and the Ghostly* (Cambridge University Press, 1994), p. 50.
13. Neil Gaiman, *American Gods* (London: Headline, 2001), pp. 127–34.
14. Gaiman, *American Gods*, p. 140.
15. Jeff Vandermeer, *City of Saints and Madmen* (New York: Bantam, 2006).
16. Robin Hobb, *Assassin's Apprentice* (New York: Bantam, 1995), p. 1.
17. Ibid., p. 1.
18. Ibid., p. 2.
19. Ibid., p. 22.
20. Ibid., p. 22.
21. Ibid., p. 27.
22. Ibid., p. 39.
23. Ibid., p. 9.
24. J. R. R. Tolkien, 'On Fairy Stories', in *The Monsters and the Critics and Other Essays* (London: Allen and Unwin, 1983 [1947]), pp. 109–61, p. 132.
25. Kate Forsyth, *Interview*, 27 January 2010.

5

MICHELENE WANDOR

Writing drama

Writing drama appears in various guises on creative writing courses: as 'screenwriting', 'scriptwriting', 'playwriting', 'writing for performance'. Often two or more of these categories are conflated: 'writing for stage, film, radio and TV', as if the media-specific skills were simply interchangeable.

This chapter is very deliberately entitled 'Writing drama', in order to mine a clear path through these attempts to pinpoint the third of the core genres of imaginative writing: prose fiction, poetry and drama. It's important to do that in order to understand what is involved in writing drama, in the distinctive ways it circulates from imagination to page to stage to page to imagination. These ways are radically different from prose fiction and poetry. I will argue also (contentiously for some, but argument is always a good thing) that, like prose fiction and poetry, writing drama is a discrete literary activity and process. This is notwithstanding the necessity of performance in relation to drama as a fictional genre.

Publication and pedagogy

Unlike the novel and poetry, where publication is on the page and in the book, writing drama reaches its audience through performance (live or recorded) before (if ever) attaining publication in print. Indeed, this is part of the excitement of writing drama – a passion for the power and magic of performance. Performance excites the drama-writing process, and ways of thinking about performance have expanded considerably in recent decades. However, these very expansions, while illuminating many aspects of performance, have also served to confuse and mystify the imaginative and material role of the dramatist.

Creative writing was established in American universities in the early decades of the twentieth century. Teaching drama played a significant role in those early years; at Harvard, George Pierce Baker set up a course called 'The Technique of the Drama' in 1906. In 1919 he published *Dramatic Technique*, based on lectures first given in 1913.[1] Creative writing took much longer to arrive in the UK – well after the end of World War II – and while drama is not exactly the poor relation, it is the least developed and understood genre, despite its popularity.[2] In the UK, drama (on the page and as a method of teaching) was important in educational developments in schools, well before it was incorporated in university Literature departments. When English Literature became a university subject towards the end of the nineteenth century, the written dramatic text was incorporated as a part of 'literature'; exemplified best, perhaps, in the way Shakespeare was studied as much as poet as dramatist.

The study of drama as a genre in its own right began when drama departments were set up in universities, pioneered by Bristol University, in 1947. This coincided with the revival of the professional theatre after World War II, and a recognition that drama was an important enough category to warrant its own area of study. Inevitably, this was linked to increasing interest in performance, as well as the written text.

In the late 1960s, Raymond Williams observed that there is 'a confusion, both theoretical and practical, in our contemporary understanding of the relation between a dramatic text and a dramatic performance'.[3] Despite a great deal of important work on drama and performance since then, the confusion has remained, and it has come to the fore in a new way with the success story of Creative Writing.

Performance theory

Williams's comment came at a pertinent moment: as attitudes to studying drama were once more in the process of radical change. In response to technological increases in television, film and theatre, together with new ideas in anthropology, cultural theory and semiology, performance studies and performance theory came into being. The very idea of 'performance' came to apply to more than the specially prepared occasion. Extrapolations from Erving Goffman's 1959 book, *The Presentation of Self in Everyday Life*, created interest in the rituals and ceremonies of day-to-day experiences, which were reconfigured as a series of roles and performances. Richard Schechner developed this thinking, comparing the assumptions of western theatre with other performance cultures. As he put it: 'Ritualised behaviour extends across the entire range of human action, but performance is a particular heated arena of ritual, and theatre, script and drama are heated and compact areas of performance.'[4] At the same time, he also acknowledged the specificities of artistic production/performance: 'drama is what the writer writes; the script is the interior map of a particular production; the theatre is the specific set of gestures performed by the performers in any given performance; the performance is the whole event, including audience and performers (technicians, too, anyone who is there)'.[5]

Censorship and after

New kinds of performance developed rapidly after the end of theatre censorship in 1968. Until then, there were serious restrictions on live staging. Plays had to be vetted by the Lord Chamberlain for approval before being rehearsed and put on. Representations of royalty, religious and historical figures, sexuality and 'bad' language were all strictly scrutinised. Performances could be visited by incognito inspectors, to make sure that there was no ad-libbing, or anything too risqué in the gestures or actions of the performers.

After 1968, the changes were no less than revolutionary; new writing could encompass virtually all subject matter and approaches. Studio spaces, informal performance venues in pubs or community halls and basements – any space could become a theatre. Called 'fringe', 'alternative', 'political', 'underground', this movement developed new relationships with audiences, and was strongly influenced by discussions about culture and politics. Some theatre groups/companies took radical change into the working practices of theatre, aiming to make the process more democratic. Important as this was, there was a curious outcome as a result of assumptions about what was seen as the traditional, putatively tyrannical authority of the individual dramatist and director.

A loose and largely haphazard form of apprenticeship for would-be theatre dramatists came about as some theatres took on responsibility for helping to encourage new writing. It is now fairly usual for theatres to have a dramaturg, part of whose role might be to run workshops and have contact with writers, in the way script editors work in television and film. Also after censorship, some companies partly or totally devised plays, either trying to write together, or bringing in a dramatist to work alongside them, all benefiting from sharing ideas, improvisation, and rehearsal. There is no doubt that as a learning device these have been valuable as part of an industrial apprenticeship, helping to make the writer's work less solitary. But, of course, that is not the whole story. French cinema in the 1960s coined the concept and term *auteur*, to ascribe authorship to the primary and central role of the director, who in some cases also wrote the film script, thus combining the two major artistic functions.

The dramatist

Somewhere within and across all these, the dramatist was being moved around: re-placed, replaced, displaced, challenged, afforded new opportunities, but also often sidelined and, to a degree, undervalued. Even while the post-1968 theatre movement encouraged many new playwrights, parts of the collectivising culture unconsciously colluded with performance theory to divert attention away from the complexity of the drama-writing process.

The function of the author/writer of drama has been concealed behind this attention to performance. On the surface, this seems to make a kind of sense. In performance, all the creative and technical elements are fused into one. The complex division of labour involved in preparation results in a moving (in more than one sense of the word) work of art. On stage it is live and ephemeral, in recorded form it is equally seamless and fixed, attaining a status as an 'object' which is more akin to book publication than live performance. The independence of the various skills and their hierarchy in terms of order of precedence and artistic importance has become harder to discuss, and in some ways, this has made drama writing harder to define and teach. In a further spark of irony, Roland Barthes's resonant slogan of 'The Death of the Author' might appear to apply more to the dramatist than to other kinds of authors.

Imagination–page–stage–imagination

In order to reconstitute drama writing as a discrete literary process, it needs – temporarily – to be separated from its fusion with performance, and allied more with prose fiction and poetry as writing procedures. It needs to be reconceived for what it is: a literary, practice-based form: from imagination to page and back again, with its own formal characteristics. This does not in any way entail a rejection of performance, or a refusal to acknowledge the complexity of what happens in 'production'. It is important in order to focus on the writerly element in the complex division of labour which – eventually – produces performance. Ironically, as we shall see, whatever it is the writer does produce, it is *not* performance; and yet it is essential *for* performance. There's the paradox. There's the excitement. A conflation of terminology has further clouded the issue in juxtaposing the 'dramatic text' (written) with the 'performance text' (production). The term 'text' suggests that there is some sort of straightforward equivalence between the two, when the reality is that they are distinct. Terry Eagleton has succinctly summarised this relationship: 'A dramatic performance is clearly more than a "reflection" of the dramatic text; on the contrary ... it is a transformation of the text into a unique product, which involves reworking it in accordance with the specific demands and conditions of theatrical performance ... what has intervened ... is a transformative labour."[6]

The dramatic text: incomplete?

As a consequence of the foregoing, there are four received clichés which serve to render the dramatic text as incomplete.

Blueprint for performance, and therefore incomplete until realised in performance

This characterises the dramatic text as a kind of outline, a blueprint, a series of codes, a musical score, a scenario; whichever of these it is (and they each undoubtedly involve skill), they are seen as unfinished, 'incomplete' until other skills complete them by creating performance. This applies to all media; Robert McKee has remarked about film, 'A screenplay waits for the camera.'[7]

The written text is commonly seen in this way: as a 'strange – incomplete – object'.[8] The notion of 'completion' is not merely something which offers to make the written text 'whole'. It has serious aesthetic consequences, suggesting that the written text has no established or discernible meaning, until it becomes transformed into performance. Performance studies has rightly focused on the ways meaning is created through performance, concentrating largely on the visual elements. The dramatist is left in a limbo of hermeneutic expectation.

S/he is assumed/expected to write something inherently 'incomplete', leaving it to others to complete. The written text becomes relatively secondary, consisting of hints to be interpreted or realised into something finished by others, out of which they make meaning.

The text is not incomplete.

Writing drama is a collaborative art/process

Even where theatre may be devised, perhaps improvised, or where a director might be intensively involved with the 'development' of a text, as long as there is one person designated as the author, the crucial process happens between the writer's imagination and the page. This is not to undermine the importance of good writer–director relationships; difficult to achieve, rewarding when they happen. Textual changes may be made during rehearsals (hopefully always with the agreement of, or in response to corrections from, the writer) or after discussion with the director, but the dramatist is never simply a scribe to whom changes are dictated, and who just follows instructions. However sensitive a director's reading of a text may be, however subtly the director may be able to discuss the text, the director does not write, any more than the dramatist directs (unless they are one and the same person).

In the vast majority of instances, the fundamental conceptual, imaginative and writerly work has been completed before the director is on board, even if the latter responds to drafts. The work always returns to the imagination and skills of the dramatist. It is not collaboratively 'thought', even if there are shared enthusiasms and concerns. The practice of 'committee' writing in movies, or the procedure of scripts being shifted from writer to writer before producers are happy with the final product, is more a comment on the power structure of the film industry, than on the nature of the writing process itself.

The text is not incomplete.

Writing drama is a visual art; stage directions

This is perhaps the most obviously misleading element in the bouquet of clichés. Because performance privileges the visual (rather than the written or heard), it may appear that the dramatist writes a visual text. This is not so. The dramatist writes dialogue, and it is into dialogue that the major conceptual, aesthetic and imaginative energy is directed. Stage directions (which is where the 'visual' is assumed to be) are specifically stylised descriptive prose passages interpolated into the dramatic text. But they are historically enormously variable, and they are, finally, dispensable.

Shakespeare's plays have hardly any stage directions; those of George Bernard Shaw, for example, are wonderfully fulsome. Many paragraphs could easily come from a novel. Imagine you could remove all the stage directions from a Shaw play. The drama remains intact, utterly stageable. Reverse the process, and remove the dialogue. There is no drama. Do the same with a film script, and the results are more or less the same. Even though film scripts tend to have more 'directions' dotted around, even if theatre stage directions might be 'visualised' on the page, they are always provisional, and no drama is ever accepted for production (in any medium) on the grounds that its stage directions are brilliant. The drama is in the dialogue. In practice, in any case, once work on any form of performance starts, the stage directions are the first things to go out of the window. Indeed, they *must* go out of the window, since the dramatist does not have the required skills, and cannot be responsible for what direction and performance will bring. These are different skills in the complex division of labour which produces performance.

At best, only a very small amount of what goes into stage directions can function as realistic, practical hints for production. By contrast, dialogue on the page is voiced, appears on the air, spoken, performed, as it is written, whereas stage directions are not and cannot be. Two small examples illustrate this: a stage direction calls for a table. What kind of table? Even if the stage direction is very precise: 'A pine table, one metre square, with straight legs' may sound precise, but there can never be enough detail. Besides, a table may turn out not to be necessary or desirable. Harold Pinter's carefully placed pauses create a subtle rhythm on the page and in the reading, and they are often held up as sacrosanct, utterly vital to the text. He wrote them. They must be. But how long is a pause? How long is one pause compared to another? What happens if a pause is missed out? What happens if one is added?

The dramatist does not 'write' the production, any more than the director 'writes' the play. While a dramatist writes, it may make the process more enjoyable or more pointed to write elaborate stage directions, as if s/he is imagining (visualising) the production as s/he writes, but this is misleading as a guide into what is involved in writing drama, and it misunderstands the nature of the text in relation to performance. An understanding of what happens in production is more than helpful – indeed, vital – and something the dramatist needs to internalise. But it doesn't mean that dramatists have to 'see' what they are writing. The material of the dramatist's trade is imagination and dialogue, dialogue and imagination.

The text is complete.

The written drama text is intrinsically difficult to read; prose or drama?

This takes us into the heart of what makes drama distinctive as a form of imaginative writing. I referred above to stage directions as 'descriptive prose passages interpolated into the dramatic text'. The operative word here is 'prose'. It is fundamentally in relation to prose that the autonomy of the dramatic text asserts itself. This is not just a matter of mere technique (linked, continuous sentences as against dialogue). It is critical in terms of what goes on in the mind, in the imagination itself, and the ways in which fictionalising as an imaginative process must necessarily be directed into a specific convention/genre.

The assumption that the dramatic text is intrinsically hard to read derives from our dominant fiction-reading habits. It is no exaggeration to say that by far the dominant literary form in our cultural world is that of the novel. By comparison, the dramatic text might seem puzzling: there are no paragraphs of introduction to people/places/back story; there are no passages of description of people/places/inner life. And finally, there is no single voiced narration (first or third person) to 'guide' the reader into and through the text, via the device of a single point of view, or even from changing individual points of view. In fiction the singular reader meets the singular narrator, a neat one-to-one. Dialogue in the novel is a minority event; it highlights immediate moments, lends variety and pace and tone, but it is, nevertheless, a minority event, subservient to the dominance of the narrative.

It is not entirely surprising that people might view the drama as a novel *manqué*: hard to read, apparently full of gaps and absences, lacking all those deictic elements which locate the reader in place and time. However, in principle, even if it takes some adjustment for a novel reader, it is entirely possible to grasp every aspect of the dramatic fiction simply from reading the text (dialogue) on the page: narrative, characters, chronology, etc. Indeed, that is exactly what a good director must be able to do, even before they begin to approach it for performance. It is also exactly what people have done during all those years of studying drama-on-the-page. The dramatic text was studied and analysed on and from the page, *because it could be.*

The dramatic text is complete in itself.

The argument that the dramatist is entirely responsible for the complete dramatic text is not a return to outdated concepts and assumptions. It doesn't ignore performance studies, and it isn't a justification for a mere return to the days when it was thought that the drama-on-the-page was 'just' literature. In any case, this chapter is not merely about study and scholarship; it is about the drama-writing process.

On writing drama: from imagination to page to stage to page to imagination

The dramatist writes only dialogue and dialogue is all. The dramatist does not write prose. The dramatic text has real autonomy as a distinctive product of the dramatist's imagination. There is nothing but dialogue, there is only dialogue and the dialogue is all. This is the challenge: to filter all the imaginative aspects of fiction (narrative, story, plot, character, theme) into and through dialogue.

In drama there is no single narrative voice in the technical sense – no 'I' or 's/he' to lead the reader. Of course, there is an authorial 'voice' which permeates drama just as much as it does the other genres – the imagining, shaping mind of the real author – the individual stamp/style which each dramatist gives to their text.

Drama is multivoiced. The dramatist creates voices engaging in dialogue with each other. Even where there is a great deal of physical action in a drama, it is grounded in what happens through and in dialogue. Because of this, dialogue, by its very nature, creates, and is about, relationships. Now, of course, relationships are between individuals; in the territory of performance, each performer 'plays' an individual 'character', but one who only exists in relationship with other characters. While it is true that there can be no relationships without individual characters, it is equally true that in drama there are no characters without relationships. The stress on 'character' makes important sense for the individual performer preparing his/her role, but does not chime in the same way for the dramatist.

Whereas prose fiction evokes the existential and experiential 'self', through its single-voiced narration, the drama returns us to the social experience of the self as *relational*, as constructed through and in relationships. Discussions about whether 'action' or 'character' drive the story/plot have threaded their way through history, since Aristotle. The dichotomy is, in any case, at best misleading. As Henry James commented, writing about prose fiction: 'What is character but the determination of incident? What is incident but the illustration of character?'[9]

Writing relationships

In general, while many people may not be comfortable with writing drama as a conscious fictional genre, everyone is familiar with conversation, with the verbal exchanges which are so important in our daily lives. Most people can write something which looks like conversation, and this can be a first step towards conceiving dialogue, structured into scenes. Often people are concerned that they might be writing 'just talk', and there are important issues behind this concern. However, at one level, it is necessary to understand that the idea of 'action' so often invoked in relation to drama, also applies to the dialogue. Indeed, speech/dialogue itself is 'a kind of action, *a compression and extension of action*. When a man [*sic*] speaks he performs an act.'[10]

Two characters in a scene constitute one relationship (from two points of view): A + B. As soon as a third character enters, the relationship configuration expands to seven relationships in all: A + B; A + C; B + C; AB + C; AC + B; BC + A; ABC. It will help to understand this by getting three people to stand up in a room, and counting out the permutations! Four characters account for a total of twenty-five relationships in different numerical permutations and combinations.[11] And so on. No matter how the dialogue is allocated in any given scene, all relationships are always active. Each character is voiced, and then interacts with other characters in dialogue.

Dialogue is predicated on cumulative exchange; each speech, line, phrase, word is also, and at every point, a reaction and response to the sum and the detail of everything which has gone before. This is the case, even with apparent non sequiturs. There is an acting exercise which highlights this:

each performer must repeat the last word or phrase addressed to him/her, before replying. For example:

A: I thought I asked you to cook spaghetti.
B: (*cook spaghetti*). You did, and I forgot. I'm sorry.

This cements the 'join' between the two speeches, as it were, enabling B to experience the way in which his/her first words must operate as apparently spontaneous response. This helps to confirm the accumulative inevitability of dialogue. From the opening line of any drama, a highly structured verbal edifice is built, in which each speech can only be understood in relation to a series of reactive eddies outwards into the rest of the text. Drama is not made up of isolated speeches, any more than everyday conversation is.

The work of Bakhtin has recently attracted attention because of the way his sociolinguistic insights have influenced critical approaches to the novel. The term 'dialogism' has become a shorthand formulation for the ways in which 'Dialogue is an obvious master key to the assumptions that guided Bakhtin's work.'[12] Arguing that there is a complicated relationship between the world and the individual, Bakhtin suggested that there is a 'dialogic' process taking place (consciously and unconsciously) within the literary work itself. This incorporates notions of intertextuality – influences, models and literary conventions. In a usefully ironic sense, writing drama also reinforces this. Dramatic dialogue inevitably demonstrates relationships in reactive, social interaction, in a constant state of responsiveness. 'Response' is the only inevitable condition of dialogue, since every line must be a response to what has gone before.

Given this fact, I have found it profoundly ironic that all the how-to-write-drama books I have read virtually ignore dialogue, or refer to it very briefly and late on in the discussion. Indeed, some even warn against writing dialogue 'too soon', as if it carries dangers with it. If speech (dialogue) is understood as one of the forms of action, and if action is held to be at the core of drama, then the art of writing dialogue must be given its rightful prominence – at the centre of how to learn to write drama.

It is common for drama writing to be taught by getting students to spend a great deal of time mapping out synopses, scenarios, plans, character studies, monologues, apparently designed to help 'create' characters and develop plot/story before they think of writing dialogue. I wouldn't for a moment discount the usefulness of any of these procedures, but there is an inherent intellectual problem which arises out of working this way. All of the above entail imagining and writing prose; effectively, a series of short stories. It is only then that students are encouraged/allowed to imagine/write in dialogue.

Imagination–page

Over many years of teaching creative writing it has become very clear to me that each of the core fictional genres – prose, poetry and drama – engages the imagination in different ways. In my teaching, the emphasis is almost exclusively on writing dialogue as a way of shaping the imagination into the form on the page. Classes consist of a similar, developing pattern of work. Students begin by writing a short scene of dialogue between two people (10–15 minutes). There are two 'rules', which operate throughout all classes: no stage directions and no monologues. Reasons for this are explained in a later session. The scenes are then read out; each student can choose to be in their scene, or hand it over to two other people. Students choose their own subject matter, and all they are initially asked to do is write one scene. Although there is no time for conscious planning, it is extraordinary how every single time intriguing scenes are produced, full of potential.

The classroom space doubles as a space which replicates the basic conditions of performance. Sitting down and reading is merely just that: sitting and reading. As soon as people stand up in space, the whole body is engaged, the way pages are held enables direct eye contact, since all drama is about dialogue between people. No more and no less. Drama *is* dialogue; dialogue *is* relationships. Every scene is enacted on the floor, immediately after it is written, and then again, in sequence, later on. Whether or not students have acting experience is irrelevant. The class is not about learning to act, but about understanding from experience what happens in performance, in embodying the dialogue. This is essential, so that students can begin to internalise the relationship between imagination–page–stage, and then return to the imagination. After each class, students type out their scenes, making enough copies for further reading in future sessions.

Over following weeks, more scenes accumulate, and are gradually read out in sequence. This means that everyone's work is read in each session, and all discussion of theoretical, technical, etc., issues, emerges from discussion of the texts. In these classes, students do not bring in extracts of dramas on which they are working at home. This is reserved for independent work for assignments, using skills, understanding and expertise acquired in class.[13]

It is always difficult to give an accurate account of class-based discussions. At first, this centres on the development of narrative/story, and the development of relationships. This can never be predicted; each initial scene of dialogue is the beginning of a process, since even the tiniest exchange implies both narrative (back – and forward – story) and some sort of relationship (with a history and a future).

A: I saw you drop it.
B: What are you talking about?
A: You know exactly what I mean.
B: No, I don't.

Discussion of narrative possibilities first.

A: I saw you drop it. *Something has just happened. Is it something that's broken? Something precious? Something thrown away?*
B: What are you talking about? *B may genuinely not know, either through real ignorance, or because s/he doesn't want to admit something. Or B may be pretending.*
A: You know exactly what I mean. *The word 'exactly' here suggests something very specific – as if A may have evidence. It also suggests that A may know B well enough to assume (rightly or not) that s/he knows.*
B: No, I don't. *B is sticking to his/her guns. What happens if s/he does or doesn't know what it's about? The story can move in one of two different directions at this point.*

The student is pointed towards deciding what may have been 'dropped', about why there is some 'conflict' between these two, what is at stake for each of the speakers, and whether they are male or female. Discussions of gender are always fascinating and revealing, even from a snippet of dialogue, such as the above.

If A is female, B might be male, and defensive; if A is male, B might be worried or frightened. Do these possibilities suggest gender stereotypes? Social expectations? Cultural assumptions? Are they both male/female? What is the relationship between them? A couple? Siblings? How old might they be? It may be too soon to decide, but the matter has been aired, and possibilities (always with reference to possible clues in the text) have been raised.

What about the gender/cultural background/ethnicity of the students as writers? This is not an occasion for interpersonal exploration, but intended to raise questions about how each of our perspectives (choices of subject matter, point of view, etc.) may be determined by our own cultural position in the world. Generally, this is a discussion which is left until much later on in the work process.

The following week in class, students write *either* the preceding, *or* the following scene. This is the beginning of thinking about structure, the order of scenes, cause and effect. The idea that one thing happens 'because' of something else, as opposed to just 'after' something else, is always interesting, and never necessarily obvious. During all discussion, students must pay careful attention to the text, *listening* to the live 'performance' of the dialogue, rather than *reading* the scenes on the page.

At some point, generally after three or more scenes have been written, students write out a brief plan for a drama of between five and seven scenes, with a one-line description of what happens in each scene. They are limited to a maximum of five characters. They must incorporate the scenes written so far. Again, discussion about plot/story, order, causality, become pertinent. At every stage there is exploration and flexibility. Often it is fascinating to experiment by changing the order of scenes, and seeing how the storyline could change.

Discussion is never based on whether or not scenes are good or bad or how they might be rewritten. That is because, while each play is for real, as it is built up, each play is also a self-generated exemplar on the basis of which all the distinguishing features of writing drama can be explored and understood. When the end of this process is reached, and everyone has completed a 15–20-minute play, each is run complete, and there are discussions about theme and message. It is not necessarily, or even finally, just about what the student would like their play to be about, but what the text reveals, and how others may interpret it. Again, all discussion takes place with close reference to the text. Above all, the imagination is constantly directed towards building relationships through dialogue. This is writing drama.

Writing exercises

There is an inherent difficulty with suggesting discrete exercises for writing drama, which does not apply to prose fiction and poetry. My insistence on the *completeness* of the conceptual and imaginative writing process in drama is consistent with the fact that performance (live or recorded) is one of the forms in which the writing is seen/read/'consumed'. In my brief account of a classroom process, I have stressed the importance of enacting each scene, so that the dialogue is experienced both on the page and on the air, and then analysed. This is the meaning of the journey from imagination to page to stage to imagination. The following exercises are suggestive, rather than complete. They are intended to generate writing, to suggest some ways of thinking about writing drama, and to encourage the development of aural acuity – listening skills.

1. Choose any play by George Bernard Shaw. Read it silently to yourself. Choose four or five pages, and type out two versions: (a) just the stage directions, and (b) just the dialogue. Then read each separately. What are the differences? In style, layout, language? How do these affect the

way you read? If you had to choose just one to rehearse, which would it be and why?

2. Set aside half an hour for this exercise. Take a notebook and pen, leave home, and go wherever you wish, making sure it is somewhere where there are people. Choose somewhere to sit or stand, open your notebook, and then write down the first half dozen pieces of conversation you hear. If these happen to be continuous – that is, between two people standing or sitting near you – that's great. If not, never mind. Do *not* base your judgement on whether what they say is 'interesting', and do *not* rely on your memory for when you get home. Simply *write what you hear.*
3. At home, set aside five minutes to divide the 'lines' of dialogue between two people, and rewrite the lines in the style of dialogue from a play.
4. Commandeer two friends, and get them to read your mini-scene out loud, while you listen. Enjoy the experience, but don't ask them what they think.
5. Thank them, provide them with tea/coffee/drink, and bid them farewell.
6. Set aside twenty minutes, and continue your mini-scene into something longer. Do not write for any longer than twenty minutes.
7. A week or a month later, return to your scene, reread it to yourself. Set aside another twenty minutes and write a short story prompted by the scene.
8. Read both again, and think about whether you prefer writing prose fiction or drama, or both.

NOTES

1. Reprinted as George Pierce Baker, *Dramatic Technique* (Boston: Houghton Mifflin, 1983).
2. For comparative histories of Creative Writing in the US and the UK, see Michelene Wandor, *The Author Is Not Dead, Merely Somewhere Else: Creative Writing Reconceived* (Basingstoke: Palgrave Macmillan, 2008).
3. Raymond Williams, *Drama in Performance* (Harmondsworth: Penguin, 1972), p. 4.
4. Richard Schechner, *Performance Theory*, 2nd edn (London and New York: Routledge, 2003), p. 296.
5. Ibid., p. 87.
6. Terry Eagleton, *Marxism and Literary Criticism* (London: Methuen, 1976), p. 51.
7. Robert McKee, *Story: Substance, Structure, Style and the Principles of Screenwriting* (London: Methuen, 1999), p. 394.

8. Simon Shepherd and Mick Wallis, *Studying Plays*, 3rd edn (London: Hodder Arnold, 1998), p. 1.
9. Walter Besant and Henry James, *The Art of Fiction* (Chapel Hill, NC: Algonquin Press, 1900), p. 69.
10. J.L. Austin, J.O. Urmson and Marina Sbisà (eds.), *How to Do Things with Words*, 2nd edn (Oxford: Clarendon Press, 1975), p. 18.
11. For diagrams, see Michelene Wandor, *The Art of Writing Drama* (London: Methuen Drama, 2008), p. 135.
12. Michael Holquist, *Dialogism: Bakhtin and His World* (London: Routledge, 1990), p. 15.
13. See discussion of the workshop in Wandor, *The Author Is Not Dead.*

6

BRONWYN LEA

Poetics and poetry

Introduction

Poetry, our oldest language art and perhaps the most recognisable, should be easy to define. And yet seemingly it isn't. Poetry cannot be defined, or so Borges says, without oversimplifying it: 'it would be like attempting to define the colour yellow, love, the fall of leaves in autumn'.[1] In this albeit idealised view, poetry is more than a set of formal features. It is something to be experienced. Part of the problem, then, in defining poetry is that it seems to refer to two distinct things: a verbal artefact and something that is more difficult to define because it is less determinate. Poetry, as Paul Valéry points out, also 'expresses a certain state of mind'.[2] Perhaps this is what Emily Dickinson meant when she famously remarked: 'If I read a book and it makes my whole body so cold no fire ever can warm me, I know that is poetry. If I feel physically as if the top of my head were taken off, I know that is poetry. These are the only way I know it. Is there any other way?'[3]

Of course not all poems aspire to nor achieve the spectacular effects, however metaphorical, that Dickinson describes. Light verse, for instance, is happy enough with a laugh. But Dickinson's observation has endured because those who love poetry know something of what she is gesturing at. The poem, with its roots in ritual, brings speech and vision together in such a way that the person experiencing it might be transported into an alternative awareness. For Les Murray this is the raison d'être: 'the poem exists', he says, 'to contain the poetic experience'.[4]

But whatever else it may be, W. H. Auden argues, 'a poem is a verbal artefact that must be as skilfully and solidly constructed as a table or a motorcycle'.[5] Many poets today, raised on a diet of anything goes, have had to rely on their wits in order to work out how to make a poem stand up or to turn it on and make it go. Sometimes they get lucky. But poets are learning that a grounding in the nature and forms of poetry can help them to write better poems. This chapter lays out some of the concerns central to composing poetry today. Contemplating these ideas, along with a lot of reading and practice writing poetry, can help you to develop your own sense of what you think a poem should be and do. It will help you to develop your own poetics.

So much depends upon the line

'The line', as James Logenbach contends, 'is what distinguishes our experience of poetry as poetry.'[6] Whenever we see, or more importantly hear, language arranged in lines we know we are entering the gallery of the poem. White space and silence frame the poem and alert us to its language. Consider the difference between William Carlos Williams's 'The Red Wheelbarrow'[7] set as prose – 'so much depends upon a red wheel barrow glazed with rain water beside the white chickens' – and the same words set in lines:

so much depends
upon

a red wheel
barrow

glazed with rain
water

beside the white
chickens.

As prose, the sentence moves swiftly so that its essential meaning can be easily grasped. But set in lines, language slows down: each word in the poem is clarified, intensified and raised in stature. The words are experienced not only as signifiers but as objects in themselves. At a reduced pace meaning opens up and multiplies. The portmanteau 'wheelbarrow', for instance, is cleaved so that we are encouraged to contemplate the word 'barrow', which can refer not only to a cart but also, perhaps, to a burial mound. This is not to argue that 'burial mound' is the preferred reading in this particular poem, but rather to show how a word, when isolated, can be unmoored from its strict context so that its alternative meanings might come into play.

In prose, a sentence has a single beginning and an end, but set in lines beginnings and endings are abundant. Each line in a poem refracts into additional beginnings and endings inside the sentence, which grants not only heightened significance through emphasis – the start and end of a line are always hotspots – but lines also offer a sense of equivalence in which words and phrases can be weighed, or balanced, against other words and phrases. Michael Dransfield's 'Pas de deux for Lovers'[8] offers an excellent example. The poem opens with a statement that 'Morning ought not / to be complex' but the sun, the poet observes, has been 'cast at dawn into the long / furrow of history'. The poet appears to be weighing this ideal of detachment against a dawning attachment to a lover:

To wake
and go
would be so simple.

Yet

how the
first light
makes gold her hair

We can imagine the poet looking down as he completes the image in the next stanza: 'upon my arm'. The poem spins on the word 'yet' which stands in isolation at the heart of the poem as a single-word line (and stanza). An otherwise small and almost insignificant word, 'yet' is granted primacy of placement and as such it demands to be taken as central to the poem's meaning. It punches above its weight and undoes both the argument and the poet, who is helpless against his growing emotion for his lover: 'Day,' he concludes, 'is so deep already with involvement.'

The end of the line

Determining where a line ends – or breaks – is the art of the poet. 'There is at our disposal', as Denise Levertov argues, 'no tool of the poetic craft more important, none that yields more subtle and precise effects, than the line break if it is properly understood.'[9] Essentially there are two types of line breaks: 'end-stopped' in which the line ends with a clear and natural pause created by punctuation; and 'enjambed' in which the phrase, clause or sentence continues across a line break to decrease the pause and speed up the rhythm and flow of the thought.

As we've seen, the interplay between the line and the sentence creates a dynamic unique to poetry. Sometimes, in the case of end-stopped lines, the line and the sentence correspond exactly, as in the opening lines of 'Under One Small Star' by Wisława Szymborska:

My apologies to chance for calling it necessity.
My apologies to necessity if I'm mistaken, after all.
Please, don't be angry, happiness, that I take you as my due.
May my dead be patient with the way my memories fade.[10]

The structure of the line is simple and clearly marked out for the ear by punctuation. The directness of the line accords a sense of formality to the poem that proceeds as a list of transgressions so human we would absolve the poet immediately, if we could. Szymborska achieves audible interest, however, in the middle of the poem and again at the end, as seen here, by extending the sentence beyond a single line:

> Don't bear me ill will, speech, that I borrow weighty words,
> then labour heavily so that they may seem light.

Here, the end-stopped lines maintain balance and form, but the smaller pause of a comma contrasts with the longer pause (and breath) signalled by the full-stop to achieve a graceful fluency and increased flow.

But more commonly in contemporary poems – and as seen in the Williams and Dransfield poems above – a poet will aim for a more dramatic line break by using enjambment. In Sharon Olds's heavily enjambed poem, 'I Go Back to May 1937',[11] the poet imagines her parents 'standing at the formal gates of their colleges' in the late May sunlight:

> I see my father strolling out
> under the ochre sandstone arch, the
> red tiles glinting like bent
> plates of blood behind his head, I
> see my mother with a few light books at her hip
> standing at the pillar made of tiny bricks with the
> wrought-iron gate still open behind her, its
> sword-tips black in the May air . . .

Olds's trademark narrative energy moves not just horizontally with the line but plunges down the page, her lines breaking on prepositions, articles, adjectives and pronouns, forcing the reader to leap ahead, dizzily, for the noun or the verb. Sometimes the ride through an Olds poem is so violent it feels as if the poet has taken a pen in her fist and torn it down the page. Such heavily enjambed lines invigorate with their wilful incursion into the sentence, even if their liveliness comes at the cost of being harder for the ear to hear the structure.

Enjambment offers the additional quality of allowing the poet to spin meaning on its head. Working in a highly condensed form, poets often celebrate the possibility of generating multiple meanings from a single statement. In Robert Hass's 'Meditation at Lagunitas',[12] for example, the poet offers the idea that desire is full, amplified, but this meaning holds only for a moment before it is shattered in the next line:

> Longing, we say, because desire is full
> of endless distances.

When the syntax resolves we discover that we haven't so much misread the first line but that the bittersweet enjambment has allowed two separate meanings to run concurrently.

The length of the line

Short lines, as seen in the Williams and Dransfield poems above, frequently can be found in contemporary free verse, where the poet determines line length based on a desire for equivalence, hesitation, emphasis and other strategic effects. But sometimes a poet wants a more fulsome line: lines we can carry around in our bodies in the hope that we may summon them at a later date for the wisdom, consolation, wittiness, or joy they offer. Shakespeare's 'To be, or not to be: that is the question', for instance; Emily Dickinson's 'Tell all the Truth but tell it slant –'; or Elizabeth Bishop's 'The art of losing isn't hard to master'.

The success of these lines, and countless others, may have something to do with the way we think. In their article, 'The Neural Lyre: Poetic Metre, the Brain, and Time',[13] Frederick Turner and Ernst Pöppel make a case for a remarkable congruency between poetry and the human nervous system. After examining a sample of metrical poetry from about eighty different cultures – from Africa to North and South America, Asia and Oceania – they found a predominance of lines that take on average about three seconds to articulate. For Turner and Pöppel, this is no accident: 'the three-second period', they argue, 'roughly speaking, is the length of the human present moment'. In English a line of iambic pentameter corresponds most consistently – though not exclusively – with the three-second duration of our experience of the present moment. Which may account for the tremendous popularity the ten-syllable line has had with poets through the ages.

Poets have used other parts of the body – the lungs in particular – to determine the length of their lines. Walt Whitman famously took his line to the end of the human breath, which in turn inspired Allen Ginsberg to conduct his own experiments with the line as a unit of breath. Each line in 'Howl',[14] for example, is designed to be read in one breath:

> I saw the best minds of my generation destroyed
>   by madness, starving hysterical naked,
> dragging themselves through the negro streets at dawn
>   looking for an angry fix . . .

Ginsberg's line pulls the reader to its natural end. The lines are ecstatic to read, especially aloud, as the poet, like a puppeteer, pulls the strings on the reader's body. Similarly, in his seminal essay, 'Projective Verse', Charles

Olson formalised the idea of a 'breath-line'[15] – in so doing, he hoped to connect the poem again to the human body.

Writing exercise

Take a stanza from a well-known poem and restructure the lines using a different pattern of line breaks. If lines are enjambed rewrite them as end-stopped lines, and vice versa. Read aloud the original poem and the restructured version, paying attention to how the line breaks interact with the sentences. What is lost and what is gained?

Not too far from music

'Music and rhythm', Plato claims, 'find their way into the secret places of the soul.' It may sound esoteric, but it speaks to the very human part of us that loves and responds to rhythm. Think of Gerard Manley Hopkins's 'The Windhover' – 'king- / dom of daylight's dauphin, dapple-dawn-drawn / Falcon' – or e. e. cummings's 'anyone lived in a pretty how town' – 'bird by snow and stir by still / anyone's any was all to her' – and try not to be swept up by the sounds. Rhythm grants a poem a deeply satisfying and coherent whole, helping to lock it in memory and imbue it with emotion. Children don't worry too much about what a poem (or nursery rhyme) means; it is enough for it to sound good. And, in many ways, it is still enough for all of us. While the possibilities for different types of music made by language have opened up in recent years, the insistence on poetry's rhythmical elements endures. Just as 'music rots when it gets too far from the dance', as Ezra Pound expounds, 'poetry atrophies when it gets too far from music'.[16]

Rhythm is all about pattern: its essence is repetition suggesting a forward movement. This allows us to anticipate, with pleasure, what will come next. The most common way to create rhythm in English is through attention to the patterning of stressed and unstressed syllables. English is a stress-timed language; that is, stressed syllables appear at a roughly constant rate, and non-stressed syllables are shortened to accommodate this. Native speakers generally know which syllables to stress: for instance, we must say **By**-ron, not By-**ron**, if the listener is to grasp that we are referring to the English Romantic poet. Stressed syllables provide the audible beat, or cadence, to the line. For example, in his poem 'Envoi' James McCauley describes his view of the Australian national character: 'The men are independent but you could not call them free.'[17] The line, even skimming lightly over the 'bumps', is inherently percussive. Close attention to the alternating unstressed and stressed syllables reveals a back beat against which the natural speech rhythms can vary expressively: 'The **men** are **in**depen**dent but** you **could** not **call** them **free.**'

The music of poetry, to state things simply, privileges stressed syllables and aims for as few unstressed syllables as possible. Take, for example, the famous line from Shakespeare's *As You Like It*: '**All** the **world's** a **stage**', which is composed of three stressed and only two unstressed syllables. Without the contraction – '**All** the **world** is a **stage**' – we get an additional unstressed syllable, which breaks Shakespeare's rhythmic pattern. While both lines mean the same thing, Shakespeare's version is more dynamic. It is less like prose – where the pattern of stresses is of less consequence – and more, for its rhythm, like poetry.

Metrics

Metre allows a poet to more easily organise patterns of sound. We could say, for instance, that a sonnet is composed of 140 alternating unstressed and stressed syllables. But such a large number is unwieldy and makes keeping count during composition tricky. It is more useful to say that a sonnet is composed of fourteen lines of ten syllables each. Or more specifically, and to employ the language of metrics, a sonnet is fourteen lines of five iambic feet, otherwise known as iambic pentameter.

Poetic metre, then, is built on a sequence of feet – a foot being a group of two or more syllables – that march across a line. It's worth remembering, however, that feet are units of rhythm not units of sense. Sometimes the divisions of feet coincide with divisions between words, as in the first line of Emily Dickinson's poem 'Because I Could Not Stop for Death':

> Be-**cause** | I **could** | not **stop** | for **Death**,
> He **kind**- | ly **stopped** | for **me**.
> The **Carr**- | iage **held** | but **just** | Our-**selves**
> And **Im**- | mor-**tal**- | i-**ty**.[18]

But scanning (dividing into feet) the rest of the stanza, we see that subsequent feet are not so tidy: 'kindly' in line 2 straddles the division between the first and second foot, as does 'Carriage' in line 3. 'Immortality', stretching across three feet, provides a pleasurable interplay between foot and word.

Feet can be divided into two basic types: rising rhythms (in which the stressed syllable comes last) and falling rhythms (the stressed syllable comes first). Rising feet include the two-syllable iamb (da-**dum**) and the three-syllable anapest (da-da-**dum**); while falling feet include the two-syllable trochee (**dum**-da) and the three-syllable dactyl (**dum**-da-da). Finally, the spondee, composed of two stressed syllables (**da-da**), rounds out the five classic feet in English metred verse:

- Iambs: 'The **whis-**| ky **on** | your **breath**' – Theodore Roethke, 'My Papa's Waltz'
- Trochees: '**Like** a | **po**-et | **hid**-den' – Percy Bysshe Shelley, 'To a Skylark'
- Anapests: 'The in-**vis**-| i-ble **worm**' – William Blake, 'The Sick Rose'
- Dactyls: '**Won**-dering, | **list**-ening' – Ralph Hodgson, 'Eve'
- Spondees: '**Break, Break, Break**' – Tennyson, 'Break, Break, Break'

Iambs, which follow most closely the patterns of natural speech, are the most well known of English feet and are thought to convey a sense of building and solemnity. Trochees, conversely, are more tripping, less at ease, than iambs and offer a lighter touch. Anapests and dactyls, which have come to be associated with light verse, are experienced as more impetuous and rapid than their two-syllable counterparts. And, finally, spondees are almost never used as the sole metre of a poem due to their overly insistent percussive qualities, yet inserted sporadically they can lend drama and variety to a metre.

In addition to the arrangement of syllables, metre is further distinguished by the number of feet in each line, from monometer to hexameter. Lines composed of only one to three feet are comparatively rare; however, trimeter, when alternated with tetrameter, forms a ballad stanza (see Dickinson's stanza above). Iambic pentameter is by far the most common in English metred verse: it is the stately metre of epics, odes and elegies.

Writing exercise

The following lines engage strong rhythms but are not slave to them. Scan them to discover the variations:

1. . . . How do they come to the
   come to the come to the God come to the
   still waters, and not love
   the one who came there with them – 'Sex Without Love' by Sharon Olds
2. summer autumn winter spring
   reaped their sowing and went their came
   sun moon stars rain – 'anyone lived in a pretty how town' by e. e. cummings

Reason for rhyme

The making of a successful rhyme leads to a literary affect that is something like the satisfaction of a hunger. Rhyme gratifies at the deepest level of response by engaging our delight in separation, at the same time as engaging our delight in union; equally, a tired or weak rhyme can arouse anger in that it disappoints our drive for gratification. Most often rhyme is used at the end of the line, but some poets, finding this placement too predictable, have preferred to embed their rhymes in the middle of the line. 'Eurydice on Fire' by Robert Adamson[19] offers an example:

> The mist
> parts as it **rolls** across
> a channel **pole's** yellow marker

Broadly speaking, rhyme can be categorised as masculine when only one syllable rhymes (rolls and pole's) or feminine when the rhyme extends across multiple syllables. Hip-hop artists make a feature of feminine rhyme, or 'multis' as they call it: Eminem, for example, rhyming 'maniac in action' with 'brainiac in fact son' in his lyric 'Infinite'. Long before hip-hop, however, Byron made comedic use of feminine rhymes in Don Juan:

> But – Oh! ye lords of ladies **intellectual,**
> Inform us truly, have they not **hen-pecked you all?**[20]

But rhyme needn't always be clever to be effective. In fact simple repetition – itself a type of rhyme – can generate powerful rhythms. Elizabeth Bishop's 'At the Fishhouses'[21] contains a heady example of the scheme known as epistrophe (repetition of words at the end of a line):

> I have seen it over and over, the same sea, the same,
> slightly, indifferently swinging **above the stones,**
> icily free **above the stones,**
> **above the stones** and then the world.

Technically only the first two repetitions in Bishop's poem employ epistrophe. The position of the third repetition makes these lines, taken together, an instance of anadiplosis (repetition at the end of a clause and at the beginning of another). More frequently, however, poets use repetition at the beginning of the line in a scheme known as anaphora. Here's an instance from T. S. Eliot's 'The Waste Land':

> **After the** torchlight red on sweaty faces
> **After the** frosty silence in the gardens
> **After the** agony in stony places[22]

Other types of sound repetition include: assonance (repetition of vowels); consonance (repetition of consonants); and alliteration (repetition of consonants specifically at the beginning of words). Just two lines of Robert Lowell's highly stylised 'To Speak of the Woe that Is in Marriage' contain instances of all three:

My h*o*pp*ed u*p* husband dr*o*p*s his home dis*p*utes,
and hits the streets to cruise for *pr*o*stitutes.[23]

Writing exercise

1. Write a poem using end rhyme. Restructure it so the rhyme moves to the beginning of the line.
2. Use anaphora to create a list poem. Try varying the repeated phrase in sets of five.

Form and feeling

Poetic form refers to the set of rules – such as metre, lineation, rhyme scheme, stanzaic structure and so on – established by poems of certain types. The form a poet chooses makes up part of the language act: 'meaning', therefore, is not only found in the words but is shaped by their patterning as well. A poet's ability to stay within self-imposed rules, and yet transcend their limitations, can push ordinary ideas and ordinary speech into an extraordinary poem: restraint frees the imagination, as Picasso puts it. Poetic forms, while a respected inheritance, are never fixed and always invite innovation.

Sonnet

If love together with argument is bothersome in real life, they make good bedfellows in the sonnet. All poets know instinctively, perhaps, that seduction requires persuasion. Of course the sonnet is open to a variety of subjects, but it works best when it doesn't just describe intense feeling but when it reasons as well. Poets are attracted to the power of concentration the sonnet offers. As Edward Hirsch writes: 'The sonnet is a small vessel capable of plunging tremendous depths. It is one of the enabling forms of human inwardness.'[24]

The sonnet is built from fourteen lines arranged as three quatrains and a concluding couplet. Typically, the first quatrain introduces an idea, the second quatrain complicates it, and the third quatrain launches a thematic or imagistic 'turn' known as the volta. The epigrammatic couplet usually resolves the idea or introduces a fresh take on the theme. The contemporary sonnet is recognisable often by merely the presence of fourteen lines, although sometimes the traditional features endure as a ghostly imprint. The Shakespearean sonnet, the most enduring variation in English, uses the following rhyme scheme:

a-b-a-b // c-d-c-d // e-f-e-f // g-g

Villanelle

The villanelle, to borrow André Breton's phrase, 'is a room of marvels'.[25] Or perhaps, given its preoccupation with the repetition of phrases, so characteristic of a mind in grief, it might well be a little house of sorrow. Its power derives from the braiding of two lines that are repeated throughout the poem, always at a small remove, until the fated couplet locks together in an epiphany. It works not on forward movement but on inevitability.

The villanelle is built from nineteen lines, comprising five triplets and a concluding quatrain. Lines 1 and 3 of the opening stanza are repeated alternately in the last lines of each succeeding stanza, coming together as a couplet in the final stanza. In the contemporary villanelle the lines are repeated with delicate shifts of emphasis, so that they may acquire faintly different meanings from different contexts. The repeated lines rhyme, as do the second lines of each stanza. Using capitals for the refrains and lowercase letters for the rhymes:

A1-b-A2 // a-b-A1 // a-b-A2 // a-b-A1 // a-b-A2 // a-b-A1-A2

Sestina

The sestina is all about obsession. Which makes it not only a perfect vessel for its traditional subject, love, but also a spectacular showcase for a mind under pressure. The form creates an intricate constellation of six totemic words that the consumed poet revisits, with varying emphases, across seven successive stanzas. Despite its complexity and its requisites of wit and ingenuity, the sestina has a natural, almost conversational feel that lends itself to narrative.

The sestina is built from thirty-nine lines, comprising six six-line stanzas and a three-line concluding stanza called an envoi. Each of the end words of the first stanza are repeated in a set pattern in five subsequent stanzas, with two per line in the envoi. Using numbers to represent the repeated end-words:

1–2–3–4–5–6 // 6–1–5–2–4–3 // 3–6–4–1–2–5 // 5–3–2–6–1–4 // 4–5–1–3–6–2 // 2–4–6–5–3–1 //+ envoi: 2,5–4,3–6, 1

Haiku

The haiku, the most philosophical of poems, wants to corral the mind, however briefly, in the strict present tense. A strong advocate of nature, the haiku insists on an allusion to the current season: blossoms to indicate spring; mosquitoes for summer; snow for winter and so on. Eschewing the indulgences of metaphor and other comparisons, haiku are built solely from concrete physical detail in the hope that poet and reader will finally 'get it': they will experience a moment of illumination in which the distractions of past and future vanish.

The haiku, in its traditional Japanese form, comprises three lines totalling seventeen syllables. The form cuts into two parts: an imaginative distance separates the sections but each is enriched by the other. In English, the cut appears at the end of the first or second line and is marked by a colon, dash, or ellipsis. Contemporary haiku often dispense with the syllable count, with the proviso that the entire poem not exceed seventeen syllables. Using numbers to represent syllables per line:

5-7-5

Ghazal

The ghazal intoxicates. It is true that love – and its attendants: loss and suffering – is the ghazal's traditional subject, but this is no ordinary love. The ghazal privileges feeling that is truly inspired, whether it be earthly or divine, feeling so deeply felt that there is no story to tell, no need for persuasion, just fervency shaped into couplets. Agha Shahid Ali compared each ghazal couplet to 'a stone from a necklace' that should continue to 'shine in that vivid isolation'.

The Persian ghazal is composed of between five and fifteen thematically autonomous couplets. In the opening couplet, both the first and second lines end with a word or phrase that becomes the refrain in the second lines of subsequent couplets. Illustrating that anonymity is inimical to passion, the poet's name (or its derivative) is built into the final couplet. English writers tend to interpret the conventions of the ghazal idiosyncratically, but many observe some or most of its native characteristics. A five-couplet ghazal using capitals for the refrain:

A-A // b-A // c-A// d-A // e-A

Open form

'Wild form's the only form', Jack Kerouac wrote, 'that holds what I have to say.'[26] Although he was not talking about poetry specifically, Kerouac's idea holds resonance for poets who feel they must, to borrow from William Blake, create their own system or be enslaved by another man's. Open form is the choice of poets who desire the freedom to say whatever they have to say the way it needs to be said. In abandoning the strictures of intricate and inherited patterning, open form is the least ritualistic and, perhaps, the most maverick and secular of forms.

But open form is not a free for all. As T. S. Eliot, playing on the open-form synonym 'free verse', famously remarked: 'No verse is free for the [poet] who wants to do a good job.'[27] Open form retains links, however nebulous, to traditional forms by borrowing, as needed and desired, established patterns and tropes. It largely observes the convention of the poetic line, at least on the page, and makes good use of parallelism and juxtaposition. Many poets retain the use of the sonnet's volta, inserting it three-quarters of the way through the poem (or in the last line). Simon Armitage's poem 'The Shout'[28] provides an example. In the first six tercets, the speaker recalls an experiment he and another schoolboy conducted to see how far the human voice could carry: 'He called from over the park', the poet says, 'I lifted an arm'. The poet then zooms twenty years forward to describe the boy's death in Western Australia by a gunshot wound to his head. The dramatic disclosure provides the energy required to change person and address the boy directly. The poem ends with the epigrammatic volta:

> Boy with the name and face I don't remember,
> you can stop shouting now, I can still hear you.

It is for these opportunities and latitudes that open form has become the dominant form in contemporary poetry.

> **Writing exercise**
>
> Take a poem you admire and distil its formal features to use as a template for your own poem.

The pleasure of ulteriority

Part of what makes poetry interesting is its indirectness. Or, as Robert Frost puts it, the ulteriority of figurative language.[29] Language that departs from its denotative usage does not merely provide a way for us to talk about how we think, reason and imagine: it is also constitutive of our experience. Figurative language, if cultivated and refined, startles and enlivens the mind; although admittedly clarity may suffer from its overuse.

Metaphor is an implicit comparison between two otherwise unlike things. It carries the connotations of one thing (the vehicle) to another thing (the tenor). Whereas Aristotle considered the skilful use of metaphor a sign of genius, Edgar Allan Poe argued for its sparing use due to the 'excess of suggested meaning' – an idea that still holds resonance for many contemporary poets.[30] In Auden's

'Funeral Blues'[31] the metaphorical outpouring of love and dependency is corralled in the penultimate stanza to dazzling effect:

> He was my North, my South, my East and West,
> My working week and my Sunday rest.

Simile, by contrast, is an explicit comparison between two unlike things, usually introduced by a phrase beginning 'like' or 'as'. Because the two compared things are held side by side, not superimposed as in metaphor, similes require less interpretive effort. Similes are particularly effective in building up to metaphor. Pablo Neruda's 'Sonnet XVII'[32] provides an example:

> I love you as the plant that doesn't bloom and carries
> hidden within itself the light of those flowers.

Like anything enduring figurative language is subject to fashion. Personification – the attribution of human qualities to an animal or idea – is waning in popularity these days. It works best for comedic purposes – as in the opening stanza of Jane Hirshfield's 'This Was Once a Love Poem':

> This was once a love poem,
> before its haunches thickened, its breath grew short,
> before it found itself sitting,
> perplexed and a little embarrassed,
> on the fender of a parked car ...[33]

However, irony – the use of words to express the opposite of their literal meaning – remains popular. It drips from the final stanza of Dorothy Parker's 'One Perfect Rose' in which the speaker wonders why no one has ever sent her 'one perfect limousine':

> Ah no, it's always just my luck to get
> One perfect rose.[34]

Writing exercise

1. Write a poem using similes that contrast with the poem's subject. For instance, if writing a love poem use war similes.
2. Write a poem that avoids metaphor until the last two lines.

Motifs and movements

While motifs in poetry are unlimited in subject and number, a concentrated view might see contemporary poetry revolving around just three: nature, the individual and language. With roots in the idealised pastoral poetry of the ancient Greeks, poetry about nature has long been a vital part of the literary tradition. In England, the eclogue took hold in the sixteenth century: nature was depicted as pleasant and serene, and the rural life free from the corruption of civilisation. Later, in the hands of the Romantics, nature poetry became a form of meditation, and poets went to lengths to describe natural phenomena with accuracy. Wordsworth saw nature as a positive force, the source of all human joy, faith and goodness, while Shelley, in contrast, lamented that nature could destroy as easily as it creates. Perhaps because nature appears increasingly the underdog in a contest against civilisation, contemporary poets have tended to see and depict nature in a positive light. Much like Chinese depictions of the human as infinitesimal against the expansive landscape, nature poets often try to move the human – and the first-person pronoun – to the margins of importance. Nevertheless the poem remains a human construct, and even a covert speaker can never fully vanish: rather they might be seen to crouch, as if in long grass, careful not to disturb the scene.

While lyric poets throughout the ages have written as individual voices, it was of course the Romantics – their influence once again asserting itself – who elevated the status of the individual to its zenith. The belief that what is special in a human is to be valued over what is representative led to the Romantic poet's frequent delight in self-analysis. But what they found was not always pretty. By the late nineteenth century the *poète maudit*, replete with a life of drugs, insanity and violence, anguished at society's outskirts. No wonder, then, that the Confessional movement surfaced in the mid to late twentieth century. Characterised by intimate, sometimes painful subject matter, an emphasis on the self, and the artifice of honesty, so-called confessional poems, for all their popularity, are not infrequently maligned as mawkish and overly personal. But Galway Kinnell argues convincingly for the power of introspection in poems: 'when you go deep enough within yourself, deeper than the level of personality, you are suddenly outside yourself, everywhere'.[35]

Finally, and perhaps foremost, poetry at all times has been about language. One manifestation of this has been the development of the vernacular tradition. Dante on the continent, as Chaucer in England, were among the first to break the standard of publishing only in Latin, thereby opening their poetry to a wider audience. It became a matter of style for Wordsworth who consciously composed his poems, which he calls 'experiments' in the Preface to the *Lyrical Ballads*,[36] in conversational tones and accessible vocabulary. The Modernists in their own way also aspired to reform language – Eliot's dictum to 'purify the dialect of the tribe'[37] – through experiments in aesthetic innovation. Taking language reform to the extreme, contemporary Language poets make mandatory the complete emphasis on the language of the poem, with the invigorating if alienating aim of divorcing language from its referents so that the word might be experienced as an object unto itself. In the end, poets, whatever else they may be, are the caretakers of language, Auden concluded late in life, with only one political duty: 'to love the Word and defend it against its enemies'.[38]

Binding it all together: a study in process

Legend says that foot-binding began in tenth-century China when a prince became infatuated with his concubine's tiny feet. She wore them tightly bound in bandages so she could toe-dance on a lotus-shaped platform, which gave rise to the metaphor of high praise: 'lily feet'. A tiny foot – the ideal being only three inches long – in time became the mark of a wealthy and well-born woman.

I'm not sure where it came from – perhaps a childhood image of Cinderella's dainty and diminutive foot – but prior to writing a poem on the subject I had the mistaken and indeed absurd idea that the lily foot was maintained in perfect miniature through the growth-inhibiting effect of constrictive bandaging. Only in researching my poem, which I entitled 'The Chinese Foot',[39] did I learn that foot-binding was in fact the devastatingly painful art of crushing almost every bone in a young girl's foot. The deformed foot, as x-rays have revealed, is shortened only because it is permanently folded in half.

The first five lines of 'The Chinese Foot' describe the process in a deliberately unembellished tone. I gambled that an objective description of the binding would be more effective than one that contrived to manipulate through sensationalist language:

> The bandage wraps figure eights
> around her heel, across the crest
> of her foot and tightly over her toes
> (which are black and pressed
> to her sole) so that her arch breaks

I wanted the poem itself to feel tightly bound, almost claustrophobic, with the sentences wrapping around the line breaks like bandages. This was not a subject, I thought, that would benefit from the airiness of white space, so I decided early on that it would be confined to a single stanza. Such a serpentine opening sentence needed its line endings accentuated with a light and irregular touch of end-rhyme: 'crest' and 'pressed', for example, 'eights' and 'breaks'. I had in mind a seven-syllable line but held to this ideal only loosely, varying the count where necessary to align the poem visually or to emphasise particular words through enjambment: 'breaks', I thought, was particularly fortuitous in falling at the end of the line.

My initial thought was that I would follow the line of the bandage to frame the lily foot. It would be telling if the bandage were the subject of the sentence, not the woman. But with the arrival of the word 'break' a strange thing happened. Although I was repulsed by the mutilated and rotting foot I was constructing, an unexpected adverb appeared to describe the precise way in which the woman's arch breaks. I could hear the bones in her foot fracture with each syllable: 'magnificently'. As I wrote it down I was suddenly outside of myself and inside the mind of someone else. The long opening sentence concluded with the poem's first of only two similes, which to my surprise was one of venerated beauty:

> . . . so that her arch breaks
> magnificently with the steep pitch
> of a temple.

The perspective was not mine, yet neither was it the woman's. I could feel the erotic charge building in the poem. Her husband was in the room, and the woman was proffering her foot: 'She lets her husband / touch it'.

The poem relies heavily on the reader's presumed knowledge: the title and the bandage are the only clues to its subject. I was determined that 'foot-binding' not appear anywhere in the poem, although I do use 'lily foot' but without defining it. It was not lost on me, however, that my oblique approach risked a diminishing of the reader's attention. I needed to get across the freakily small dimensions of the woman's foot, but I was reluctant to be discursive. Sitting at my writing desk, I put down my pen and used my thumb to measure three inches along the fist of my other hand. My head swayed in disbelief. I watched then as the husband used the same measure along his wife's foot. But he was more pleased with himself than amazed. He assessed his wife's foot the way a satisfied owner of a new Porsche might buff a sparkling side mirror with his sleeve. The poem continues:

> He uses the measure
> of his thumb-tip-to-first-knuckle
> along her lily foot and counts one,
> two, three and smiles.

The image that follows arose from the uncovering of a particularly gruesome fact: the bound foot was perpetually awash in blood, rotting flesh, pus and sweat. Not uncommonly girls died from infection. But when the bandages were unwrapped to bathe the foot, the foul fluids were collected in a vial and savoured as an intoxicating male aphrodisiac. With this in mind, I wrote:

He brings it
to his lips, inhales, and thanks
the ancestors, who also smile
and wish him many sons.

These lines might drip with patriarchal Confucianism, but from the husband's perspective, at least, they are not ironic. He is in love, and he worships his wife at the temple of her broken foot. I allowed these lines, steeped in reverie and falling right at the heart of the poem, to settle into the soothing rhythms of iambs. Elsewhere I ruthlessly broke iambic feet to compose a more violent music. The first line of the poem, for instance, was initially written in iambic tetrameter – 'The **ban-** | dage **wraps** | a **fig-** | ure **eight**' – but I excised the indefinite article to unsettle the iambic cadence. In selecting vocabulary, I favoured spondees: 'arch breaks', 'steep pitch', 'silk shoes', and 'white cloud'. Sometimes I managed three consecutive stressed syllables: 'courtyard like', 'long braid blue', and of course 'one, two, three'. But here it seemed right to echo the husband's heartbeat in language, while the dark perfume of his wife's foot transported him into deep memory the way only the sense of smell can. The poem continues:

He has
loved her since first he saw her,
swaying in the courtyard like
a little tree, her long braid blue
under the moon, her lily feet
dressed in green apple silk shoes.

The imagery, as seen through the eyes of the husband, is evocative of a Chinese landscape painting. Excepting the moon, each image – the temple, the little tree, green apples – is, by design, figurative rather than concrete. But as such, each image is ultimately illusory, and I took pleasure in watching each one vanish under my close inspection. I wanted the beauty that the husband sees in his wife's maimed feet – likewise in the prison of her immobility – to be shown up for the construction it is. None of it is natural, nor yet real: he has been seduced by his own mind.

But natural or not, one thing was clear: the husband's desire had taken my poem by siege. The shift to the past tense of memory provided the volta needed to energise the poem towards conclusion, but it had arrived with gusto ahead of the classic three-quarters placement I would have preferred. My poem, like the wife's foot, was in jeopardy of breaking in two. I knew I had to get out fast, but I also needed to maintain unity. Scanning the poem I noticed that following the first two sentences – which began 'The bandage' and 'She lets', respectively – a light pattern of anaphora had developed.

Unconsciously, or even by chance, three successive sentences opened with the masculine subject pronoun: 'He uses'; 'He brings'; 'He has'. I knew then that a variation of this repetition could hold the poem together while it signed off. And what better way, I thought, to begin the final sentence in a poem about foot-binding than with the possessive masculine pronoun. In contrast to the serpentine opening image, I bookended the final image with the end-stopped lines to accord it formality and a sense of closure:

> His mouth fell open at the sight,
> but he was careful when he
> exhaled not to blow her over
> with the white cloud of his breath.

NOTES

1. Edward Hirsch, *How to Read a Poem: And Fall in Love with Poetry* (Boston: Mariner Books, 2000), p. 299.
2. Władysław Tatarkiewicz, 'The Concept of Poetry', *Dialectics and Humanism*, 1 (2) (1975), p. 13.
3. Mabel Loomis Todd (ed.), *Letters of Emily Dickinson* (Mineola, NY: Dover, 2003), p. 265.
4. Les Murray, *A Working Forest: Selected Prose* (Potts Point, NSW: Duffy & Snellgrove, 1997), p. 373.
5. Victoria R. Arana, *W. H. Auden's Poetry: Mythos, Theory and Practice* (New York: Cambria Press, 2009), p. 156.
6. James Logenbach, *The Art of the Poetic Line* (Minneapolis: Graywolf Press, 2008), p. xi.
7. A. Walton Litz and Christopher MacGowan (eds.), *The Collected Poems of William Carlos Williams*, vol. 1: *1909–1939* (New York: New Directions, 1991), p. 224.
8. Michael Dransfield, *Streets of the Long Voyage* (St Lucia: University of Queensland Press, 1970), p. 26.
9. Denise Levertov, 'On the Function of the Line', *Chicago Review*, 30 (3) (1979), p. 30.
10. Wisława Szymborska, *Poems New and Collected: 1957–1997*, trans. Stanisław Baranczak and Clare Cavanagh (Boston: Mariner Books, 2000), p. 142.
11. Sharon Olds, *The Gold Cell* (New York: Knopf, 1987), p. 23.
12. Robert Hass, *Praise* (New York: Ecco, 1990), p. 4.
13. Frederick Turner and Ernst Pöppel, 'The Neural Lyre: Poetic Metre, the Brain, and Time', *Poetry*, 142 (5) (1983), pp. 277–307, pp. 296–7.
14. Allen Ginsberg, *Howl and Other Poems* (San Francisco: City Lights, 2001), p. 9.
15. Charles Olson, *Projective Verse* (New York: Totem Press, 1959), p. 3.
16. Ezra Pound, *ABC of Reading* (New York: New Directions, 2010), p. 61.
17. James McCauley, *Collected Poems: 1936–1970* (Melbourne: Angus & Robertson, 1971), p. 6.

18. Emily Dickinson, *The Complete Poems* (New York: Back Bay Books, 1976), p. 712.
19. Robert Adamson, *The Golden Bird: New and Selected Poems* (Melbourne: Black Inc., 2008), p. 242.
20. George Gordon Byron, *Don Juan* (New York: Penguin, 2010), p. 51.
21. Elizabeth Bishop, *The Complete Poems 1927–1979* (London: Hogarth Press, 1983), p. 65.
22. T. S. Eliot, *Collected Poems, 1909–1962* (San Diego: Harcourt, 1991), p. 66.
23. Robert Lowell, *Selected Poems* (New York: Farrar, Straus & Giroux, 1977), p. 132.
24. Hirsch, *How to Read a Poem*, p. 309.
25. Ibid., p. 32.
26. Jack Kerouac, *Selected Letters*, vol. 1: *1940–1956* (New York: Penguin, 1996), p. 371.
27. T. S. Eliot, 'The Music of Poetry', in *On Poetry and Poets* (London: Faber, 1957), pp. 26–38, p. 37.
28. Simon Armitage, *The Shout: Selected Poems* (Boston: Houghton Mifflin Harcourt, 2005), p. 1.
29. Robert Frost, 'The Constant Symbol', *Atlantic Monthly*, 170 (8) (October 1946), p. 50.
30. Edgar Allan Poe, 'The Philosophy of Composition', in David H. Richter (ed.), *The Critical Tradition: Classic Texts and Contemporary Trends* (New York: St Martin's, 1989), pp. 371–8, p. 377.
31. W. H. Auden and Edward Mendelson, *Selected Poems* (New York: Vintage International, 2007), p. 48.
32. Pablo Neruda, *100 Love Sonnets: Cien Sonetos de Amor*, trans. Stephen Tapscott (Austin: University of Texas Press, 1986), p. 39.
33. Jane Hirshfield, *Given Sugar, Given Salt: Poems* (New York: Harper, 2002), p. 16.
34. Dorothy Parker, *Complete Poems* (New York: Penguin, 2010), p. 62.
35. Galway Kinnell, *Walking Down the Stairs: Selections from Interviews* (Ann Arbor: University of Michigan Press, 1978), p. 6.
36. William Wordsworth, *Lyrical Ballads* (New York: Routledge, 2005), p. 49.
37. Eliot, *Collected Poems, 1909–1962*, p. 204.
38. Quoted in Lewis P. Simpson, *The Man of Letters in New England and the South* (Baton Rouge: Louisiana State University Press, 1973), p. 229.
39. Bronwyn Lea, *Flight Animals* (St Lucia: University of Queensland Press, 2001), p. 7.

7

KÁRI GÍSLASON

Travel writing

Introduction

This chapter introduces techniques that are used in travel writing to create a strong sense of place and a meaningful, engaging narrative of a journey. I raise and briefly define well-established terms of modern rhetoric – that is, exposition, description, narration – with the aim of showing that a distinctive and enduring feature of travel writing lies in the ways it mixes these modes of writing. For example, Clive James, who has built a brilliant career working across genres (from poetry to novels to reviews and essays), has commented that it was in travel writing that he was able to bring his various skills as a writer together.[1] He was able to do so, I think, because the best travel writing is a combination of forms – as Rory Stewart has pointed out, the staple of travel books today is 'the blend of reported speech, historical digressions, landscape portraiture, theorizing and . . . comedy', what he sees as a kind of patchwork 'burlesque'.[2] As in theatrical burlesques, travel writing is often an extravaganza of parody and mixed forms, and so comes with a playfulness that offers great freedom to writers.

However, like all blends, the key lies as much in finding a strong unifying element as it does in the choice of the component parts. Towards the end of the chapter, I will suggest that humour and analysis offer the travel writer ways of effectively joining the different styles they use, and of establishing an engaged, humanist attitude to the people and places they encounter, even if the journey has been a difficult one. Finally, you will find writing exercises drawn from the key techniques that I suggest.

Difficult journeys are best

The acclaimed travel writer Paul Theroux once wrote that it is the worst trips that make the best reading, and that comfortable travel 'becomes in the telling little more than chatting'.[3] It is a maxim that many travel writers have understood, and so it is not uncommon to see travel writing focus on, and perhaps even exaggerate, the perilous or difficult moments of a journey. Many travel writers actively seek out danger and difficulty:

> I had grown up dreaming of big-game shooting and exploration, and was determined, now that I was back in Africa, to get away into the wilds. I had brought a rifle out with me. One day, standing on the Legation steps during a lull in the [Ethiopian] coronation festivities, I asked Colonel Cheesman, the well-known explorer, if there was anywhere left in Abyssinia to explore.[4]

This is from Wilfred Thesiger's classic, *Arabian Sands*. Clearly, for him, travel is about exploration, and the function of the travel book is to witness a journey that readers would find difficult to make themselves. He describes something we can't possibly have seen, and informs us about a world that is hidden in 'the wilds'. Unifying his account is the desire for adventure, and a seeming hope for the worst trip the writer has ever had.

Thesiger is almost giving us an apology or justification for the aims and directions of his trip, a feature that has its roots in the eighteenth and nineteenth centuries, when travel writers often included a preface that explained their book's contribution to knowledge. At the heart of these explanations was a concept of the travel book as expository – it was providing information to governments, traders, armies and future travellers. While the aim of travel has since changed, and although we may no longer think of travel books as semi-official documents, we nevertheless still read them in order to learn about the world around us. That is, if the travel writer is motivated by a passion to explore, such as will get them through the difficulties of travel, then the reader will be, too.

The Road to Oxiana by Robert Byron is a famous example of what we could call a 'no-excuses' approach to including the reader: he expects *us* to keep up with him, and not necessarily the other way around. Byron travelled to Afghanistan in 1933 in search of the origins of Islamic architecture, and he regularly interrupts his travel narrative with detailed descriptions of buildings, and lengthy expositions on the history of Islamic architecture more generally. He is on a difficult and uncomfortable journey through a remote and sometimes dangerous part of the world. Behind the task lies great passion, which motivates the reader to join in on what might otherwise feel like a personal obsession.

> While the cadent sun throws lurid copper streaks across the sand-blown sky, all the birds in Persia have gathered for a last chorus. Slowly, the darkness brings silence, and they settle themselves to sleep with diminishing fluttering, as of a child arranging its bedclothes. And then another note begins, a hot metallic blue note, timidly at first, gaining courage, throbbing without cease, until, as if the second violins had crept into action, it becomes two notes, now this, now that, and is answered from the other side of the pool by a third. Mahun is famous for its nightingales. But for

> my part I celebrate the frogs. I am out in the court now, in the blackness beneath the trees. Suddenly the sky clears, and the moon is reflected three times, once on the dome and twice on the minarets. In sympathy, a circle of amber light breaks from the balcony over the entrance, and a pilgrim begins to chant.[5]

As we see here, Byron is a rich stylist, and this also helps us to join in. His description is based on a number of alternations, each one tracing the border between day and night, and between his perception of and involvement in the world. It becomes dark, there are shadows, and then the moon appears and an 'amber light breaks from the balcony'; the birds settle, but are replaced by frogs, and then by religious chanting; to begin with, the narrator is somehow to the side of the scene, but then is 'out in the court' to see the light on the buildings, which are his reason for travel. The overall effect is a demonstration of passion through heightened sensitivity. The result is that we want to understand not only the life behind the emotional intensity, but the details of the obsession, as well.

Alongside the richness of Byron's descriptive writing comes a seductive combination of forms. *The Road to Oxiana* quite explicitly reproduces the quality of a travel diary, interweaving a central narrative with scenes of dialogue, summaries of Byron's reading and intense observations of landscape: this is the blend that I referred to above. As in a travel diary – or perhaps more commonly today, a blog – the order of the content is determined by a wide range of experiences, internal and private, as well as external and public. As a result, the account of the journey often seems more like a patchwork than a unified story. The interesting thing about travel writing is that for the reader this mixed modality can be a source of great pleasure, rather than frustration, as it might be in forms with a more definite sense of dramatic unity.

There is, of course, a catch. The journey itself – the core content – must, as in *The Road to Oxiana*, make it all worthwhile; and so the first question for a travel writer remains whether the journey is, at some level, difficult enough. What are you challenging yourself to do that makes it worthwhile for the reader to join you?

- A difficult destination. Here, it is the fact of getting somewhere and/or the mode of transport that poses the difficulty. Are you the first person to write about this journey? If you are following in someone else's footsteps, is there nevertheless an area or aspect that remains unexplored? Examples include Jason Elliot's *An Unexpected Light*[6] and Rory Stewart's *The Places in Between*,[7] both about trips in Afghanistan.
- Settling in. You are attempting to live in a new place for an extended time, and the process of adaptation is in some ways a fraught one, even if it is based on a love affair with the place. Work of this kind includes Sarah

Turnbull's *Almost French*[8] and Bill Bryson's *Notes from a Small Island*,[9] which I discuss in more detail at the end of this chapter.

- A complex question or situation. The trip requires you to confront demanding questions about yourself, culture or society, even if the logistics of the travel are quite straightforward. This is an important aspect of my own writing about the journeys I have made to my birthplace Reykjavík, in which I have grappled with the complicated process of returning home after a long while away.[10] Other examples include *The Snow Geese*[11] by William Fiennes (about illness and homecoming), *An Omelette and a Glass of Wine*[12] by Elizabeth David (about food and cultural influence), or *Blue Highways*[13] by William Least Heat-Moon (about back roads, slow travel and personal recovery).

Later, I will suggest three subgenres of travel writing that relate to the type of challenges I have listed here (see below, 'Finding a thread'). Those familiar with the works I've cited above will realise that the best travel books often combine two or all three of these writing challenges, and we will see that the subgenres of travel are often mixed as well. First, though, we should turn to the common elements of travel writing.

Never, 'just the facts'

If we were to think of exposition as a currency, we would say that its base unit is the *fact*. While many types of writing struggle with how best to incorporate facts – science fiction, with its imagined worlds, is perhaps the most obvious example – readers of travel writing have generally been fairly relaxed about the 'info dump'. After all, if one is interested enough in a place to buy a book about it, it is always worthwhile getting the facts one needs better to understand the place: events in a travel story don't occur in isolation of their social context, and sometimes that context needs simply to be summarised clearly.

The most exposition-heavy forms of travel writing are also probably the most visible, often populating large sections of our bookshops. Travel guides such as those produced by Lonely Planet are in the main functional texts intended to ease the traveller's mind and guide them through the attractions they will meet. They tend not to include much about the reviewer's own journey, and in fact are often multi-authored and written over the course of many trips. As in most instructional literature, the perceived importance of the information determines its order and organisation – rather than, say, anything that the reviewers have learned about a place. As a result, few of us would buy a guidebook unless we were intending to visit the place it covers, and it is unusual to keep them once the information they store has begun to date.

This is different from travel stories, which often retain their importance after the practical information in them has become obsolete. While it's true that readers don't want to be lectured by a travel book, there are methods for making your use of exposition more than a mere accompaniment to the main thread.

- As often as possible, tie exposition to a specific point in the journey. If, for example, there is a famous poem you want to discuss, do so when you are approaching the place in which it was written or is set. Relate the content of the poem to your impressions of the place, and, if the journey goes well, how reaching the place has helped you to reach into the poem.
- Multitask. Use facts to convey not only information but theme. That is, how do the facts enrich our sense of the difficulty in your journey?
- Retain local flavour. If you are explaining a religious custom, use the specific terms that the culture uses. This will give your writing credibility, and allow you to use exposition as a vehicle for mood.
- Accentuate the human element. When possible, relate a historical event from an individual's point of view. This can mean interviewing those who remember or were affected by the events; reading accounts written at the time; or interviewing experts who you can place in an expository paragraph as characters in their own right.

In his *Nine Lives*, William Dalrymple uses a conversation to inform the reader about oral traditions in India:

> I found the old lady sitting on a cane chair on the veranda of an inner courtyard. The rani was a poised and intelligent octogenarian whose fine bones were obscured by thick librarian's glasses ... She told me that she had been born into the palace Deogarh, from which her father had ruled his huge semi-desert principality. The purdah system – the seclusion of women – still operated then as much for aristocratic Hindu women as for Muslim ones, but in 1957 the rani had shocked her family by emerging from the *zenana* (women's quarters) and standing for the Rajasthan Assembly.
>
> 'The area where the story of Dev Narayan was set was in my father's principality and in my own constituency,' she said. It was during her time in the assembly that she became interested in the epic, which she feared was under threat from television and the cinema.[14]

Notice how the interviewee's concerns about changes in oral culture are harnessed to the narrator's travel experiences, and how it is the interviewee's life that becomes the departure point for what Dalrymple sees as necessary exposition about the epic in which he is interested. Rather than the exposition hanging over the narrative, it is anchored to two specific moments (the conversation now, and the interviewee's past) and then integrated into the overarching shape of the journey, which in the case of this book is Dalrymple's search for spiritual life in modern India.

The poet W. H. Auden, who twice visited Iceland and who, like Dalrymple in India, felt a strong spiritual connection when there, presents some of his information in list form – across nonfiction genres one of the most common methods of exposition. Yet even a list, if well handled, can work surprisingly well in travel writing, perhaps because they so often appear in our actual travel documents (place names, itineraries, foods, things to buy and do before the journey begins, and so on). In Auden's list are collected some of the more unusual remarks made by earlier travellers to Iceland, including these:

> *The Icelanders are human*
> 'They are not so robust and hardy that nothing can hurt them; for they are human beings and experience the sensations common to mankind.' – Horrebow[15]
>
> *Concerning their kissing*
> 'I have sometimes fancied, when they took their faces apart, that I could hear a slight clicking sound; but this might be imagination.' – Howell[16]
>
> *First sight of Iceland*
> 'We were delighted at seeing some new faces, in spite of their nastiness and stench; and their grotesque appearance afforded us much amusement.' – Hooker[17]

As we will see later, humour can be used to unify the different writing styles in travel writing, and establish an empathy that exists between the traveller and the people he/she meets. Auden's use of it here helps to establish what his contribution to knowledge will be: he won't be reproducing the rather scathing accounts of Iceland written before him. And the first step will be to reproduce the worst (and funniest) of them. The end result is that Auden gets to use his background reading, inform us and entertain all at once.

Both Dalrymple and Auden know and trust their readers, in Auden's case to see that he will have a different response to Iceland, and in Dalrymple's to share his desire to properly contextualise the nature of his search. And, though writing many years apart, they both also trust that the free form of the travel book can nevertheless carry theme, something we will also see in descriptive writing.

Creating space

If the core unit of exposition is the fact, then in descriptive writing it is *space*. Naturally, travel writers are concerned with creating a feeling for a place and a strong, physical impression of it, and so a distinctive and evocative descriptive style is seen as a key reflection of your level of engagement with an area.

For example, Clive James gives his descriptive writing individuality through a rich turn of phrase and an analytic element that helps his descriptive writing develop momentum. Here is a passage from his first return visit to his hometown of Sydney in 1976:

> The late Kenneth Slessor, in his prose as much as in his poetry, probably came nearest to evoking the sheer pulchritude of Sydney harbour. But finally the place is too multifarious to be captured by the pen. Sydney is like Venice without the architecture, but with more of the sea: the merchant ships sail right into town. In Venice you never see big ships – they are all over at Mestre, the industrial sector. In Sydney big ships loom at the ends of city streets. They are parked all over the place, tied up to the countless wharves in the scores of inlets ('You could hide a thousand ships of the line in here,' a British admiral observed long ago) or just moored to a buoy in mid-harbour, riding high. At the International Terminal at Circular Quay, the liners in which my generation of the self-exiled left for Europe still tie up: from the Harbour Bridge you can look down at the farewell parties raging on their decks.[18]

Many well-known features of James's nonfiction are present. His reference to cultural figures offers him a way into an analytical paradigm that suggests theme: the Australian poet Slessor, 'a British admiral', and Venice give the descriptions the quality of an argument, and through this a sense of movement. Venice, of course, is used for contrast, but also for the introduction of James's irony: Sydney is 'Venice without the architecture' with ships 'parked all over the place', the latter the kind of off-key metaphor that marks the James style. He is present ('my generation of the self-exiled') but not really physically: presence is implied rather than shown, another sign that James's analytical rather than physical point of view will dominate.

Travel writing requires the full arsenal of descriptive techniques – metaphor and simile, sensory language, imagery and specificity.

- If possible, reflect movement and change: how, for example, is the landscape altering as the journey goes on? Does your descriptive writing highlight an aspect of the people and culture that is specific to where you are in the journey, or your understanding of the place at that moment? Colin Thubron's *The Lost Heart of Asia*[19] manages this superbly.
- Relate your physical point of view to the *type* of travelling you are doing. This will give your descriptive writing a chance to carry theme, and allow the point of your journey to emerge more organically out of the places you encounter. Is theme best served by an intimate, close point of view, or is it important to get to the high ground and establish panoramas? Look at D. H. Lawrence's *Sketches of Etruscan Places*[20] for his shifts in point of view.
- Use research in your description as much as you do in exposition. Particularly in the case of travel writing, where you will be discovering

> new environments, descriptive writing relies on precise, accurate terms. For example, populating 'a field of flowers' with three or four local names for the species will not only clarify the image but also establish for the viewer the nature of your gaze.

Almost a decade after Clive James returned home, Jan Morris fell in love with Sydney for the first time. Here is part of her attempt at catching the visual impact of the harbour:

> Yet it is one of the most beautiful cities in the world, specifically because it is Australian. That winding, nooky, islanded, bosky harbor thrillingly reminds one always that Sydney stands on the shore of an island totally unlike anywhere else on earth. The pale pure light of the Sydney winter seems to come straight from the bergs and ice mountains of Antarctica. The foliage of Sydney's parks and gardens is queerly drooped and tangled, apparently antediluvian fig trees overshadow suburban streets, and the perpetual passing of the ships through the very heart of the city gives everything a tingling sense of remoteness. The water goes down the plug-hole the other way in Australia, and it really is possible to imagine, if you are a fancifully-minded visitor from the other hemisphere, that this metropolis is clinging upside-down to the bottom of the earth, so subtly antipodean, or perhaps marsupial, is the nature of the scene.[21]

You can almost feel Morris solving an analytic problem here: how do you define Sydney if, in fact, your idea of Sydney is simply that it is very Australian? The answer, it seems, is to enjoy the circularity of that definition – Australianness defines Sydney and Sydney defines Australia. As such, specific and quite dense descriptors of the visual experience – 'winding, nooky, islanded, bosky', 'pale pure light', 'queerly drooped and tangled' – merge with Australian specialties like 'marsupial', 'antipodean', 'remoteness' and 'upside-down' to produce a passage of writing in which 'a fancifully-minded visitor from the other hemisphere' is seen to be overwhelmed.

If we contrast the James and Morris extracts with Bill Bryson's picture of Sydney, we will see more clearly how subtly James and Morris include themselves, and how the distinctiveness of the Bryson approach, which has earned him enormous success as a travel writer, is largely about how he places himself as narrator.

> Life cannot offer many places finer to stand at eight thirty on a summery weekday morning than Circular Quay in Sydney. To begin with, it presents one of the world's great views. To the right, almost painfully brilliant in the sunshine, stands the famous Opera House with its jaunty, severely angular roof. To the left, the stupendous and noble Harbour Bridge. Across the water, shiny and beckoning, is Luna Park, a Coney Island-style amusement park with a maniacally grinning head for an entrance. Before you the spangly water is crowded with the harbour's plump and old-fashioned ferries, looking for all the world as if

> they have been plucked from the pages of a 1940s children's book with a title like *Thomas the Tugboat*, disgorging streams of tanned and lightly dressed office workers to fill the glass and concrete towers that loom behind.[22]

Bryson's leisurely phrasing – 'to begin with', 'life cannot offer many', 'you can understand' – moves him to centre stage, as does his steady, central point of view – 'to the left', 'to the right', 'before you'. Sydney Harbour is expanding before him, not so much in response to an idea about what Sydney stands for, but simply in response to his particular way of seeing the world. Thus, 'as if they have been plucked', 'jaunty', 'spangly', and 'disgorging' give us as much a sense of Bryson as of Sydney, and reflect the role of narrator in relating a sense of place.

Stories and journeys

Here is the opening to Rory Stewart's *The Places in Between*:

> I watched two men enter the lobby of the Hotel Mowafaq.
>
> Most Afghans seemed to glide up the center of the lobby staircase with their shawls trailing behind them like Venetian cloaks. But these men wore Western jackets, walked quietly, and stayed close to the banister. I felt a hand on my shoulder. It was the hotel manager.
>
> 'Follow them.' He had never spoken to me before.
>
> 'I'm sorry, no,' I said. 'I am busy.'
>
> 'Now. They are from the government.'
>
> I followed him to a room on a floor I didn't know existed and he told me to take off my shoes and enter alone in my socks. The two men were seated on a heavy blackwood sofa, beside an aluminum spitoon. They were still wearing their shoes. I smiled. They did not. The lace curtains were drawn and there was no electricity in the city; the room was dark.[23]

As we see here, narrative techniques used in memoir and novels can be used in travel writing as well. In this passage, Stewart is adapting the action novel in order to create a sinister feeling of suspense: there are mysterious commands from shadowy figures; there is short, sharp dialogue; there is the presence of a threat from an unclear source.

As in other forms of narrative, the core unit of narrative in travel writing is *time*: the representation of the journey across a temporal axis that is different from the 'real' time it takes to make a journey. Consider, for example, the opening of chapter 2 of Bruce Chatwin's *The Songlines*:

> In my childhood I never heard the word 'Australia' without calling to mind the fumes of the eucalyptus inhaler and an incessant red country populated by sheep.
>
> My father loved to tell, and we to hear, the story of the Australian sheep-millionaire who strolled into a Rolls-Royce showroom in London; scorned all

> the smaller models; chose an enormous limousine with a plate-glass panel between the chauffeur and passengers, and added, cockily, as he counted out the cash, 'That'll stop the sheep from breathing down my neck.'
>
> I also knew, from my great-aunt Ruth, that Australia was the country of the Upside-downers. A hole, bored straight through the earth from England, would burst out under their feet.
>
> 'Why don't they fall off?' I asked.
>
> 'Gravity,' she whispered.[24]

Through his use of narrative, Chatwin begins his journey to Australia during childhood. And through what feels like the semi-mythical perspective of a child, the book begins with the inner world of imagination, as much as with Chatwin's contact with the real place. As perhaps only narrative has the capacity to do, the anecdote very quickly establishes a relationship between reader and author. From the very beginning of the book, Chatwin has established a point of view that charms. There are a number of other narrative devices that do the same.

- By stating what you hope to achieve from your travels, you establish a narrative arc for the work as a whole. The reader has the opportunity to become a part of your search, and this creates empathy.
- What sort of traveller are you? A discoverer, a hero? Or is your self-characterisation more along the lines of a mock epic? Deciding this early will help the reader understand the type of narrative you have undertaken. Michael Palin's everyman approach, which is perhaps more immediate on television than in his writing, is an example here.
- Who do you meet? Recall that many narrative forms are based around a central character's interaction with others. Can you incorporate other characters' points of view to distinguish your own and add another element to the story?

One of the most popular forms of travel writing is the travel memoir, which relies almost exclusively on narrative as a way of representing experiences abroad. Books like Gerald Durrell's *My Family and Other Animals* (1956),[25] Peter Mayle's *A Year in Provence* (1989)[26] and Frances Mayes's *Under the Tuscan Sun* (1996)[27] have been adapted to film or television, an adaptation that is made easier because of the dominance of narrative in these books.

Finding a thread

The way you combine the writing styles I have discussed will reflect your aims as a traveller, and help position your writing within a subgenre of travel writing, from the narrative-heavy approach of the travel memoir to more descriptive forms such as the essay. Regardless of the subgenre you choose, it is important to be sure of what, above and beyond the place itself, unites the travel story.

- The *travelogue* format reproduces the author's own travel journal almost in its entirety. In this case, the formal structure of days passed and miles covered creates a sense of unity in the writing. This form is best suited to journeys that are in some sense extraordinary in their own right, or to accounts that are intensely personal. Lawrence Durrell's *Prospero's Cell*,[28] which is worth reading alongside his brother Gerald's account of life on Corfu, is structured in this diary form.
- The travel essay often replaces the difficulty of the physical travel experience with a complex analytical task. For example, getting to Naples might not be difficult, but understanding the mix of cultural influences there may take a lifetime. The essay tends to privilege exposition and description, because these carry argument more efficiently than narrative. In this case, the account is unified by your question or set of questions about a place. Julian Barnes's *Something to Declare*,[29] a collection of essays about France, often includes travel episodes that serve the overall, analytical purpose of the collection.
- Comedy. This has long been a part of travel writing – one of the most famous travel books of all time, after all, is *Gulliver's Travels*,[30] a fictional parody of the tall tales that had preceded it, and which are no less a part of the travel writing scene today. Humour can hold an otherwise disparate set of experiences and concerns together.

Earlier, I looked at Bill Bryson's description of Sydney Harbour, and, before I turn to travel writing exercises, I'd like to look at two passages from his English book, *Notes from a Small Island*.[31] Bryson is very much a *wit*: his humour lies in pointing out the ridiculousness of society, and importantly he includes himself in that critique. But for Bryson the travel writer, humour also functions as a holding agent for his very wide-ranging concerns.

Bryson is a collector of information, and packs his books with historical and social descriptions. There is usually also a strong narrative element in his work. Unifying these aspects of his writing is a silliness that both charms the reader and connects Bryson, his interests, and his engagement with place. And that, ultimately, is the function of any unifying device in travel writing: it forms the necessary insight into why you travel and how you experience travelling.

> There are certain idiosyncratic notions that you quietly come to accept when you live for a long time in Britain. One is that British summers used to be longer and sunnier. Another is that the England football team shouldn't have any trouble with Norway. A third is the idea that Britain is a big place. This last is easily the most intractable.

> If you mention in the pub that you intend to drive from, say, Surrey to Cornwall, a distance that most Americans would happily go to get a taco, your companions will puff their cheeks, look knowingly at each other, and blow out air as if to say, 'Well, now *that's* a bit of a tall order,' and then they'll launch into a lively and protracted discussion of whether it's better to take the A30 to Stockbridge and then the A303 to Ilchester or the A361 to Glastonbury via Shepton Mallet.[32]

Despite the sharp wit, Bryson's *tone*, or the attitude of the narrator to the subject material, is rather loving. He is trying to understand the British because he loves them, and if he finds them a little insane, it's an insanity he clearly hasn't tired of. His bemusement is Gulliver's, but his attitude remains self-aware and ironic in something more like the Clive James approach that we saw earlier. If there is a superiority to the writing, it is matched by what Thomas Hobbes once called the superiority to 'the self formerly': Bryson knows that he, too, is capable of being mocked. Here he is walking us along to a British Ordnance Survey map:

> In my idle perusal, I noticed that a mile or so to the west there stood a historic obelisk. Wondering why anyone would erect a monument in such a remote and challenging spot, I struck off along the crest of the hill to have a look. It was the longest mile I can remember walking. I passed through grassy fields, through flocks of skittish sheep, over stiles and through gates, without any sign of my goal drawing nearer. Eventually, I arrived at a modest, wholly unremarkable granite obelisk. The weathered inscription revealed that in 1887 the Dorset Water Board had run a pipe past this point. Well, yippee, I thought. Pursing my lips and referring once more to my map, I noticed that just a bit further on was something called the Giant's Grave, and I thought: 'Well, that sounds interesting.'
>
> So I plodded off to see it. That's the trouble, you see. There's always some intriguing landmark just over the next contour line.[33]

Both analysis and good humour establish our interest in a place, and a willingness to uncover a shared humanity – sometimes, too, just a willingness to become lost. The reasons we want to know and the reasons we laugh are not, in travel writing, so far apart. The difficulty of travelling is the same as the difficulty of writing: we are being drawn out of ourselves and into the world. If, in the process, you refine your sense of engagement with others, I think you have come a long way in producing a great worst trip.

Exercises

1. What sort of a traveller are you? Do you start conversations with strangers, or are you more likely to hold back and watch the world go by? Write two accounts of a recent journey: in the first, you are the main character, while in the second you are present merely as a set of eyes.

2. Write a 100-word description of someone you met during a trip. Try to include their appearance and mannerisms, the reason for them being in the place you met them, and some dialogue that catches their way of speaking and thinking about the world.
3. Collect a series of photographs that best capture the feeling of a trip. Describe what you see in those photographs as accurately and specifically as possible. Is there a common theme emerging through the descriptions? Or would the photographs be more easily connected by a narrative?
4. Use one of the descriptions from Exercise 3 as the basis of an expository paragraph about the place you visited. That is, use the physical environment as the start of an explanation of an aspect of the society's history or culture.
5. Choose one photograph for close study. Compose a list, using specific terms, for the things you see. For example, for the photograph of Sydney Harbour below, you would need to be able to give specific information about the architectural and landscape features, the time of day and what that meant for the appearance of the city, and so on.

1. Sydney Harbour Bridge, copyright Kári Gíslason

6. Imagine you are in the photograph above, in a ferry that is about to pass under the bridge. Write two descriptions, one which takes a

commanding point of view of the scene as a whole, the other tied to your movement in the ferry.

7. Use a map to describe a journey you've made. Where did the journey slow down and/or intensify? Why do you think you spent more time in a particular place? Was it because you had planned to, your interests drew you there, or because of events that occurred during the journey itself? Thinking about these questions will help you pace your travel narrative.
8. What have you learned about yourself during travels you have undertaken? Use the answer to that question as the underlying theme of a travel story. This will mean developing a narrative about the place you visited as a way of highlighting a change in you. However, remember that when writing about yourself a light touch is often best, and that although the piece as a whole is moving towards greater self-understanding, at the paragraph level the writing can focus mainly on others.

NOTES

1. Peter Thompson [interviewer], *Talking Heads*, Clive James [interviewee], available online at www.abc.net.au/talkingheads/txt/s1995349.htm, accessed 25 March 2011.
2. Rory Stewart, 'Preface', in Robert Byron, *The Road to Oxiana* (Oxford University Press, 2007).
3. Paul Theroux, in Nicholas Parsons (ed.), *Dipped in Vitriol* (London: Pan Books, 1981), pp. 65–7, p. 66.
4. Wilfred Thesiger, *Arabian Sands* (London: Penguin, 2007), p. 21.
5. Byron, *The Road to Oxiana*, p. 183.
6. Jason Elliot, *An Unexpected Light: Travels in Afghanistan* (London: Picador, 1999).
7. Rory Stewart, *The Places in Between* (London: Picador, 2004).
8. Sarah Turnbull, *Almost French: A New Life in Paris* (Sydney: Bantam Books, 2002).
9. Bill Bryson, *Notes from a Small Island* (London: Black Swan, 1996).
10. Kári Gíslason, *The Promise of Iceland* (St Lucia: University of Queensland Press, 2011).
11. William Fiennes, *The Snow Geese* (London: Picador, 2002).
12. Elizabeth David, *An Omelette and a Glass of Wine* (London: Penguin, 1986).
13. William Least Heat-Moon, *Blue Highways* (New York: Back Bay Books, 1999).
14. William Dalrymple, *Nine Lives* (London: Bloomsbury, 2009), p. 94.
15. W.H. Auden, *Letters from Iceland* (London: Faber, 1967), p. 61.
16. Ibid., p. 63.
17. Ibid., p. 68.

18. Clive James, 'Postcard from Sydney', in *Flying Visits* (London: Picador, 1985), pp. 15–22, pp. 17–18.
19. Colin Thubron, *The Lost Heart of Asia* (London: Penguin, 1995).
20. D. H. Lawrence, *Sketches of Etruscan Places* (London: Penguin, 1999).
21. Jan Morris, 'Over the Bridge', in *Journeys* (Oxford University Press, 1985), pp. 3–20, p. 5.
22. Bill Bryson, *Walkabout* (London: Doubleday, 2002), pp. 297–8.
23. Stewart, *The Places in Between*, p. 1.
24. Bruce Chatwin, *The Songlines* (London: Vintage, 1998), p. 5.
25. Gerald Durrell, *My Family and Other Animals* (London: Penguin Books, 2006).
26. Peter Mayle, *A Year in Provence* (London: Pan Books, 1990).
27. Frances Mayes, *Under the Tuscan Sun* (London: Transworld Publishers, 1999).
28. Lawrence Durrell, *Prospero's Cell* (Mount Jackson: Axios Press, 2008).
29. Julian Barnes, *Something to Declare: Essays on France and French Culture* (London: Picador, 2002).
30. Jonathan Swift, *Gulliver's Travels* (London: Penguin, 2003).
31. Bryson, *Notes from a Small Island*.
32. Ibid., p. 29.
33. Ibid., pp. 115–16.

8

HAZEL SMITH

Creative writing and new media

From page to screen, from human to computer

Writing has always involved forms of technology, whether the pen, the typewriter or the computer. But the growth of new media technologies is offering many exciting possibilities for experimentation and innovation in creative writing. In new media writing – or networked and programmable writing, e-literature or digital writing as it is variously called – the screen replaces the page. In such writing environments we can make words kinetic, pursue new forms of interactivity and link disparate web pages. We can also interweave text, sound and image, and create environments in which readers/viewers transform texts through their bodily movements. Most radically, we can program the computer to compose fiction or poetry, thereby shifting our conception of authorship. Consequently, new media writing is a very diverse and challenging field which stretches from animated poetry and interactive fiction to computer-generated text and computer-interactive installations.

However, new media writing does not constitute a break with the literary tradition, rather it shows the influence of twentieth-century experimental writing from the modernists to the postmodernists. It incorporates techniques drawn from modernist collage, and visual and sound poetry, as well as the syntactical dislocations of American Language poetry.[1] It can project alternative storylines like those we find in postmodern fiction, though to a higher degree of complexity, and its linking system provides an excellent environment for cross-genre writing, that is writing which mixes prose and poetry or critical and creative writing. Most fundamentally, new media writing is a development of approaches to writing which are *algorithmic*: that is they apply a set of rules to a particular writing task. Such approaches to writing have been evident in the twentieth and twenty-first centuries even on the page.[2] For example, members of the French group Oulipo developed writing techniques which applied constraints – the novelist Georges Perec in 1969 set himself the task of writing a 300-page novel without the letter *e*.[3] Historically, many genres of writing have been algorithmic – when pre-twentieth-century poets adopted a rhyme scheme, for example, they were writing in relation to certain rules or algorithms. The difference now is the variety, complexity and fluidity of the algorithms used, and the employment of computer code to formulate and implement new ones.

However, there are also many non-literary influences upon new media writing, and its links with sonic and visual art are particularly strong. In fact, some practitioners in the field, such as Simon Biggs, are primarily visual artists who also apply their technological expertise effectively to writing, and new media writing sometimes appears in the context of art galleries or musical performances. Another major influence is games: some interactive fictions are designed in game-playing terms so that a problem has to be solved to further a story or to progress to the next level of the text: see, for example, the work of Jason Nelson, Kate Pullinger and Chris Joseph.[4] New media writing also interfaces with popular activities such as social networking sites, blogs and texting. These do not require skills in creative writing but can benefit from them, and are making the concept of the author more fluid and ubiquitous.

Creative writing in new media means working with computer code as well as language, and creates a triumvirate between the writer, language and programming.[5] Some practitioners in the field have expertise as computer programmers; however, technological sophistication is not essential. It is possible to create works with user-friendly programs such as Quicktime, Processing, Flash or iMovie, or alternatively through collaboration with peers who have programming skills. Nor is it necessary to relinquish print-based writing, as it can be productive to mediate between page and screen. Stephanie Strickland, for example, has on occasion published a work as both a book and a new media piece, thereby exploring the unique possibilities of both forms and their overlap.[6]

The history of new media writing has been well documented elsewhere, for example by Katherine Hayles,[7] and I will touch on it here only briefly. It is open-ended because the field is still changing at an astonishing rate as new software appears. Of early importance were the hypertext novels in the late 1980s and early 1990s by authors such as Michael Joyce,[8] Shelley Jackson[9] and Stuart Moulthrop.[10] In these novels readers activated hyperlinks to open up alternative pathways through the narrative, producing a different text on each occasion. Hypertext novels were followed by, and overlapped with, animated poems, often written in Flash, of which Brian Kim Stefans's *The Dreamlife of Letters* is the classic example.[11] These animations sometimes morphed words into other words, or created kinetic rearrangements of letters, words and phrases. They extended ways of reading since words were scattered round the screen, and reading speed was sometimes deliberately pushed to unreadable limits.

Over a period of time, particularly from the late 1990s, higher degrees of interactivity were introduced: mouse actions, for example, would open up different parts of the screen, or cause text or images to transform or disintegrate: Talan Memmott's *Lexia to Perplexia* is an ingenious example of such writing.[12] Other interventions – known as codeworks – by authors such as Mary-Anne Breeze (mez) or Memmott, were notable for the way they fused language and computer code.[13] Mez even developed her own language known as mezangelle, a hybrid of code and English, including also puns, neologisms and quirky punctuation.[14] Fiction writing continued, sometimes – as in *Afterimage* by M. D. Coverley – creating a strong fusion between the narrative and the poetic.[15] The desire for a different approach to narrative also fuelled interactive fiction (IF) – a genre which originated in adventure stories and pre-dated hypertext fiction.[16] In IF the user/reader responds to prompts in order to further the story and control characters in a simulated world, as in the work of Jon Ingold and Nick Montfort.[17] Creative writing in new media also became increasingly multimedia in the twenty-first century, so that the narrative or poetic content was conveyed through images and sounds, as well as through words.

Most of these types of writing still continue, but other new media interventions have also developed. Recently an important trend has been text generation, that is, the use of computer programs to compose text. Text generation is central to the work of Daniel Howe, Fox Harrell, Judd Morrissey, Simon Biggs and others. Despite the difficulties it poses in terms of composing a text which is – when desired – grammatically and semantically cohesive, text generation is arguably the most radical form of new media writing and likely to be very influential in the future. A complete refutation of the romantic idea of art as the expression of creative genius, it heightens 'emergence', that is the autonomous evolution of the text.[18] When we talk about emergence as authors, we mean our feeling that a piece of our writing is evolving in a way that we would never have anticipated. However, this sensation becomes much stronger when authors partially hand over the task of writing to the computer, because one computational event will continuously trigger another and take the text in its own (albeit programmed) direction.

Text generation sometimes involves changing a given text by substituting or adding words from a database or constellation of databases, to the point where the original text becomes almost unrecognisable and a new one emerges. Sometimes, as in Daniel Howe and John Cayley's *The Readers Project*,[19] texts are generated by 'reading through' a pre-existing text – algorithmically selecting words from a prior text so that they form a new text. Alternatively, text generation can be a process of evolving combinations of words, phrases or sentences, and may operate in response to user input (that is, the writer or reader types in a word, or set of words, which change the text output). Fox Harrell, in *The Girl with Skin of Haints and Seraphs*,[20] employs GRIOT, a computer platform he has developed in which the writer inserts keywords into specific thematic domains. The domains are extensive databases of related words and concepts, but the same keyword will trigger alternative combinations of words, creating a different text each time. The programming architecture in GRIOT produces high levels of organization and integration at the semantic, syntactic and narrative levels. Harrell's stated intention is to intertwine the computational, cultural and cognitive, and he balances highly improvisatory strategies with some control over meaning.[21] Harrell, an African American, has argued that many computer games encourage stereotyping of racial and gender identity, and that in new media work we must underpin technical innovation with cultural and socio-political commitment. In *The Girl with Skin of Haints and Seraphs* some of the keywords are Africa, Europe, demon, angel, black, white, juju. The thematic domains are organised so they respond to these keywords by generating texts which dismantle racial stereotypes. So the GRIOT platform is set up to maximise convincing text generation, but also to ensure that the text addresses issues of racial identity.

Other recent experiments in new media writing produce a complex and new relationship between print and screen sometimes referred to as 'augmented reality'. In the work *Between Page and Screen*, by Amaranth Borsuk and Brad Bouse, readers open the pages of a handmade book in front of a computer screen.[22] The pages contain geometric shapes and these trigger software which causes word animations to appear on the screen. New media writing also increasingly takes the form of performances or installations. A good example is Simon Biggs's *reRead* which he has documented through video.[23] Biggs describes the transformations the body of the viewer effects as it passes through the installation, which includes close circuit video, a mirror, video sensing and software for text generation:

> On entering the work the viewer finds themselves electronically reflected in a life-size video projection composed of orthogonally opposed and reversed texts. The texts are constantly writing themselves into being, adapting their content and form in response to the viewer's movements. This visual field is sensitive to the movement of the viewer, distorting as the viewer moves, creating an elastic surface in which the viewer is reflected. The system only writes when there is a reader/viewer present. When the viewer departs the area between the projection and the mirror the system enters a state of stasis ...

Creative writing in new media therefore raises pertinent issues about reciprocation between humans and computers, a process Katherine Hayles calls intermediation.[24] In text generation a person undertakes the programming and can be selective about the output, but the process does considerably loosen authorial intention and control. Many questions suggest themselves for the future: will it be possible for people with very little literary education to create work? Will writing be identified with a range of writing environments (the screen, the gallery, the virtual reality cave) rather than just the page? Will multimedia artists supplant writers? Already we can see significant changes in the figure of the author, who is not necessarily a lone writer committing words to print. Rather the author may be a writer–programmer, or a writer who is working with programmers, musicians and visual artists.

The technological as the sociopolitical: some case studies

This section will focus on works by Jason Nelson, Roger Dean and myself, and M. D. Coverley. These pieces have technical features that you may be able to implement in your own work, but also link those features to significant contemporary and historical themes.

Jason Nelson's *Wide and Wildly Branded*[25] and *Birds Still Warm from Flying*,[26] written in Flash, combine interactivity with animated elements. *Wide and Wildly Branded* consists of a circle which is a compass, but also looks like a globe or a wheel with highly coloured axes. As the mouse activates alternative points on the compass, different texts appear. The texts are divided between those above the circle labelled 'poetic', and those below labelled 'subpoetic', and are fragmented and decontextualised. The textual fragments sometimes seem to belong together but at other times seem to be coming from different hemispheres or conceptual frameworks. Nelson constructed these texts by recording from ABC radio using speech-to-text software, and then reforming 'the resulting strange sentences and garbled grammar'.[27] The circle is superimposed on a looping video which pans backwards and forwards over an (Australian) landscape, and a repetitive looping soundtrack accompanies the words and images. So circularity is written into the piece on a number of different levels, though it is often interrupted.

The symbolic resonances of the piece are rich and ambiguous. The compass is a navigational instrument, but also an instrument for drawing circles. Furthermore, the navigational compass has been replaced recently by the Global Positioning System (GPS), so the inclusion of it brings the instruments of the past into focus with present technologies. The relationship between the top and bottom of the circle implies the division between north and south, both real and illusory. Nelson points to the geographical implications in his accompanying note, alluding indirectly to his new home Australia (he is American) and ironically debunking stereotypical views of it, 'To the south we are distant and other, lesser and undeveloped, we are the wild and widely branded pioneer, the known and unknown hemisphere. This digital poem is a compass to these bottom lands, a winding journey into the artificial side of opposite'.[28] In an email to me Nelson wrote: 'the work represents Australia's strange multi-direction spin, its confusion about how it sees itself, its indigenous past and future, its relationship with either its neighbours in Asia or its western-world counterparts in Europe and North America'.[29] *Wide and Wildly Branded*, like other works by Nelson, problematises dichotomies, including that between north and south. The use of the terms poetic and subpoetic suggests multilayered tensions hinted at in the textual fragments: for example between conscious and subconscious meaning, between continent and subcontinent, and between the historical and the contemporary.

Birds Still Warm from Flying consists of a cube with text projecting at different angles. The cube can be rotated, distorted and multiplied (though it springs back into a single structure). At any angle certain texts will be invisible, indecipherable or inverted, though others will be readable and new ones may appear. And, of course, the texts can be read in any order. Once the player/reader starts to disrupt the cube, it can only be recuperated in its original form by beginning the piece again. The cube also progressively fills with videos which flicker and excite, but cannot be fully viewed.

The text often seems to be torn from larger contexts and to contain fragments of narratives: the phrase 'heartless discussion between flights' is typical. Like most of Nelson's pieces the lines refer to many different contexts, including medicine and architecture. But Nelson says that the thematic/poetic background to the piece is the difficult process of travelling overseas from Australia: 'even short trips become complex extended journeys involving multiple borders and navigations'.[30] For him the cube reflects 'the puzzle of travel, of leaving and arriving from/to this southern island continent'.[31] Many of the lines can also be read as metatexts (that is as referring to the work itself) since they involve the idea of disruption and breakage which underlies the cube structure. A repetitive looping soundtrack, whose insistence contrasts with the looseness of the cube, accompanies the images and texts.

Instabilities 2, by Roger Dean and myself, is a piece designed for performance: it will be different each time it is performed, but you can nevertheless view it in a recorded, fixed version.[32] The screen is divided into three sections which echo and foreshadow each other. The top section is a Quicktime movie I made of twelve short texts which scroll at readable speed. These texts are both disjunct from each other and also interconnected, and in writing them I employed a broad palate of genres including the reimagining of well-known speeches, parodies, discontinuous poems, surreal metaphors, short narratives, allegories, commands and statements. They include many different metaphors for instability – linguistic, psychological, economic, political, geographical and technological – but the metaphors are continually realigned so that, for example, mental instability is sometimes represented in economic terms, sometimes in political terms. Instability, however, emerges as both negative and positive, and is viewed as a trigger to change, not just as a precursor to disintegration.

The middle screen section consists of the same material processed as image in the program Jitter/MAX/MSP by Roger Dean. Blocks of the text are subjected to a series of processes: stretching, multiplication, enlarging, compression, overlaying and overwriting. The order of the processes forms a sequence which remains the same for each performance of the piece; the order of the texts, however, is determined according to mathematical probabilities and will be different each time the piece is performed. The Jitter manipulation treats the text as a visual object, introduces some colour, and speeds up the text so that it is sometimes readable, sometimes not.

The third part of the screen results from work with our Verbal Interactivity Project, a project dedicated to computerised text generation. It includes the Text Transformation Toolkit (TTT) devised and created in the computer language Python by David Worrall and Roger Dean, with additional input from Michael Bylstra and Jon Drummond (all four are musicians and programmers). The purpose of TTT – which is under continuous development – is to generate text by gradually transforming it, especially in real-time interactive and performance contexts. TTT, in which the processing algorithms for *Instabilities* 2 were written, permits both live coding and manipulation of a graphic interface. It also uses several other substantial research and programming endeavours, such as the Free Association Database, Wordnet (a very sophisticated dictionary which tags parts of speech so that it can, for example, find synonyms and antonyms for words), and the Natural Language Toolkit (a computer platform for analysing, building and transforming grammatical structures).

The same texts – together with others which do not appear in the top movie – are processed in real-time by Roger Dean in the computer platform Python, using a variety of forms of word, character and sentence manipulation. TTT can substitute nouns and verbs for other nouns and verbs, either by recourse to a specific database of specially compiled words or by using Wordnet. It can shuffle, append or merge sentences, excise vowels, swap characters, insert caps in the middle of words, and so on.

In addition, computer-synthesised voices add an aural dimension and undergo the same processes. The voices are some of those available on the Macintosh, and they are heard individually and in combination. Sometimes the words are distinct and audible, sometimes the voices form a dense sound texture. The voices read the texts in their original form, but they also give voice to the transformed text, often morphing from one to the other. This means they are sometimes in and sometimes out of synch with the written text.

The soundtrack for this version is a 'comprovisation' (that is, an improvisation with a composed structure) written by Roger Dean especially for the piece. The music is designed to give a strong emotional undertow and is an important element of the multimedia blending of word, sound and image. Here the acoustic improvisation (performed by Sandy Evans, Phil Slater and Roger Dean) is gradually over-run by the electroacoustic sound (performed by Greg White) but then re-emerges. This mirrors the processes the text undergoes, since fragments of text are constantly replaced by other fragments, but also often reappear, sometimes in a transformed state.

M. D. Coverley's *Accounts of the Glass Sky*[33] is written in Flash and has strong narrative trajectories, but is also highly poetic. Like much of Coverley's work it includes photographs; this gives the piece an aura of historical authenticity even though it is fiction, and also means that the poetic and narrative elements pass across different media. The words and photographs are fragments; they suggest larger contexts, characters and stories.

Coverley is American, and the central image is of a skyscraper projected upon the image of a stone circle; the photographs are in turn superimposed upon the glass windows of the skyscraper. The photographs can be viewed by activating them with the mouse, but there is also an alternative mode of navigation. All the photographs have rolling captions which appear and then disappear, and the photographs tend to disintegrate and abstract as we look at them. The timing of the words and images is critical, there are pauses which allow us to dwell on a text and image, but we may also sometimes need to open a window more than once to have time to read everything. The haunting soundtrack comprises recorded sounds of northern lights, sounds of breaking glass, and a heartbeat linked to the navigation icon.[34] The sound changes with each window, is sparse, and occurs in well-judged and highly evocative bursts.

In the accompanying notes Coverley reveals that the piece, begun before the bombing of the World Trade Center, changed in its aftermath. It became an attempt to understand how prior historical events which might seem unconnected with 9/11 – such as the Vietnam War or the Great Depression – were actually moving towards it. But the images of sky and glass central to the piece are indicators not only of historical change but also of how history is represented. The sky undergoes a transformation from liquid to more solid, 'going hard round the edges', from lightness to shadow and darkness, from sky to glass. Coverley says:

> The images of the sky and the glass are part of a multifaceted metaphor (kind of a layered metaphor). At one level, glass replaces the sky in many of our modern, urban landscapes – when you look up you see walls of glass where sky used to

> be. Along that line, the sky is also obscured with air pollution where I live – giving a claustrophobic, closed-in feeling, as though the sky were covered with something like a glass darkly.
>
> On the symbolic level of a total metaphor, the replacement of sky with 'glass' represents the increasing opaqueness that intrudes between observed reality and the 'picture' of the world that is created by the media (in conjunction with the government and big business) . . .[35]

This progression from clear sky to muddied glass is written into the photographs and their inscriptions. A snapshot of children at a birthday party in the 1920s is accompanied by a caption 'the sky was just there. No one worried about it.' However, the disintegration of that image is accompanied by the idea that 'the sky is turning', with some doubts about what the cause is and what its effects will be: 'it's hard to tell if the glass is dirty or the images have been reduced'. The 1950s are a prosperous time, but 'on some days the glass seems filled with light – other days, shadowy images appear'. By 1964 the skies have become international but 'under the bell jar of the sky, we sense the tracings of an outcome we cannot imagine'. These are the skies of global communication which, in turn, brings the false representation created by media intervention: by 1984 all that remains of the sky is a simulacrum of it. 'A copy of the real sky has been projected on the glass; we must be grateful.' Coverley says:

> Although these segments are not in chronological order, they trace some moments in time that I thought were significant. The photos were chosen for the way they depict that 'innocent' state that we remember. In the earliest photo, 1924, we have a world that seems to be exactly the way it looks (the sky is clear enough to know it is there!) – but moving through time, other windows refer to military adventurism (including the Vietnam War and other arms-for-money deals) and aspects of media mind control (including the use of psychological coercion as part of our culture).[36]

Overall, Coverley's piece demonstrates how the interlinking of images, words and sounds can produce a wealth of narrative and poetic possibilities for engaging with contemporary social-political events.

The process of writing: technologies and techniques

Effective artworks occur when artists interact strongly with the medium in which they are working. Writers do not usually have preconceived ideas which they then mechanically express in language; rather they find or transform ideas as they write. Creative writing in new media writing presents the opportunity to engage simultaneously with language and with computer code as a way of shaping ideas, and in this section we focus on techniques which can facilitate that process. Some types of writing already mentioned require high levels of programming to implement: if you have programming experience, or intend to collaborate with someone who does, such work may be within your range. However, I will draw attention here to some basic techniques which can be used to sophisticated ends without such expertise. In general, these techniques will be most effective if used to subvert or displace print-based modes of writing while also demonstrating continuities with them. You are also more likely to employ the technologies innovatively if you write directly into them, rather than producing a page-based text which is then 'translated' into a technological object, though you can approach the task both ways.

One of the main characteristics of new media writing is its capacity for kineticism, so we will look first at techniques for the animation of words using a program such as Flash or Processing. A major consideration in any animation is how fast the words move, because the author metaphorically turns the pages of the book for the reader and dictates how quickly the words are read. You can use animation techniques to place words on the screen at an average reading speed, but such techniques can also be used to redirect the way we read, for example by pushing reading speed beyond the norm, or by drastically slowing it down. Similarly, writing in new media can challenge western reading habits of reading from left to right, since words may be scattered anywhere on the screen, and also rapidly change their position and formation. In animations, letters, words, phrases or blocks of text can be rearranged, added or subtracted in such a way as to continually generate new words or arrangements of words. For example, word animations can create connections between words which have some similar letters but are disconnected in meaning, by using the common letters as a pivot.[37] John Cayley's works employ techniques of 'transliteral morphing' whereby one text is transformed into another (and sometimes from Chinese to English or vice versa) by successive substitutions of letters.[38] A highly meditative approach to animation, in which the sound, image and words unfold slowly and repetitively, can be seen in Alan Sondheim and Reiner Strasser's *Dawn*.[39]

A second important technique in new media writing is the use of a split screen. Some experimental video makers have engaged with split screen techniques to considerable effect, for example, Will Luers.[40] Split screens allow you to juxtapose multiple narratives with interplay between the different streams. This increases the possibility for contrasting or complementary narratives to reverberate with each other. Screens can be split vertically or horizontally, symmetrically or asymmetrically, into two, three or four components. Words may appear in all the screen sections, or alternate between them; writing can be overlaid on images (as it is in *Accounts of the Glass Sky*) or alternate with them. What is critical is the co-ordination and timing between the different parts of the screens – that is, decisions about when the words will flash on and off, and whether there will be several pieces of text on different sections of the screen at once. Again issues of readability rear their head, and decisions have to be made about the degree to which the reader's ability to assimilate independent pieces of information simultaneously will be challenged. Where the intention is narrative, issues arise about how divergent narratives resonate with each other. They may be alternative parts of the same story, have features or events in common, or reveal contrasting points of view.

A third important feature is interactivity. This can be introduced through programs such as Flash and Processing, or in the case of interactive fictions, through programs such as Inform. Interactivity may be simple or very complex. It may involve activating a link or series of links (either hidden or overt) which reveal different aspects of the piece. It may be an element of a game whereby certain actions have to be completed, or problems solved, before it is possible to enter the next level. In Jon Ingold's interactive fiction *All Roads*,[41] for example, the reader has to imagine how a character can escape from being locked in a room with his hands tied before progressing with the story. In IF the reader not only has to play the game but learn how to play: in Aaron Reed's *Blue Lacuna* the reader can opt to be in story mode or puzzle mode; there is a hints page for how to solve the puzzles, and one can write to the author for advice.[42] Interactivity may also take the form of mouse movements which rearrange or recombine texts such as Jim Andrews's *Stir-Fry Texts*, co-written with Brian Lennon and Pauline Masurel.[43] So interactivity within a new media work usually serves a purpose, and would normally either produce a high level of engagement for the reader, reveal features which were previously hidden, add new levels, or further the game or narrative aspect.

Finally, a very important set of techniques is the juxtaposition and merging of text with sound and image; all the pieces discussed in the case histories section contain multimedia elements. Images and sounds can be 'found' or composed, representational or abstract, taken from the environment or synthesised. Sound includes the voice, which can be recorded and edited by a program such as Audacity, or transformed by a program like Sound Hack with regard to pitch, rhythm and timbre. Manipulation of the voice can create many salient effects including 'cross-dressing', where a deepened female voice appears male or a raised male voice appears female: see my audio collaborations with Roger Dean.[44] As a writer you may feel that you do not have the necessary technique to create images and sounds. But you can borrow them from other internet sites given the appropriate Creative Commons licence (permission to use the work in this way), shoot your own photographs, or video or record your own sounds: these sounds and images may be different from those made by professional artists or musicians but may still be very effective.

Creating interplay between sounds, words and images augments the capacities of language. In the work of Young-Hae Chang Heavy Industries,[45] for example, the rhythmic music coordinates with the speed at which the words appear, producing a new slant on the concept of verbal rhythm. In M.D. Coverley's *Afterimage*, environmental sounds and photographs deepen the sensation of the Ethiopian location evoked in the text.[46] My collaborations with Roger Dean often use words in musical ways while conversely making musical meaning evolve from text.[47] You may want to work independently with the different media and then bring them together, or move between them as you create the work. In terms of the relationship of sounds, images and text, major considerations are: (a) whether a text and an image, or a text and a sound, are working with each other (in a supporting, complementary or illustrative way) or against each other (in a contrasting, oppositional or independent way); (b) whether they appear in a relationship of superimposition, juxtaposition or fusion, and (c) the degree to which they adopt each others' characteristics, so that, for example, words are presented as visual objects using different fonts, spacings and colour.

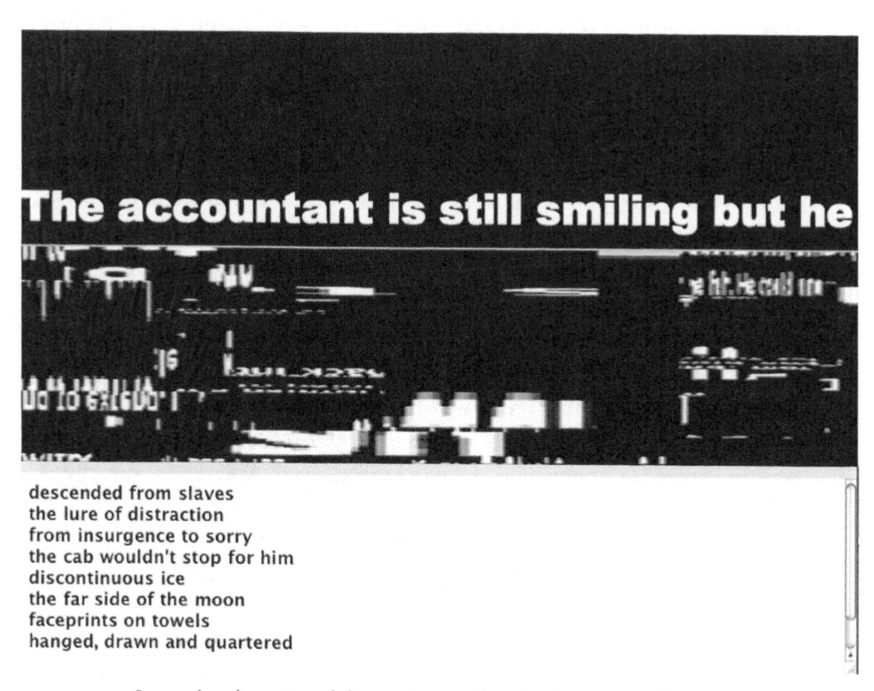

2. Screenshot from 'Instabilities 2', copyright Hazel Smith and Roger Dean

Writing exercises

In the following exercises specific computer programs are not suggested, since there are many commercial and open-access programs which could be employed.

1. Start with one word and using an animation program gradually add more words until you have built up a sentence. The words should appear out of order though in their eventual correct position, so that the reader must fill in the gaps and keep guessing what the sentence will be. Then start again with another sentence and keep building sentences until you have a short animation consisting of the successively accrued sentences.
2. Create an animation in which you start with a word and then juxtapose it with another word which is different in sense but has one or more letters in common with it. Then juxtapose the second word with a third word in the same way. Continue the process until you end up with a word which has completely different letters from the word with which you started.
3. Create a piece with a split screen. Then make two videos for the two parts of the screen, each consisting of still or moving images, and with some words superimposed on the images. How do the two different screen halves interact with each other in terms of meaning, readability and visual effect?
4. Use a game or puzzle you have enjoyed playing as the basis for forming a new media poem or a story. The reader should have to solve a series of puzzles or win successive stages of the game to progress through the piece. How have you reconciled the genre of puzzle/game with that of poem/story?
5. Take some photographs of people you know or use photographs from other websites (with permission). Write some text in response to the photographs, and then find ways of hyperlinking the texts and the photographs and/or superimposing the texts on the photographs. Sometimes link a photograph to its corresponding text, but mostly link it to an unrelated text or to several texts. Add extra text or photographs, if you wish, as the work progresses. What new meanings and relationships have you created?
6. Create a piece with any combination of text and sound in which the sonic elements sometimes illustrate the words and sometimes contrast with them.
7. Create a piece which uses any combination of hyperlinking, interactivity and animation to interlink a set of historical and contemporary

events, and personal and political perspectives on those events. You should focus on a particular theme, for example, slavery or environmental destruction.

NOTES

1. Hazel Smith, *The Writing Experiment: Strategies for Innovative Creative Writing* (Sydney: Allen & Unwin, 2005).
2. Hazel Smith, 'The Posthuman and the Writing Process: Emergence, Algorithm, Affect and Multimodality', in Nigel Krauth and Tess Brady (eds.), *Creative Writing: Theory and Practice* (Teneriffe, Queensland: Post Pressed, 2006), pp. 169–86.
3. Georges Perec, *La disparition* (Paris: Gallimard, 1990).
4. Kate Pullinger and Chris Joseph, *Inanimate Alice* (2005), available online at www.inanimatealice.com, accessed 1 August 2010; Jason Nelson, *Net Art/ Digital Poetry Games*, available online at www.secrettechnology.com/artgames.html, accessed 1 August 2010; see also the work of Noah Wardrip-Fruin and Pat Harrigan (eds.), *First Person: New Media as Story, Performance, and Game* (Cambridge, MA: MIT Press, 2004).
5. Many aspects of this triumvirate are discussed in Adalaide Morris and Thomas Swiss (eds.), *New Media Poetics: Contexts, Technotexts, and Theories* (Cambridge, MA: MIT Press, 2006).
6. Stephanie Strickland, *V: Waveson.Nets/ Losing L'una* (New York: Penguin, 2002); Stephanie Strickland, *V: Vniverse with Cynthia Lawson* (2002), available online at http://vniverse.com, accessed 31 July 2010.
7. N. Katherine Hayles, *Electronic Literature: New Horizons for the Literary* (University of Notre Dame Press, 2008).
8. Michael Joyce, *Afternoon: A Story* (Watertown, MA: Eastgate Systems, 1990).
9. Shelley Jackson, *Patchwork Girl* (Watertown, MA: Eastgate Systems, 1995).
10. Stuart Moulthrop, *Victory Garden* (Watertown, MA: Eastgate Systems, 1991).
11. Brian Stefans, *The Dreamlife of Letters* (2000), available online at www.ubu.com/contemp/stefans/dream/index.html, accessed 1 August 2010.
12. Talan Memmott, *Lexia to Perplexia* (2000, republished 2006), available online at http://collection.eliterature.org/1/works/memmott__lexia_to_perplexia.html, accessed 31 July 2010.
13. Rita Raley, 'Interferences: [Net.Writing] and the Practice of Codework', *Electronic Book Review* (2003), available online at http://www.electronicbookreview.com/thread/electropoetics/net.writing, accessed 31 July 2010.
14. Mary-Anne Breeze, *_][Ad][Dressed in a Skin C.Ode_* (2001), available online at www.cddc.vt.edu/host/netwurker, accessed 31 July 2010.
15. M. D. Coverley, *Afterimage* (2001), available online at http://califia.us/Afterimage/, accessed 31 July 2010.
16. Nick Montfort, *Twisty Little Passages: An Approach to Interactive Fiction* (Cambridge, MA: MIT Press 2005).
17. Nick Montfort, *Homepage: Nick Montfort*, available online at http://nickm.com/, accessed 31 July 2010; Jon Ingold, *All Roads* (2001, republished 2006), available

online at http://collection.eliterature.org/1/works/ingold__all_roads.html, accessed 31 July 2010.
18. Smith, 'The Posthuman and the Writing Process'.
19. Daniel C. Howe and J. Cayley, *The Readers Project: Documentation and Video* (2010), available online at http://rednoise.org/readers/video.php, accessed 31 July 2010.
20. D. Fox Harrell, 'GRIOT's Tales of Haints and Seraphs: A Computational Narrative Generation System', *Electronic Book Review* (2008), available online at www.electronicbookreview.com/thread/firstperson/generational, accessed 31 July 2010.
21. Ibid.
22. Amaranth Borsuk and Brad Bouse, *Between Page and Screen* (2010), available online at http://betweenpageandscreen.com/, accessed 31 July 2010.
23. Simon Biggs, *reRead [Video from the Installation, with Description and Specification]* (2009), available online at www.littlepig.org.uk/reRead/reread.htm, accessed 31 July 2010.
24. Hayles, *Electronic Literature*.
25. Jason Nelson, *Wide and Wildly Branded*, *SoundsRite*, 1 (2009), available online at http://soundsrite.uws.edu.au/soundsRiteContent/volume1/NelsonInfo.html, Accessed 31 July 2010.
26. Jason Nelson, *Birds Still Warm from Flying*, *SoundsRite*, 1 (2009), available online at http://soundsrite.uws.edu.au/soundsRiteContent/volume1/NelsonInfo.html, accessed 31 July 2010.
27. Jason Nelson, email to Hazel Smith, 21 July 2010.
28. Notes accompanying Nelson, *Wide and Wildly Branded*.
29. Nelson, email to Hazel Smith, 21 July 2010.
30. Ibid.
31. Ibid.
32. Hazel Smith and Roger T. Dean, *Instabilities 2: Drunken Boat* (2009), available online at www.drunkenboat.com/db12/06des/smith/index.php, accessed 25 March 2011.
33. M. D. Coverley, *Accounts of the Glass Sky* (2002, republished 2006), available online at http://collection.eliterature.org/1/works/coverley__accounts_of_the_-glass_sky.html, accessed 31 July 2010.
34. M. D. Coverley, email to Hazel Smith, 25 July 2010.
35. Ibid.
36. Ibid.
37. For Strategies of this kind see Stefans, *The Dreamlife of Letters*, or Chris Funkhouser's word animations, *Homepage: Chris Funkhouser*, available online at http://web.njit.edu/~funkhous/, accessed 31 July 2010.
38. Hazel Smith, 'Affect, Emotion and Sensation in New Media Writing: The Work of John Cayley, M.D. Coverley and Jason Nelson', in Anthony Ulhmann, Helen Groth and Paul Sheehan (eds.), *Literature and Sensation* (Newcastle Upon Tyne: Cambridge Scholars Press, 2009), pp. 300–12; Hazel Smith, 'Textual Variability in New Media Poetry', in Annie Finch and Susan M. Schultz (eds.), *Multiformalisms: Postmodern Poetics of Form* (Cincinnati: Textos Books, 2008), pp. 485–516.
39. Alan Sondheim and Reiner Strasser, *Dawn* (2005), available online at www.eliterature.org/collection/1/works/strasser_sondheim__dawn.html, accessed 1 August 2010.

40. Will Luers, *Taylor Street Studio*, available online at www.taylorstreetstudio.com/, accessed 1 August 2010.
41. Ingold, *All Roads*.
42. Aaron Reed, *Blue Lacuna* (2009), available online at www.lacunastory.com/, accessed 31 July 2010.
43. Jim Andrews, with Brian Lennon and Pauline Masurel, *Stir-Fry Texts* (2006), available online at www.eliterature.org/collection/1/works/andrews__stir_fry_texts.html, accessed 30 July 2010.
44. Hazel Smith and Roger Dean, *The Erotics of Geography*, book and CD-Rom (Kaneohe, Hawaii: Tinfish Press, 2008), and homepage: *austraLYSIS*, available online at www.australysis.com, accessed 6 August 2010.
45. Young-Hae Chang Heavy Industries, *Homepage: Young-Hae Chang Heavy Industries*, available online at www.yhchang.com/, accessed 31 July 2010.
46. Coverley, *Afterimage*.
47. Homepage: *austraLYSIS*.

9

FIONA SAMPSON

Creative translation

Why Bottom, thou art translated!
– William Shakespeare, *A Midsummer Night's Dream*

Why should the emerging creative writer bother with translation? Or to put it another way, why is translation 'creative'? Surely it simply repeats what's already been written by someone else: reproducing their ideas, their imagery and insight in a way that's almost mechanical? And moreover, wouldn't one need to be an accomplished linguist to do this?

Many writers in English avoid translation because of their assumptions about what's involved. Literary translation forces us to shift our literary worldview a little – and that, of course, is one of its benefits. British schools still teach a curriculum that can make it seem as if English Literature and literature itself are synonyms. I remember how the public library where I got my real literary education reinforced this impression: lined with English-language novels, it had a single set of shelves for foreign literature. I was into my teens before I stopped believing that 'literature' was one of those things, like cricket, that Britain did well but many other countries not at all. Ridiculous, yes. Yet while today's emerging writer may be more widely travelled than ever before, he or she often has no sense of entering a *particular* tradition within the *world* context. Quite aside from social or existential consequences, this matters creatively.

For having some sense of what's going on among your peers in the rest of the world not only opens up a world of creative alternatives: paradoxically, it can also serve to throw your own literary tradition into sharper relief. Seeing what other ways of writing do is a way of seeing what your own practice leaves out. It helps focus creative choices, especially those to do with register and form. This is particularly true for poets. Poetry's scale and density both make it ideal for the kind of literary translation that fits into a writing life, rather than becomes a full-time career. After all, it's reasonable to expect to make a first working-draft translation of a poem in an afternoon; that and subsequent drafts will be the result of many of just those close reading choices and creative strategies that poem redrafting uses – and which make literary translation such a rich way of practising creative writing. For all these reasons, this chapter concentrates on poetry.

> At this point, make a list of poets or poetries you'd like to know more about. For example: Aimé Césaire is the father of literary 'negritude' – you have family links to the Caribbean but don't know the francophone tradition at all. The German Romantics – Goethe, Schiller – are set in classical *Lieder* and you've always wished you knew what the songs were saying. *Beowulf* is among the Anglo-Saxon and Norse epics you know informed J. R. R. Tolkien's *Lord of the Rings*.

Artists and art students have always copied great paintings. In doing so, they talk about composition and form: as they copy, they observe closely, learning *how* the original artist structured the work. It makes sense for poets to do the same. As T. S. Eliot said,

> Immature poets imitate; mature poets steal; bad poets deface what they take, and good poets make it into something better, or at least something different. The good poet welds his theft into a whole of feeling which is unique, utterly different than that from which it is torn; the bad poet throws it into something which has no cohesion. A good poet will usually borrow from authors remote in time, or alien in language, or diverse in interest.[1]

'Going through the motions' by translating a poet you admire, or whose work you want to know better, works like this. It's a form of literary curiosity. All writing is carried on in dialogue with other writing, whether or not canonical, which we *think towards*, whether formally or as a kind of characterising presence. 'Attentiveness is the natural prayer of the soul', as Paul Celan said, taking up a phrase of Walter Benjamin's.[2] But translation's also the closest of close readings, and the best way to 'steal': to make a form, trope or idea your own so that you can incorporate it into your own work. Translation doesn't just provide an enriched international context for your writing; it offers a masterclass in the thing itself. As you solve the same problems – those smudges of ambiguity, or the search for a consistent music – the original poet resolved in the original language, you find out where you can do the same: and where you can't.

Since so much of creative writing is in fact rewriting, translation allows us to carry on our own work in another form. This means that translation is particularly useful in practical terms. At the writing desk, it solves the familiar problem of wanting to write but having nothing particular to write about. It prevents the writer from resorting to arbitrary exercises, the kind that produce exercise-y, non-essential texts. Translation is real writerly engagement, given authenticity by your enthusiasm for the original. It is also a strategic professional skill – and a good way, especially for early-career writers, to be published in serious outlets (though in today's Britain it's harder to get *books* of translations published). For useful evidence of this, browse the contents of established poets' collections: many include one or more translations of some kind – we'll talk more about such 'kinds' later in this chapter.

Translation informs English language culture. Brainstorm the translated texts – from camera manuals to favourite TV series, great novels to religious or spiritual texts, guide books to songs – which are part of your life at the moment. How aware are you that they're translated? Do you have access to any of them in alternative versions? Do you notice some of these examples being particularly flawed, or successful, translations – and if so, how?

What, though, is translation itself? What makes for good practice? This is something about which there's always been anxiety. The biblical story of the Tower of Babel, in which God punished human hubris by splitting the original language of Eden into multiple languages, causing incomprehension and chaos, is a reflection of this anxiety (Genesis 11: 1–9). A translation 'carries something across': but, as this chapter's Shakespearean epigraph reminds us, there is always a degree of *transformation* in that process. Indeed, the most formative translations in English culture are also interpretations. Anglophone literary culture has its roots in translated traditions. Most obviously and recently, they include the rich, and multilingual, traditions both literary and oral, from Africa, Australia, the Caribbean, India and North America, that have been translated into English-language writing. These demonstrate how translation, unless handled with care, can be a form of appropriation. Gayatri Chakravorty Spivak writes with scrupulous intellectual integrity about the importance of the translator's 'surrender to the text' – finding its specific and pleasurable self rather than *normalising* the text into forms *acceptable* to British publishers, markets or scholars. As she points out, that is 'a betrayal of the democratic ideal into the law of the strongest. This happens when all the literature of the world gets translated into a sort of with-it translatese.'[3]

But even without colonial appropriation, written English culture is historically largely the product of two active traditions of translation. The classics and Christianity dominated British education, and so literary imaginations, until the middle of the twentieth century. Here too translation has been an active form of reception. A model of the translation of classical literature, Ovid's mythopoeic narrative *Metamorphoses* have been seen as literary exercises at least since the eleventh century, but they've been disseminated even more widely as ideas, stories and images: from the sixteenth-century paintings of Titian to the twentieth-century music of Benjamin Britten and Richard Strauss. The Bible's 'Vulgate' translation into Latin in the fourth century, and into English in the seventeenth century (Welsh in the nineteenth century, and so on), could not avoid exegesis – since translation decisions had to be made on doctrinal grounds: 'They trusted in him that hath the key of David, opening and no man shutting' as the Preface to the King James Bible has it.[4] But more than that, biblical translation is *itself* an expression of a different relationship between audience and text. Translated into a language the audience understands, a text becomes less a symbol, with mystical or magical properties in itself, and more a messenger conveying meaning. As Martin Luther said of his translation of the Bible into German, 'I would rather do injury to the German language than deviate from the word. Oh, translation is not an art just anyone can do, as the mad holy ones believe . . .'[5]

So one way to think about translations is as cultural *processes*, or as texts *in process*. Translation is clearly a form of cultural dialogue – it might even be a model of good practice in such dialogue. It is certainly always involved in the new. Every translation, even a retranslation, is a new, and to some small extent reframed, reading of the original text. One of the reasons works like Dante's *Divine Comedy* or Homer's *Iliad* and *Odyssey* are repeatedly retranslated isn't just that they are literary summits for ambitious new translators – it's that translations *date*. They are ways of reading the original which match it with contemporary ideas of equivalent literary style, and may even draw out the particular ethical, political or other thematic aspects which resonate more strongly with the thought of their day. A translation is always a new reading; and so is always at the cutting edge of cultural reception. When, in 1971, Elaine Feinstein was the first to publish Marina Tsvetaeva in translation,[6] she introduced English readers to a whole new set of poetic possibilities (and, especially, possibilities for women's poetry). In doing so, she helped shift British prosody itself.

> Use Google, Amazon, libraries and anthologies to find out as many different versions as you can discover of a well-known text – anything from the *Tao Te Ching* to the much-quoted opening of the *Aeneid*. How do they compare formally – with each other and with the original? How many versions, especially from more than twenty years ago, do you think are still readable? Which elements estrange you, and which cause you to trust the translator? How important is *pleasure* in your reading of these translations, compared to the pleasure you expect to get from reading poetry in general?

Despite, or perhaps because of, these ramifications literary translation struggles to convey *both* the meaning and the innate character of a text. This struggle arises because sometimes, as in all writing, meaning and character seem to compete. An obvious example is the way rhyme can cut across intention during the writing of a poem. The workshop wisdom is that rhyme forces you to think beyond what you first felt was the destination of a line or verse: it helps you avoid the obvious. But this is complicated in translation, where the line's destination *is* predetermined. If, like the exiled Russian poet Joseph Brodsky, you have a firm belief – as most poets do, when it comes to their own work – in the impossibility of separating a poem's meaning from the words it uses, then you may find yourself, as he did, trying to use the *same* formal devices, such as strict metre and full rhyme, in the host language as in the original. Yet English, even in conversation, has a music totally different from Russian's: to say nothing of the differences in those linguistic resources which make rhyme easier (more organic) or more difficult (producing more arbitrary distortions).

If on the other hand you believe with Vladimir Nabokov, another great Russian prosodist exiled to the US, that the music–meaning relationship is contingent on the specifics of the original, and that it's masterful to an extent unlikely to be reproduced by a translator, then you will conclude, with him, that:

> 1. It is impossible to translate [Pushkin's *Eugene Onegin*] in rhyme.
> 2. It is possible to describe in a series of footnotes the modulations and rhymes of the text as well as its associations and other special features ... I want such footnotes and the absolutely literal sense ... for all the poetry in other tongues that still languishes in 'poetical' versions, begrimed and beslimed by rhyme.[7]

To put it another way, translation is always anxious about authority. Much translation theory is preoccupied with trying to think up ways to make the process of translation itself untransformative, transparent or scientific. This is particularly true of research by non-literary translators such as, in the 1950s, the logical philosopher Willard V. O. Quine or Roman Jakobson, pioneer of structuralist linguistics, each of whom one can't help but feel was trying to solve other, more general questions of language, using translation as a laboratory. But literary translation is, as we shall see, by definition unscientific: it is a series of special cases. It's as if such translation theory has heard an ideal reader asking, 'Says who?'

That question can paralyse an emerging writer's original writing, too. Translation reveals the truth in the cliché that a piece of writing is never finished, only abandoned; it creates a mode in which writing is process as much as product. It gives permission for what's contingent and partial in another way too. Translation also reminds us about the *particular* character of English. Unlike many languages, including Russian, English is not derived from a single root, then garnished with loanwords. Because it's split at the root by Germanic and Romance origins, it's relatively difficult to unify with matching sounds. It's no coincidence that the aurally integrated indigenous forms of half-line assonantal verse, Anglo-Saxon and Welsh-language *cynghanedd*, pre-date the Norman Conquest and the linguistic bifurcation that accompanied it. On the other hand, that split does make English a language of greater musical *range*. And, because its multiple roots offer so many synonyms to choose between, English literary language is characterised by those choices, and inflected by register and style to a greater extent than more unified literatures. So important are these choices that another way to think about English vocabulary might be to say that there is no such thing as a synonym. A *brook*, for example, isn't a *stream*. A brook is a slightly archaic, certainly specifically picturesque, pastoral phenomenon. A stream can appear in any setting and, although it can be a very small river, its second life as a verb of fast, vigorous movement means that it can also name the current in something larger. However small, it's clearly moving onward: unlike the brook, with its onomatopoeic suggestion of gurgling against small resistances, and its own second life as a verb that pauses (to hold, endure or enjoy).

The consequences of this for translation move in both directions. The point of English language poetry can be wholly lost in translation that fails to take account of both context and qualification. In Les Murray's poem about his life as a professional translator,

> The trade was uneasy about computers, back then:
> if they could be taught not to render, say, *out of sight*
> *out of mind* as *invisible lunatic*
>
> they might supersede us – not
> because they'd be better. More on principle.[8]

Perhaps more difficult though is the importance to English-language translation of taking responsibility for selecting the right vocabulary and register from an almost-too-open field of what at first glance seem like equivalents. So, where to start?

If you are bilingual, or studied languages, or have learnt one or more languages in adult life, you will already have a feel for *negotiating* between two or more vocabularies and conceptual worlds. If your language studies were part of formal education, you may well already have done some literary translation. But this chapter assumes that the emerging writer is no such special case. I have to imagine that you, like me, left school with very little expertise – and still less confidence – in any language other than English. Yet you love literature, have a healthy literary curiosity, and have a feel for language.

Don't be put off by the scholars and specialist translators who, clutching their language skills to their chests, claim that only they should translate or – worse – that we should all read literature in the original tongue. That's a privileged, bourgeois dream: do you have the wherewithal to learn a new language to the highest, literary level? I know that I spend my every free moment making time to write. It's also extraordinarily narrow. If I learn Italian so I can read Petrarch, do I not need to care about Dostoevsky or Tolstoy, should I assume the Koran has nothing to teach, or turn my back on contemporary Chinese experimental poets of witness, like Bei Dao and Yang Lian? Obviously not. All the same, it makes sense to start with translations about which no one can claim you don't know enough. For the non-polyglot, these are from dead languages – finite bodies of knowledge, all of which can *be looked up* – and co-translation, done in dialogue with the original author.

In the latter case, the original author isn't the 'real' translator. If poetry is, glibly, what's lost in translation, then literary translation is arguably what rediscovers the poetry – whether by trying to produce a new finished poem in the target language or by publishing a literal version with Nabokovian footnotes. Whatever its presentation, the nuanced, complex, choices that finish off a translation are the ones that make it 'literary'. A European or Asian intellectual with good 'conversational' English can't *write poems* in English; and so can't translate poems into English. But he, or she, can respond to detailed questions about intention, shades of meaning, form and register: about whether his 'brook' is in fact a 'stream'.

Co-translation has many advantages. It cements translation as a process of friendship. It allows the translating writer to make a deep and practical creative relationship with a writing peer. And it gets round the most difficult of problems, which is that very few individuals who are gifted enough to be established literary writers have that degree of command equally in more than one language. (Nabokov did: Brodsky, arguably, did not.) Political exile made translators out of the poets George Szirtes and, from an earlier generation, Ewald Osers. Poets like Marilyn Hacker (in Paris) and Herbert Lomas (in Finland) have lived and taught in the languages they translate from for many years. But these are the exceptional circumstances. Co-translation is one way to circumvent the problem that a little knowledge is a dangerous thing; allowing a full range of literary knowledge about both languages to come into play.

Here is a translation from a language I don't speak, Anglo-Saxon:

Saturn's Riddle
from *Solomon and Saturn*

What wonder travels this world
unstoppably, razing foundations,
raising tears, often victorious?
Not star nor stone nor ostentatious gem,
water nor wild beast, deflect it one whit,
but into its hand go hard and soft,
small and great. Into it
every single earth-dweller, air-skimmer, sea-swimmer –
three times thirteen thousand of them –
will fall.[9]

Like other contemporary poets, I chose to include some translations in my latest poetry collection. Like them, I wanted to vary the book's reading texture, and also to gather together what I felt was the best of my recent work. Besides, the 'Riddle''s theme fitted well with that of the rest of the book. The piece is a reasonably straightforward translation; yet the poem itself doesn't exist – at least not in this form. It's an extract from the second of the two long 'Dialogues of Solomon and Saturn' – this one is 336 lines long – which exist, with prose, among the surviving Anglo-Saxon wisdom poetry. I've always been fascinated by the wisdom poetry: it's gnostic, and clearly transitional. Here, for example, two pantheons meet in a dialogue in which the old Roman god is the more human protagonist – flawed, questioning – while the Abrahamic Solomon has the answers.

When Solomon answers *this* question of Saturn's, his surprising answer is not death, but the ageing process:

On earth, age overpowers everything
with press-gang prison-irons.
That great chain yaws wide,
a long line capturing all it desires.
It uproots trees and breaks branches,
shakes the standing stem,
gorges on soil, then gobbles down
the wild bird; it overwhelms the wolf.
It outlives stones, it outstays steel,
it eats up iron with rust: does the same to us.

For Saturn is not really setting Solomon a riddle; in fact this is speech searching for meaning; and in fact one of the marks of the surviving piece as a whole is the way in which Solomon and Saturn have differing, yet overlapping, perspectives. But taken out of context, the speech becomes a riddle.

I'd been commissioned to translate some of the Second Dialogue for an anthology compiled by a poet, Greg Delanty, and an Anglo-Saxonist, Michael Matto.[10] The editors made sure I had the original:

> Saturnus cwæð:
> 'Ac hwæt is ðæt wundor ðe geond ðas worold færeð
> styrnenga gæð, staðolas beateð 105
> aweceð wopdropan, winneð oft hider?
> Ne mæg hit steorra ne stan ne se steapa gimm,
> wæter ne wildeor wihte beswican,
> ac him on hand gæð heardes and hnesces,
> micles and mætes; him to mose sceall 110
> gegangan geara gehwelce grundbuendra,
> lyftfleogendra, laguswemmendra,
> ðria ðreoteno ðusendgerimes.'

And at least one crib:

> Saturn said: But what is that strange thing that travels through this world, goes on inexorably, beats at foundations, causes tears of sorrow, and often comes here? Neither star nor stone nor eye-catching jewel, neither water nor wild beast can deceive it at all, but into its hand go hard and soft, small and great. Every year there must go to feed it three times thirteen thousand of all that live on ground or fly in the air or swim in the sea.

and a glossary.

My first step was a word-by-word translation, ignoring the crib but using both the glossary and notes from another edition:

> Saturn said,
> But what is that wonder that through this world fares/travels,
> goes on inexorably, beats down foundations,
> awakes weep-drops, wins often here?
> Nor may star nor stone nor the conspicuous gem,
> water nor wild beast one whit it deflect,
> but into its hand go hard and soft,
> little and big. To him shall marsh/bog
> certainly go every single earth-dweller,
> air flyers, sea swimmers,
> three times thirteen thousand in number.

My next step was to look for ways in which I could paraphrase what was very literal into more conventional contemporary idiom:

Saturn said,	
But what wonder travels [through] this world,	strange thing
[going on] inexorably, flattening foundations,	unstoppably
causing tears, often winning?	victorious
Neither star nor stone nor conspicuous gem,	outstanding
water nor wild beast, can deflect it one whit,	
but into its hand go hard and soft,	
small and big. To it [bog]	
every single earth-dweller, air-flyer, sea-swimmer,	
three times thirteen thousand of them,	in number
will certainly go.	

But I didn't assume these were automatic improvements. After all, it's not only the case that Anglo-Saxon has a distinctive flavour; the poem-ness of this extract lies in its idiomatic expression.

The next step was to integrate these ways of reading: contemporary idiom and literal character. At each point I tried to choose an option which didn't 'overshoot' the rest of the piece. I didn't want to make choices which alienated the reader from the life of the poem; not only the life of its idea but the liveliness of the original sound. I found it particularly hard to get the register right for the 'size' words, *mickle and mighty* as I thought of them. Is 'big' a potentially childish word, like 'little'? By now I seemed to have committed myself to putting 'every single earth-dweller, air-skimmer, sea-swimmer' all on one line. I wanted the sense of motion and escalation this provided:

> Saturn said –
> But what wonder travels this world
> unstoppably, razing foundations,
> starting tears, often victorious?
> Neither star nor stone nor ostentatious gem,
> water nor wild beast, can deflect it one whit,
> but into its hand go hard and soft,
> small and big. Into it
> every single earth-dweller, air-skimmer, sea-swimmer –
> three times thirteen thousand of them –
> is sure to sink.

That 'sink' was a nod to the fog/marsh hovering in earlier drafts.

The poem is now nearly complete, but four changes are going to click it further into place. Conscious of the loss of assonance and alliteration from the original, I couldn't resist the sound-play of 'raising tears' straight after 'razing foundations'. 'Neither', introducing three alternatives, is ungrammatical and became 'Not'. I decided that 'mighty' was better served by 'great', and that any echo of 'all creatures great and small' was sufficiently ploughed-in by sticking to the original Anglo-Saxon word order, 'small and great'. Finally, 'is sure to sink' seemed to me too far removed from the poem's portrayal – not quite a personification – of the roving principle of ageing for a non-specialist, out of context, audience. I changed 'sink' to 'fall' and simplified the phrase to 'will fall', whose quadrupled *Ls* I thought clicked shut together, and slowed the poem's slightly speaking-rhythm into a two-foot line, heavy with closure.

Middle English, Anglo-Saxon and Latin poetry is often published in parallel text editions with a glossary (Greek, too, if you can read the alphabet). Use an edition of a poet/poetry you like and set yourself a specific short poem or short section – twelve lines is ideal – to translate. Translate every single word, looking each up in the glossary. If it has a resemblance to a contemporary English word (like the AS *mætes* – *mighty*), allow that to colour but not *determine* your thinking. Present-day vocabulary is a descendant of Latin and Anglo-Saxon, but it has been shaped by centuries of subsequent use. Now take this draft through each of the steps I took with 'Saturn's Riddle':

1. Check against a crib or existing translation, ideally more than one, for wild goose chases.
2. Paraphrase expressions and lines into conventional idiom.
3. Make a note of the music and form of the original. Is there any way you can imitate the effect (of measured metre or alliterative echo) even though you're not reproducing the form?
4. Try to integrate these separate streams of input into a single unified 'poem'.
5. Put that draft on one side, so that you can come back and see it as a whole.
6. What will tighten this draft up so it reads as an interesting text and not an exercise? Look at: sound, punning meanings, repetition/extended tropes like metaphor, diction.

Translation moves towards ownership in the final stages of this process. It's here that we need to think again about what translation can mean. And there are literal, close and loose translations, versions and homages to choose from. A good insight into this range comes from *Sappho through English Poetry*, edited by Peter Jay and Caroline Lewis, which cleverly anthologises many of the Sappho-inspired poems that have been published in English, from Sir Philip Sidney and John Donne to Michael Longley and David Constantine.[11] Comparing filmed versions of Shakespeare is a great way to see how laughably the tastes of their respective decades cut across what they assumed were neutral versions of the plays. Jay and Lewis's book does the equivalent of juxtaposing fifties kodachrome with seventies big hair and twenty-first-century star casting: Tennyson is falsely archaic in *Eleanore*, while A. E. Housman's Sappho has the folk-song metre of *A Shropshire Lad*.

In fact, though, Sappho is so widely translated that I can make a similar comparison by going to my bookshelf, where I find Anne Carson's steely filigree of Fragment 16 stanza 5:

> I would rather see her lovely step
> and the motion of light on her face
> than chariots of Lydians or ranks
> of footsoldiers in arms[12]

and Diane Arnson Svarlien's sensible problem-solving:

> How I love the way that she walks. I'd rather
> see her now in motion, the bright expression
> flashing from her eyes, than the whole assembled
> Lydian army[13]

Such comparisons remind us that translation is an act of creative ownership. But they don't in themselves seem to help us to distinguish as readers between degrees of additional creative improvisation. Poets, though, are as keen as anyone else for their work and gifts to be recognised – whether that feat is a scrupulously-close translation or a creative synthesis – and literary convention is for them to label what they do. A translation may be close or loose: so much so self-explanatory. It may also be a literal, but a *literal* literal isn't a recognisable text but a set of annotations which include the whole range of a definition, and Nabokovian footnotes about context.

Equally straightforward is a homage, which as it were strikes the original a glancing blow. A homage is a poem with its own beginning, middle and end. Its relationship to the original is tangential, if explicit. For example, it might do one of the following:

quote a famous image or trope from the original;
use the original's title;
retell the incidents of the original but from a different perspective and with a different outcome or conclusion;
borrow the form of the original (if this is distinctive);
use the persona of the original narrator.

As this list suggests, homage is a form of translation that doesn't have to involve a language barrier. It's possible, and creatively rich, to write a homage to another English-language text, or even to another art form. T. S. Eliot's *Four Quartets* are, among other things, a homage to a late string quartet by

Ludwig van Beethoven, but they're certainly not simple ekphrasis. They also pay homage to Dante (by using *terza rima*) and, through quotations, Dame Julian of Norwich and St John of the Cross – yet it's always clear that these originals have been synthesised into *new* poetry.

> Using one of the techniques above, base a homage on a poem you've recently got to know. What other strategies could you add to this list?

The most conceptually complex form of translation is the version. But it's also the kind that can be the most fruitful for the writer, since it brings together the stimulating constraints of a given original with room for manoeuvre. In other words, it is disciplined by the original, but can't rely on it as a creative alibi. This is partly because the version creates itself at *two* levels: first, by deciding the character that versioning will take and, second, by the success with which it carries it out. A version can, for example:

use a formal metre – with all the semantic changes that dictates – which differs from that of the original;
change the tense or the speaker of the original;
play with its diction – not for example by translating wholesale into dialect, which would be an act of straightforward translation, but by personifying certain speakers through slang;
transpose the work from its original setting.

> As before: are there techniques you would add to this list? Practise versioning, first of all, on the poem you translated earlier in the chapter. Now compare some of the versions mentioned below with their originals, or with straight translations of the same poems. Can you see why the poets have chosen their particular strategies in each case? Would you version one of these originals in a different way; changing the tense but not the setting, for example? Follow up your intuitions with actual versions.

Earlier in this chapter we saw how some of the most formative translation in English literary writing has been specifically transformative. Some of the most influential poetry translations in recent decades have also been versions. Robert Lowell's highly personal selection, almost a common-place book, of *Imitations* has introduced two generations of readers to a range of European poets – including Johann Peter Hebel and Umberto Saba – they might otherwise not have heard of. The book is controversial because the poet sacrifices aspects of the originals to make characteristic Lowell poems: yet from the title onwards it makes no attempt to conceal this strategy. Over the last twenty years, Christopher Logue has retold Homer in *Kings*, *The Husbands*, *War*

Music and *Cold Calls*: brilliant, often line-by-line translations but which reorder the original to tease out thematic concerns or specific substories. Among middle-generation poets, Jo Shapcott (in 'The Windows' from 1992's *Phrase Book* and 2001's *Tender Taxes*) and Don Paterson (in *Orpheus*) have each made Rainer Maria Rilke their own – and indeed his name is absent from their covers, though present on their title pages – but been faithful to the exposition of the original. As Paterson says, 'My main motivation in making this version was selfish. I wanted to make a rhymed English version for my own use, one that would, hopefully, have just a little of the self-sufficiency of the German – meaning one I could memorise, and carry round in my head.'[14]

Versioning thus exposes the pragmatic heart of translation. Like all creative practice, translation is ultimately contingent: a set of best-alternative choices given the constraints of the particular. Better practised than theorised, it is just like every other form of creative writing. Skill, techniques and awareness all need to be applied – at once – in a delicate, brilliant balancing act.

NOTES

1. T.S. Eliot, 'Philip Massinger', in *Selected Essays* (London: Faber and Faber, 1999), pp. 205–20, p. 206.
2. Paul Celan, 'Der Meridian', in Paul Celan, *Gesammelte Werke* (Frankfurt: Suhrkamp, 1983), vol. 3, p. 198, translated and cited in John Felstiner, 'Kafka and the Golem: Translating Paul Celan', in Daniel Weissbort (ed.), *Translating Poetry: The Double Labyrinth* (Iowa City: University of Iowa Press, 1985), pp. 35–50.
3. Gayatri Chakravorty Spivak, 'The Politics of Translation', in *Outside the Teaching Machine* (New York and London: Routledge, 2003), pp. 179–200, p. 182.
4. Miles Smith, 'The Translators to the Reader', in *King James Authorised Version of the Bible* (1611).
5. Martin Luther, 'Open Letter on Translation', in Daniel Weissbort and Astradur Eysteinsson (eds.), *Translation: Theory and Practice: A Historical Reader* (Oxford University Press, 2006), pp. 57–67, p. 64.
6. Elaine Feinstein, *Selected Poems of Marina Tsvetaeva* (Oxford University Press, 1971).
7. Vladimir Nabokov, 'Problems of Translation: Onegin in English', *Partisan Review*, 22 (1955), pp. 196–512, p. 512.
8. Les Murray, 'Employment for the Castes in Abeyance', in *Selected Poems* (Manchester: Carcanet, 1986), pp. 51–2, p. 51.
9. Fiona Sampson, *Rough Music* (Manchester: Carcanet, 2010), p. 36.
10. Greg Delanty and Michael Matto, *The Word Exchange: Anglo-Saxon Poems in Translation* (New York and London: W. W. Norton, 2010).
11. Peter Jay and Caroline Lewis, *Sappho through English Poetry* (London: Anvil, 1996).

12. Anne Carson, *If Not, Winter: Fragments of Sappho* (London: Virago, 2003), p. 29.
13. In Peter Constantine, Rachel Hadas, Edmund Keeley and Karen van Dyck (eds.), *The Greek Poets: From Homer to the Present* (New York and London: W. W. Norton, 2010), p. 87.
14. Don Paterson, *Orpheus* (London: Faber and Faber, 2006), p. 65.

10

PHILIP NEILSEN

Life writing

Two hundred years ago life writing was already highly popular in the form of autobiography, memoir, biography, journals, essays and diaries. It now commands a huge share of the publishing market, as there is an enormous demand from readers for narratives based directly on 'real lives'.

There is a lot of common ground between the two main forms – autobiography/memoir and biography: both require skilled storytelling (rather than listing facts and events), research and imagination. The quality of the writing itself is crucial to the impact on the reader. A person can have an exciting, worthy life but unfortunately write about it (or be written about) in a dull way. And how a person is remembered and valued can be a factor of life writing about or by them. This chapter will define and contextualise life writing, look at specific detailed examples, and offer guidance on how to write effectively.

Key concepts and strategies in life writing

These will help you think through what is required of each form, which form best suits you, and what aspects to address in your writing. Life writing is primarily a way of making an individual's life and times – either one's own or someone else's – 'matter' to others, and to reflect on what is important about that life. It makes a story about a 'self' that develops in some way. Finally, life writers use the organising principles of narrative to give shape to a life. (Biography also can be a story about a group of people, a city, animal or object.)

Memoir needs to resonate with 'authenticity', while a biographer also needs to be a sceptical detective sorting through ambiguities, prejudice, myths and false testimony or evidence. We now expect a high degree of 'openness' from life writing – though this began as early as Samuel Pepys's sexually explicit diaries (1660–9). Despite, or perhaps because of, postmodernism making us more alert to the constructed nature of identity and history, the writer's 'contract with the reader' to be truthful remains powerful. You have a great deal of choice in whom you write about – no longer is it thought, as Dr Johnson pronounced: 'Nobody can write the life of a man, but those who have eat and drunk and lived in social intercourse with him.'

All life writing imposes an illusion of coherence and establishes patterns. Questions of 'self', 'memory' and 'truth' are central to this coherence.

Self

In making a story about a 'self' you can combine the traditional, 'stable self' model with more recent concepts: of the self as formed by contingency; or by evolutionary forces such as adaptation (nature); or by childhood experience or education (nurture); or by language itself. You don't need to tick all those boxes in your life writing – but an awareness of them is valuable in your representation of individuals in all their rich layers.

As life writers we often gain perspective by maintaining some distance from our subjects and our selves. Writing as both a reflective (thoughtful, questioning) and reflexive (engaging with either one's own self or another person as 'other') process assists in this.

> It involves creating an internal space, distancing ourselves from ourselves . . . so that we are both 'inside' and 'outside' ourselves simultaneously and able to switch back and forth . . . giving ourselves up to the experience of 'self as other' whilst also retaining a grounding in our familiar sense of self.[1]

Memory

Life writing is activated by memory – either your own or the gathered memories of others. The way memory works can be painful or restorative, but always a dynamic process of seeking and remaking. It both unifies and fragments experience. It locates us as agents within our own life, which inevitably we see as a story.

In other words, what we are and know depends on what we remember, and our memory alters a remembered scene over time. Philip Roth expresses this succinctly: 'facts are never just coming at you but are incorporated by an imagination that is formed by your previous experience. Memories of the past are memories not of facts but memories of your imagining of the facts.'[2] So we need to be cautious about our memories, but also embrace the creative aspect they can bring to our writing – filling in gaps, probing in dark corners, enlarging our point of view, providing more of a sense of the elusiveness of lived experience. Toni Morrison eloquently explains how we rely on the senses in remembering:

> Writers are like that: remembering where we were, what valley we ran through, what the banks were like, the light that was there and the route back to our original place. It is emotional memory – what the nerves and skin remember as well as how it appeared.[3]

And Mark Philip Freeman links memory with our earlier key concept – the 'self': 'Memory . . . which often has to do not merely with recounting the past but with making sense of it . . . is an interpretative act the end of which is an enlarged understanding of the self.'[4]

Fictional techniques

This 'interpretative act' links life writing to fictional narrative – shaping a story. Every commentator on life writing stresses its dependence on fictional techniques, and biographer Michael Holroyd draws a boundary: 'Biographers have learned a good deal from novelists . . . Though the biographer may not invent dialogue . . .'[5] We could argue that even dialogue can be imagined, to add immediacy. But it would need to be 'plausible' in context and inference, such as dialogue based on sentiments expressed in actual letters written by the people concerned. Unlike fiction, life writing is thought of as 'falsifiable' – that is, its truthfulness can be *tested* as a representation of actual events.

As for plotting, Richard Holmes has recommended you consider 'the hope–dread axis': 'This is true of all storytelling and it's certainly true of biography. What do you hope for your subject and what do you fear for them?' This should drive the choice of how you narrate.[6]

Truth

While it is correct that no matter how truthful we aim to be, we are still creating a version of reality, and readers know the full truth is elusive, they still expect the life writer to demonstrate the *intent* to deliver truth – or not to represent invention as truth. 'Inauthentic' life writing is frowned on, as demonstrated by the vehement attacks on Edmund Morris, James Frey and Norma Khouri. The implicit 'contract with the reader' still matters.

Diction

The skilful use of language to capture emotion, including mixed feelings – is illustrated by Andrew Motion's boyhood memoir, in which his fresh diction and juxtapositions ('a shout and a secret') recast the familiar pastime of bird watching as both ephemeral and thrilling:

> When ... I kept one in focus for long enough to check the quiff on its head wasn't black at all, but green as a gun barrel, I felt I'd understood something special – something like a shout and a secret mixed together. And it meant I always ended my trips feeling disappointed, no matter how much I'd enjoyed myself. A black drop in my stomach, the same as being hungry.[7]

Precise word choice ('gun barrel', 'black drop') is crucial here in establishing tone – the variable aspect of voice.

Demonstrate don't state

We usually inform, give pleasure and provoke thought by means of showing, not bald statement. The information is as accurate as you can make it, but when conveyed by the dramatic devices of characterisation and scenes, it creates an immediacy closer to lived experience.

Characterisation

All primary individuals need to be as well realised as characters in a novel, with their own mix of social background and psychology (class, race, gender, motivation, desires, contradictions) – which lifts them above stereotype and aids insight and understanding.

Organising principles

Every form of life writing requires you to choose organising principles of writing, so as to give form and structure to the content of your narrative. The basic form of introduction, body and conclusion is the staple template – but much can be done beyond these basics.

Many narratives are still conventionally arranged in chronological order, to tell a continuous story of the subject from birth to death, or childhood to adulthood. But your arrangement may jump forward and backwards in time, sometimes returning to an event already treated, to give it a new interpretation and calling into question other episodes or views in the narrative. This approach may be closer to our lives as we experience them, rather than one smooth flow. However, there seems currently to be a return to more traditional approaches – with a strong story arc and comprehensible, 'stable' characters favoured by many readers.

Through-lines

It is extremely useful to have organising themes or 'through-lines' to aid coherence and lucidity. Common themes are: a search for identity; gaining a sense of belonging; exploring loss of various kinds; love and friendship; reconciling past and present; celebration of courage and survival; the role of circumstance and accident; the impossibility of escaping the past; the relationship with a parent or child; moving towards discovery or revelation; moving from childhood to adulthood; or understanding the importance of place. You may shape your story by repeatedly contrasting past and present situations and re-examining your own preconceptions, or use the trajectory of reaching and surviving a turning point or crisis, or achieving greater self-awareness or transformation, or preparing for and negotiating a traumatic or challenging event or condition, or being confronted by the unexpected and finding a way of coping.

Forms of life writing

Diaries

This is the most intimate form of life writing. The famous diarists (e.g. Pepys, Anne Frank) strive for self-examination. Antonia Fraser's diaries of her years with Harold Pinter are compelling because a formidable person admits her fears and limitations, even if this conflicts with other evidence of her wisdom or good judgement:

> I love Harold, I adore him, but I wonder whether I am *capable* of uprooting myself for anyone? Do I have the courage? I am quite a cowardly person, I know. Whether I have not finally and carefully constructed my own very pleasant prison [her marriage to Hugh Fraser] from which emotionally I can't escape. If only we could just go on and on being lovers . . . I fear for the effects of everyday life on love.[8]

One of her last entries pinpoints the main pitfalls in writing a diary: 'Did I go on a bit too much about my own sufferings? Diaries are self-pitying instruments. Did I criticise Harold? Diaries are also self-justificatory, q.v. the Tolstoys.'[9]

The internet and blogs have facilitated a blossoming of diary writing, though of a kind intended for an immediate reader. It is those blogs written with verve, sincerity and ingenuity that stand out from the cyber mass.

Hybrids

In her foreword to *The View from Castle Rock*, which explores the eighteenth-century world of her Scottish ancestors as well as more recent family life in Canada, Alice Munro makes it clear that she has enjoyed the imaginative blurring of the boundaries between memoir, family history and fiction. She has combined fact and invention, in pursuit of a kind of emotional or psychological 'truth':

> I put all this material together over the years, and almost without my noticing what was happening, it began to shape itself, here and there, into something like stories. Some of the characters gave themselves to me in their own words, others rose out of their situations. Their words and my words, a curious re-creation of lives, in a given setting that was as truthful as our notion of the past can ever be.
>
> ... I put myself in the centre and wrote about that self, as searchingly as I could.[10]

So narrative can contain both the truth of fact and the truth of fiction, as explained by H. Porter Abbott:

> The historian Hayden White used the term *emplotment* to describe this process of turning a mere *chronicle* of events, coming one after another, into a story with a beginning, middle and end, guided by deep structures of genre and story (*masterplots*) with all their potential freight of thought and feeling. In this way, the past is infused with meaning through the process of narrativization. Facts, in short, don't speak for themselves. They must be interpreted. And interpreting facts as they proceed in time requires turning them into a story.[11]

Before looking at each of the major forms more closely, it may be useful to offer this summary: autobiography focuses on an individual's life and tries to explore the development of that individual into what they find themselves now to be; memoir often explores in a more anecdotal and selective way the effect upon an individual of the events and people encountered by that individual; biography tries to explore the constituent elements of an individual's nature or psychological make-up and evaluate the importance of the life they lived. Of course, in practice these distinctions can be blurred.

Autobiography and memoir

Though the word 'autobiography' dates from around 1800, classical writers such as the poet Sappho (*c.* 600 BC) wrote of personal experiences. Augustine (AD 354–430) recorded his youthful imperfections, but offered himself as a model; whereas Montaigne's much later *Essays* (1595) have more faith in the credibility of idiosyncratic disclosures than in models or generalisations. As we would expect, autobiography always reflects the conception of 'self' of the period in which it is produced.

'Memoir' was a term in use from the 1500s. By the late 1700s it was established in a non-religious confessional form – not just Rousseau's philosophical *Confessions* (which many see as the start of the modern autobiography), but also 'scandalous memoirs' – including by actresses and prostitutes. Intimate confession is still a mainstay of memoir, as in Kathryn Harrison's *The Kiss* (1997), which recounts her incestuous relationship with her father, breaking perhaps the last taboo of the genre.

Memoir as powerful historical testimony for a generation is exemplified by Eli Wiesel's *All Rivers Run to the Sea*, in which he describes his survival of the Holocaust. The war memoir endures, but with some elements (such as honouring courage) remaining and other ideals subverted, as cultural values are re-examined. *The Last Enemy*, a classic by Richard Hillary, an Australian pilot in the Battle of Britain, despite its self-deprecation and occasional cynicism is also buoyed with idealism and thoughts of building a better world through gallantry:

> In a fighter plane ... we have found a way to return to war as it ought to be, war which is individual combat between two people, in which one either kills or is killed. It's exciting, it's individual, and it's disinterested.[12]

Jarhead, Anthony Swofford's account of the first Gulf War, is more extreme in its cynicism and disparagement of himself and his comrades. Hillary was killed a year after writing his memoir, while Swofford has the benefit of hindsight. Unlike Hillary he uses present tense and staccato sentences for immediacy and to mimic formally his task of stitching together fragments of memory. He suggests all war stories are essentially the same, like war movies; the differences lie in the individual. This through-line is set up in his first paragraph:

> But, no, I am not mad. I am not well, but I am not mad. I'm after something. Memory, yes. A reel. More than just time. Years pass. But more than just time. I've been working towards this – I've opened the ruck and now I must open myself.[13]

Both writers are self-consciously dealing with the common elements of memoir – the plasticity of memory, selectivity (from the 'ruck') and self-representation. Both avoid an over-lyrical style, or a tone that is self-important or flippant. Their voice is sincere and penetrating, even while playful. Swofford's voice is also open about what is going on: memoir seems to excuse this aspect of telling rather than showing, because readers expect to know what the shared task will be – such as reclaiming memory, or understanding an event.

Autobiography and memoir work best when addressing a *problem* of some kind, and achieving layers of reflection and exploration. When you start, write down a chapter plan and be prepared to revise it as the work proceeds; you may have dwelled too long on earlier years, or repeated yourself unnecessarily, or now see a pattern that has emerged, that could be made clearer.

Detailed example

Chloe Hooper's multi-award winning *The Tall Man* (2008) is a hybrid of memoir, biography of a place, and reportage. Hooper spent some time living on Palm Island off north-eastern Australia, where the death in police custody of an indigenous man had led to a riot and the police station burned down. She researched the history of the island, came to know the family and friends of the deceased man Cameron Doomadgee and also several of the police and lawyers. She attempts to be fair to both the indigenous and police perspective (both have strengths and flaws), but finally shows her keenest sympathy lies with the least powerful. Though she takes great pains to document the feelings and beliefs of others, everything is filtered through her own palpable presence and consciousness, tracing her own struggle to understand the complexity of the issues and people. Early in the book she describes Senior Sergeant Chris Hurley, the tall policeman being investigated for allegedly causing the death of Doomadgee:

> In front of him was the sea; and the mountains reared up close behind. On Dee Street one house was salmon pink, the next dark blue, then light blue and lime green and yellow; a tropical mix, bright colours to disguise that every second house had broken windows, graffiti, small children playing around beer cans. This was now Hurley's natural environment, and this was another typical day. He had become a creature of the Deep North, a specialist in places on the edges of so-called civilisation: Aboriginal communities and frontier towns in Cape York and the Gulf of Carpentaria. Places where the streets, the days, shimmered as if you were in a kind of fever – all of it, with its edge of menace, like some brilliant hallucination.[14]

Hooper's description has symbolic resonance that reinforces both the characterisation and unifying themes. On Palm Island nothing is as it seems and the tropical paradise is a prison for all – Hurley is hemmed in by mountains ('rearing up') and sea. The merrily painted houses are misleading, subtly raising the book's themes of misinterpretation and the elusiveness of 'truth' in this place, as does the imagery of 'shimmering' and the indistinctness of 'hallucination' – the distortion of perception and difficulty of seeing issues fully here. Representing Hurley as a 'creature' of this environment suggests the shared humanity and problems of the two groups, and his attempts to reach out to the people there, but also anticipates the more sinister *Heart of Darkness* and Kurz allusion Hooper will later make. The vastness of the Gulf and Cape are in ironic juxtaposition to the motif of the tall man – seen physically as a giant among these people, but dwarfed by the weight of a brutal history and a surviving culture he can not actually be part of. It is a fine example of the maxim to demonstrate and evoke rather than state.

The description of Hurley in the witness box later, when legal proceedings seem to be going badly for him, focuses on a layered psychological profile, but is again accompanied by sharp physical description and cultural context. Earlier Hooper had asked several times to interview Hurley but he had not replied:

> Penned there he looked rotten, as if there was something poisonous inside him. You could almost see the bitter rage rocking through his head.
>
> I thought of the cave painting I'd hiked to see in Cape York, showing a two-metre-tall police officer being bitten on the foot by a huge snake, perhaps the Rainbow Serpent – the totem of Doomadgee's grandmother. Hurley had told his story as a man would suck venom from a bite. His life was at stake. And this was the only antidote . . .
>
> Then, for some reason, Hurley looked over at me . . . His glare had partially erased [his eyes], had sunk them even deeper into their sockets, so it took a few seconds to realise I was its subject. I don't know if he knew who I was; I suspect he did. With a weak smile I turned away, feeling my blood surge. I did not have it in me to stare back. He was a man trying to save his life and he seemed to be saying, *How dare you judge me?*[15]

Hurley depends on his courtroom narration of events – just as our life stories define all of us – and his protective story and identity are under threat. Hooper brings herself dramatically into the scene by describing the moment the two finally face one another. She has written herself into his story, but she admits her own human frailty by being unable to hold his gaze. And her uneasiness about 'judgement' echoes the ethical predicament of all life writers. *The Tall Man* convinces through its background research, skilful deployment of literary techniques, efforts to be fair, and the through-line of a surviving indigenous culture which sustains identity. It permits much more involvement of the writer in the narrative than we would expect in biography, and acknowledges its ultimate subjectivity. The writing depends for its authority on crafting an engaging and honest voice, as well as attaching meaning to circumstance and integrating reflection, analysis, understanding and revelation. Even with an obvious inequality of power among the participants, it tries to avoid simple value judgements, or the shorthand reduction of Hurley to a *type*, despite his symbolic connotations.

Biography

It is usually said that biography progressed from exemplary Lives of saints (*types*), to more 'realistic' accounts such as Boswell's *The Life of Samuel Johnson* (1791), slid backwards with Victorian hagiography, idealised and sanitised, and went forward again in modernist experiments. However,

Aubrey's *Brief Lives* of the 1670s and 1680s look quite modern in their psychological enquiry, frankness and vitality. The sharply illustrative anecdote was just as important to biography then. Who today could resist Aubrey's account of Edward de Vere bowing to Queen Elizabeth and accidentally farting – the shame of which sent the earl into self-exile for seven years. Boswell's biography of his obsessive, intimidating, witty, truth-seeking companion is still the most famous. (It should be noted that although women's writing in print multiplied in this time – including diaries and letters – memoirs by, or biographies of, women did not. The novelist Fanny Burney had to settle for editing her father's memoirs.) Boswell was already using terms that have a twenty-first-century ring, such as 'authenticity', and both he and Johnson stressed the need for concrete and particular details to be captured.

Contemporary biography owes much to the modernists as well. As one of the finest biographers, Hermione Lee, has pointed out, they

> set out to change the way life-stories could be written ... The 'art of biography' used miniaturism, craft and craftiness, imaginative fictional tactics, irony, parody, and caricature ... The biographer could be the equal, not the respectful or awe-struck disciple of the subject. Biographers were self-conscious; biography might even be seen as a form of autobiography. Above all, biography aimed to uncover the inner self behind the public figure, with the help of the new tool of psychoanalysis.[16]

Lytton Strachey's portraits of four famous Victorians were both empathetic and iconoclastic, a mix common today. His Florence Nightingale is no less admirable for her egotism – she is a celebrity in a time when such status required extraordinary talent and achievement. But Strachey wants us to know also that myth can be more powerful than reality, and demonstrates this through public and private dramatic scenes:

> ladies, mistaken by the crowd for Miss Nightingale, were followed, pressed upon, and vehemently supplicated – 'Let me touch your shawl'; 'Let me stroke your arm' ... That vast reserve of force lay there behind her ... she might hint or threaten ... remind some refractory Minister, some unpersuadable Viceroy ... that she had only, so to speak, to go to the window and wave her handkerchief, for ... dreadful things to follow. But that was enough; they understood; the myth was there – obvious, portentous, impalpable; and so it remained to the last.[17]

Virginia Woolf stressed the importance of gaining access to the inner life of the biographical subject, and in 'The Art of Biography' (1939) she anticipated a twenty-first-century view of the biographer as having to 'admit contradictory versions of the same face' and to be prepared to subvert the biographical form itself.

But imaginative subversion is very different from distortion for cheap effect. Hermione Lee skewers the biopic film *The Hours* for resorting to stereotype:

> For all its polemical earnestness about the mistreatment of mental illness and the constrictions imposed on Virginia Woolf after her breakdown, the film evacuates her life of political intelligence or social acumen, returning her to the position of doomed, fey, mad victim. I wish, for instance, that she could have been seen setting type at the Press alongside Leonard, as she so often did, instead of wandering off for gloomily creative walks on Richmond Hill.[18]

So what are the ingredients of successful biographies today? Most can be found in the best that has gone before: well-judged tone, historical context, psychologically complex characterisation, vivid description, frankness, personally intimate anecdote and feel, realism and humour (ranging from irony to satire), a commitment to 'truth', and refraining from easy moral conclusions. The focus of the biography must not stray for long from the main subject, and selects the most telling events and decisions. A biography requires a strong narrative arc – and does not give away key revelations too soon. There is now an understanding that most individuals create a public identity for themselves that nevertheless relates to the private self. You need to be aware of these multiple identities and their intersection in your biography. A good biographer has an impressive range of abilities: they forge an imaginative bond with their subject; strike a balance between involvement and detachment (so they are neither sentimental nor boring); persevere through years of research; interview living sources and draw telling knowledge from them; and write with the storytelling skills of a novelist.

Detailed examples

Putting the record straight

Biographies are perhaps at their most exciting when, as with Tim Jeal's biography of the explorer Stanley, or Antonia Fraser's biography of Oliver Cromwell, painstaking research and the ability to step back and see the subject with fresh eyes gives us a fairer or even radically revised assessment of someone's life.

Jeal's *Stanley: The Impossible Life of Africa's Greatest Explorer* largely rehabilitates an explorer formerly condemned as a racist, a murderous imperialist who 'duped' chiefs out of their land. Through documentary evidence Jeal gives us a warts and all, but nevertheless different individual – one who is formed by his illegitimacy, abandonment by his mother and rearing in a Welsh workhouse – who invents a new persona for himself as an American, fights in the Civil War and through persistence, skill and courage becomes Britain's greatest land explorer (finding the source of the Nile and the Congo), admires the African peoples and is comparatively restrained in violent acts for an explorer of that time. (Stanley came to see explorers as buccaneers, intruding uninvited on Africa.) He emerges as a scapegoat for the excesses of those who came later to the Congo to exploit it – a 'gentler, sadder person' lacking in self-esteem and trapped into repeating for many years the imaginary background and identity that he had given himself, even in his *Autobiography*. Jeal tries to avoid preconceptions and forms a convincingly complex psychological profile of Stanley; he also has a strong through-line in the theme of invention – the Stanley who was invented by his detractors, but more importantly Stanley's own self-invention, which brought him both fame and anguish. Jeal argues that Stanley's famous words – 'Dr Livingstone, I presume?' – were a deliberate fabrication:

> It seems to me that his invention of an adoptive father, and his setting himself the task of finding Dr Livingstone long before he had interested a newspaper in the idea, were remarkable enough in their own right to merit remembrance. To go on from there to invent a greeting so memorable that it would be recognised by millions over a century and a quarter after places him in a class of his own. The fact that Stanley would be ridiculed and patronised as a direct result of this greeting, which he almost certainly never uttered, is painfully ironic. He invented it because of his old insecurity about his background. Ill at ease among the British officers in Abyssinia, he had admired their laconic, understated style and had hoped to emulate it. He had been struck especially by an anecdote in Kinglake's *Eothen* concerning two English gentlemen whose paths had crossed in the wilds of Palestine, and who had uttered no words of greeting but merely lifted their caps and walked by. Henry had thought this the height of gentlemanly insouciance. Of course, many English gentlemen would have thought it unfriendly and absurd. But how could the insecure outsider have known this?
>
> Later, when people were laughing at him for coming up with a parody of drawing room gentility at this highly emotional moment, instead of a joyful exultation, Stanley knew he had made a fool of himself, but by then it was too late to retract.[19]

Jeal has skilfully increased sympathy for his subject by satirising the very class Stanley hoped to be accepted by; and chooses the perfect anecdote (the Palestine encounter) to support his speculation as to Stanley's inspiration, as well as implying the impossibility of him overcoming entrenched discrimination against his humble past. He also maintains a tragicomic balance to preserve his tone of admiration for, but ability to criticise, his subject. In various scenes, Jeal gives us the pathos of Stanley's life, but without

3. The 'Stanley Cap' in 1885: photograph in *The Autobiography of Henry M. Stanley*, ed. Dorothy Stanley (1909), copyright not applicable

sentimentality and even with humour, as in his description of the headwear he invented; Jeal aligns it with the name his African workers gave Stanley of 'Bula Matari' – 'breaker of rocks':

> His self-designed, and unintentionally comical 'Stanley Cap' ... with its tall crown, numerous ventilation holes, cloth 'havelock' to shield the neck, and its military peak ... seems almost to have been intended to make its unsmiling, mustachioed wearer appear worthy of the name Bula Matari – in short, the ideal disguise for a sensitive and wounded man who wished to seem invulnerable.[20]

Jeal makes his own recreation of Stanley consistent by cleverly intertwining recurrent themes of recreation, inner conflict and defensiveness. But at the micro level he also turns the concrete description of an object – the cap – into a metaphor for Stanley's psychological problems.

One of the most popular biographers is Antonia Fraser. She finds a style that is sophisticated but accessible. Her biography of Cromwell also reassesses a historical figure – one who often has been vilified despite his peerless military courage and brilliance, and to a significant degree, championing of democratic ideals well ahead of their time. Fraser strips away myths and misinformation. But see how she describes his greatest failure to live up to his ideals, in the notorious battle in Drogheda:

> Oliver's own mercy was said to have been stirred by the sight of a tiny baby still trying hopelessly to feed from the breast of its dead mother. Propaganda is one thing. Personal guilt is another. It is personal guilt which interests the biographer. The conclusion cannot be escaped that Cromwell lost his self-control at Drogheda, literally saw red – the red of his comrades' blood – after the failure of the first assaults, and was seized by one of those sudden brief and cataclysmic rages which would lead him later to dissolve Parliament by force and sweep away that historic bauble ... The slaughter itself stood quite outside his usual record of careful mercy as a soldier ...
>
> And so quickly over, in the heat of the moment, in a foreign land, occurred the incident that has blackened Oliver Cromwell's name down history ...[21]

Life writing usually proceeds by creating scenes and summaries; after having given us the shocking battle scene, Fraser follows with the summary. She inserts herself into the narrative as the biographer, citing pro-Cromwell propaganda, and so by implication asking us to be wary of stories told against him, reminding us that history is continually rewritten, usually by the most powerful. She also admits the horror of his acts while suggesting that no act is inexplicable – avoiding simplistic concepts such as evil or destiny. Cromwell is swayed by his own personality (prone at times to sudden anger and precipitate action), but also the sight of his 'comrades' blood' in a 'foreign' land. Carefully chosen diction provides an undercurrent of explanation, and the 'sudden brief' and 'quickly over' phrases reduce the magnitude of the violence. Parliament is described paradoxically as a 'historic bauble' – which contrasts a positive sense of tradition and authority with a meaningless frippery. Here the tone is deliberately ironic and tells against Cromwell.

In the Hooper, Jeal and Fraser extracts, we see that the best life writing is not reductive, but instead seeks out its subjects, looking always for meaningful encounters rather than judgements.

Poetic life writing

It is well worth experimenting with this form. There is a long tradition – including Dante's *La vita nuova* (*c.* 1294), Wordsworth's *The Prelude* (written 1798–1805, published 1850), Robert Lowell, Anne Sexton, Sylvia Plath, Seamus Heaney's *Death of a Naturalist* (1966), and Ted Hughes's *Birthday Letters* (1998). Here is an extract from a narrative poem of my own – 'The Art of Lying':

When I was fifteen I told my friends that I jumped
off the Indooroopilly bridge for a dare –
by the time I was twenty-five I could describe the feel
of the water, the cold muddy shock, the soft greasy river-bed,
musky smell of weeds on the bank, drying in the sun,
cars passing over the bridge as I lay on my back.

Then my wife told my parents and the lie lurched
out of its safe cosy cave . . .
She didn't talk all the way home, just
'I bet you lie in your dreams':
What's the use of describing to her the roaring in my ears,
the pain in my back and left leg, scratched face
from the drifting debris?[22]

The poem is confessional memoir, its unifying theme the way we retell lies until they become as influential as truths, its aim to find meaning in trying to recapture a crucial experience from boyhood. The 'I' persona of the poem is less tangible than the experience of struggling from the Brisbane River – which is no less formative for being imaginary. Imagination is demonstrated to be active in constructing an emotional truth – the sensual appreciation of being alive and aware of one's surroundings. Which in turn suggests an eco-critical theme: the self of the poem feels most whole and genuine when in connection with nature – even if suburban, not pastoral.

Life writing as health therapy

The physiological and psychological benefits of life writing have been clinically demonstrated. Pennebaker argues that 'catharsis or the venting of emotions' without 'cognitive processing' has little therapeutic value and people need to 'build a coherent narrative that explains some past experience' in order to benefit from writing.[23] As Pennebaker and Seagal reason in the *Journal of Clinical Psychology*, the life-writing process:

> allows one to organise and remember events in a coherent fashion while integrating thoughts and feelings . . . [T]his gives individuals a sense of predictability and control over their lives. Once an experience has structure and meaning, it would follow that the emotional effects of that experience are more manageable.[24]

The term 'dysnarrativia' has been coined to describe the documented difficulty in constructing self-narrative among those suffering amnesia, autism, severe child abuse or brain damage. Paul John Eakin stresses the importance of self-narrative in creating our identity.[25] Most exciting for teachers and students of creative writing, there is evidence from Vicki Lindner for example, that life writing which is guided according to fundamental aesthetic principles such as structure, avoidance of cliché, and concrete descriptive detail is more effective therapeutically than less well-written work.[26] This has been my own experience in conducting life-writing workshops for those with severe mental illness. Even fictional autobiography can bestow a richer sense of self-identity, as attested by Fiona Sampson.[27] Digital storytelling – where the writer prepares a brief autobiographical script to accompany video or still photographs to illustrate a life episode – is another powerful tool.

All the forms we have looked at require a well-written narrative that constructs a self and places it in a real social context in order to make meaning of a life. And there always needs to be openness: in autobiography you need to write as frankly as you can manage; in the biography you need to be open to your subject – not try to fit them into your preconceived notions or theoretical frameworks. As life writers we investigate the choices we or others made, and we give others the opportunity to speak through us.

Writing exercises

1. Memoir can be brief and so very suitable for workshops. Begin 250 words with 'There was a time when I believed that ... But now I've changed my mind / look at it differently ...' Then read it to see if there is a framing theme or through-line; one should have emerged that you can develop when rewriting the piece.
2. One of the joys of starting a new relationship is telling your favourite anecdotes from your past. Make two lists – one of anecdotes that reflect well on you, one of those that do not. In 250 words, use one anecdote to shed light on the puzzle of yourself as a character, including the social context of the time and a relevant conflict.
3. Think of a street, house or room where you have lived, but not visited for quite a few years. For fifteen minutes make a list of things you remember that were in that place, or associations with it (smells, music, illness, a mystery, a discovery, a loss, an infatuation, books, an important person not fully understood). Write a page using your list to describe that place. Then visit the location and see what you have remembered accurately and what you have altered or forgotten. Your first version may still be the most evocative, even if you have imagined

some details. In note form, write what you think your page has illuminated about you or another person.

4. Write about the same subject in first- and then in third-person point of view: focusing on the dynamics/relationships in your immediate family; or on an event in your own life during the last year (in third person you will portray yourself as a character). Note how the voice, tone, amount of detail, level of insight and complexity have varied in the two versions. List the advantages of each narrative point of view in these two pieces of writing.
5. Study the photo of Stanley in his cap, then describe it and his related personality in a way that is entirely positive, and not comical.
6. Two major ways of structuring life writing are by recreating a specific encounter or scene (with the details dwelled upon sharply, and spanning only a short time), or by giving a summary (spanning days or even years, when you need to move your narrative along to a later time). Firstly, write a short *scene* that could be part of the chapter of a biography (choose a historical or contemporary figure who interests you, and recreate the way they behaved in a meeting or argument with another person). Secondly, provide a *summary* of the week/month/year that followed. Use 250 words each for the scene/encounter and the summary.
7. Write a first-person poem of 12–20 lines with a narrative structure. Base it on a key event or turning point from your life. Make sure the description and imagery is fresh, concrete (not abstract) and appeals to the senses. Avoid using a tone of complaint or self-absorption.

NOTES

1. Celia Hunt and Fiona Sampson, *Writing: Self and Reflexivity*, 3rd edn (New York: Palgrave Macmillan, 2006), p. 4.
2. Philip Roth, *The Facts: A Novelist's Autobiography* (New York: Vintage Books, 1997), p. 8.
3. Toni Morrison, 'The Site of Memory', in Carolyn C. Denard (ed.), *What Moves at the Margin: Selected Nonfiction* (Mississippi University Press, 2008), p. 77.
4. Mark Philip Freeman, *Rewriting the Self: History, Memory, Narrative* (London: Routledge, 1993), p. 29.
5. Michael Holroyd, *Works on Paper: The Craft of Biography and Autobiography* (London: Little, Brown, 2002), p. 26.
6. Quoted in Sara Haslam and Derek Neale, *Life Writing* (London: Routledge, 2009), p. 177.
7. Andrew Motion, *In the Blood: A Memoir of My Childhood* (London: Faber and Faber, 2006), p. 177.

8. Antonia Fraser, *Must You Go? My Life with Harold Pinter* (London: Weidenfeld & Nicolson, 2010), p. 21.
9. Ibid., p. 262.
10. Alice Munro, *The View from Castle Rock: Stories* (London: Vintage, 2007), pp. ix–x.
11. H. Porter Abbott, *The Cambridge Introduction to Narrative*, 2nd edn (Cambridge University Press, 2008), p. 155.
12. Richard Hillary, *The Last Enemy* (London: Macmillan 1942), p. 17.
13. Anthony Swofford, *Jarhead: A Marine's Chronicle of the Gulf War* (New York: Scribner, 2003), p. 1.
14. Chloe Hooper, *The Tall Man: Death and Life on Palm Island* (Camberwell, Vic.: Hamish Hamilton, 2008), p. 20.
15. Ibid., pp. 235–6.
16. Hermione Lee, *Biography: A Very Short Introduction* (Oxford University Press, 2009), p. 72.
17. Lytton Strachey, *Eminent Victorians: Cardinal Manning, Florence Nightingale, Dr. Arnold, General Gordon* (London: Chatto & Windus, 1918), pp. 152–3.
18. Hermione Lee, *Body Parts: Essays in Life-Writing* (London: Pimlico, 2008), p. 40.
19. Tim Jeal, *Stanley: The Impossible Life of Africa's Greatest Explorer* (London: Faber and Faber, 2007), p. 117.
20. Ibid., p. 242.
21. Antonia Fraser, *Cromwell: Our Chief of Men* (London: Phoenix Books, 2002), pp. 424–5.
22. Philip Neilsen, *The Art of Lying* (Brisbane: Makar Press, 1979).
23. J. W. Pennebaker, 'Telling Stories: The Health Benefits of Narrative', *Literature and Medicine*, 19 (1) (2000), pp. 10–11.
24. J. W. Pennebaker and J. D. Seagal, 'Forming a Story: The Health Benefits of Narrative', *Journal of Clinical Psychology*, 55 (10) (1999), p. 1243.
25. Paul John Eakin, *Living Autobiographically: How We Create Identity in Narrative* (Ithaca, NY: Cornell University Press, 2008).
26. Vicki Lindner, 'The Tale of Two Bethanies: Trauma in the Creative Writing Classroom', *New Writing: The International Journal for the Practice and Theory of Creative Writing*, 1 (1) (2004), pp. 6–14.
27. Fiona Sampson, 'Writing as "Therapy"', in *On Listening* (Cambridge: Salt Publishing, 2007), pp. 102–10.

PART II
Topics

11

DAVID MORLEY

Serious play: creative writing and science

Thought experiment

What are the historical connections between creative writing and science? Is it possible for science to be a catalyst for imaginative writing? To explore these issues we must first open our minds to a conjunction of knowledge and work that some might find unusual. This poem is an illustration of possibility:

Fulcrum / Writing a World

While I talk and the flies buzz,
a seagull catches a fish at the mouth of the Amazon,
a tree falls in the Adirondack wilderness,
a man sneezes in Germany,
a horse dies in Tattany, and twins are born in France.
What does that mean? Does the contemporaneity
of these events with one another,
and with a million others as disjointed,
form a rational bond between them,
and write them into anything
that resembles for us a world?

I wrote this poem and published it in a collection called *Scientific Papers*. It was later featured as posters on London's Underground trains to celebrate the 350th anniversary of the Royal Society. It is a 'found poem', an excerpt spliced from the prose of William James's *Reflex Action and Theism* then arranged into lines. It is scientific prose and it is a poem; it is the work of the living and the dead; like Schrödinger's cat it is both there and not there. It is a thought experiment. But the poem presented itself, as poems do if you're lucky or receptive. Like science, creative writing requires apprenticeship, patience and practice to allow that receptivity to begin to feel like luck.

Writing is not 'made' in the same way as science, nor does it share its purpose. Scientific ideas are the creation of many minds working inductively. Scientists analyse data for their statistical significance, not for authenticity or inevitability. Most experiments are conducted according to the philosopher Karl Popper's concept of falsifiability. This is also viewed as the point of demarcation between science and metaphysics. Sometimes, however, science requires something other than inductive logic, and that *other* is imagination: our interior landscape: metaphysics.

Receptive imagination

I live and work as a poet and ecologist. After seven years of ecological training I became skilful at 'reading' a landscape for investigation – where I might set a humane trap for the dawn flight of emerging freshwater insects; or how an angle to the wind might shift pupae carapaces on a lake. Training affected how I 'read' analyses of four-dimensional mathematical models; and how I might apply these patterns to the real world under the surface of a beck or lake. Those swarming numbers resembled the world in which these animals lived and died. They were models of the living world constructed from physical, chemical and biological events. Like William James, my task as a scientist was to examine these events with one another and with a million others as disjointed, to try to form a rational bond between them and see in what way they resembled a part of the natural world.

This process grew instinctual. In his essay 'Landscape and Narrative' from *Crossing Open Ground* Barry Lopez wrote, 'One learns a landscape finally not by knowing the name or identity of everything in it, but by perceiving the relationships in it – like that between the sparrow and the twig. The difference between the relationships and the elements is the same as that between written history and a catalog of events.'[1] Practice and experience sharpen intuition and instinct, allow them greater play in creating ideas. Eventually, by knowing something you find you know so much less about the world than you can possibly know in a lifetime. This ignorance is relative but only by discovering you 'know nothing' can you pierce a zone of heightened receptivity that allows an unconscious independence to second-guess your way into making breakthroughs, unusual correlations and counter-intuitive associations.

One of the founders of modern chemistry, Humphrey Davy, compared the scientific and poetic imagination:

> The perception of truth is almost as simple a feeling as the perception of beauty; and the genius of Newton, of Shakespeare, of Michael Angelo, and of Handel, are not very remote in character from each other. *Imagination, as well as the reason, is necessary to perfection in the philosophic mind. A rapidity of combination, a power of perceiving analogies, and of comparing them by facts, is the creative source of discovery.*[2]

The Nobel Prize-winning molecular biologist Max Perutz observed of the discoverers of DNA, 'Crick and Watson ... achieved most when they seemed to be working least ... engaged in argument and apparently idle ... attacking a problem that could be solved only by a tremendous leap of the imagination ... Imagination comes first in both artistic and scientific creations.'[3] Through a trained receptive imagination, those lucky breaks allow scientific breakthroughs. This zone of receptivity corresponds to John Keats's notion of negative capability: 'several things dovetailed in my mind and at once it struck me, what quality went to form ... Achievement especially in Literature & which Shakespeare possessed so enormously – I mean *Negative Capability*, that is when man is capable of being in uncertainties, Mysteries, doubts, without any irritable reaching after fact and reason.'[4] The zone of the receptive imagination is pierced through method and practice as well as apparent or actual idleness.

The most surprising and thorniest ideas are often simple. Simplicity of this type is reached through processes that are complex. Such ideas might seem beyond rational thought, wrung from realms of intuition and feeling. Yet, like the mind's own 'muscle' (the brain's ultra-complex synapses), fluent feeling and intuition are made ever more pliant and receptive by practice and, without exercise, they atrophy. The same can be said for creativity in any field of endeavour, including science and mathematics. We know that creative ingenuity is the product of 10,000 hours of practice combined with talent and luck. Yet in essence all our children are nascent geniuses. What they are waiting for is permission to mature their precocity. If they are fortunate, the value of a receptive imagination is encouraged and enlarged in the early years of education. But as a student moves through the educational system they are required to specialise. By early adulthood the cast of specialism is set. As part of this process the receptive imagination is undervalued or simply devalued. As Ted Hughes wrote, 'this immense biological over-supply of precocious ability is almost totally annihilated, before it can mature'.[5] This annihilation is often carried out with the best of intentions but can be deadly for the maturing complexity of the imagination's synaptic hard-wiring. Imagination needs to be wired through intelligence; intelligence to be wired through imagination.

Double helix of writing and science

At heart there is a misunderstanding of the receptive imagination and its intangible value to achievement in many fields including science and mathematics but also in the ability of humans to understand and reach out to each other. In Europe, creative writing and science, although they went by different names in the past, were seen not as poles apart but as conjugate 'lines and veins' within human knowledge. Renaissance Man found specialist thinking an exclusive and excluding position from which to develop human understanding. Francis Bacon writing in *The Advancement of Learning* (1605) argued 'that all partitions of knowledges be accepted rather for lines and veins, than for sections and separations; and that the continuance and entireness of knowledge be preserved'. By the end of the Enlightenment numerous works even combined science and poetry, including Erasmus Darwin's *The Botanic Garden* (1791) and Goethe's *Metamorphoze der Pflanzen* (1798). Tomes of this type, ballasted by footnotes, were a mode for teaching natural philosophy as well as a vehicle for play and prosodic skill.

Mark Kipperman has written,

> the Two Cultures were not so clearly distinct in the early nineteenth century, though in Coleridge and Shelley we do begin to see marks of tension. The 'sciences', however, did not at this time denote exactly our modern disciplines, and the 'arts' had not yet quite attained their dubious Wildean distinction of uselessness: history and theology, as systematic studies, were 'sciences', and engineering might be categorized as a 'useful art'.[6]

The late eighteenth and early nineteenth centuries have been dubbed eras of Romantic science as well as Romantic literature. Scientists dramatised their expeditions and experiments in public lectures and popular books. Their books were printed and promoted by the same publishing houses as poets, including William Wordsworth with whom Davy enjoyed a competitive friendship (which tells us much about the cultural status of each of them). Scientists were storytellers and brought art to explication, but they also borrowed the process of invention from the art of narration and used it to drive them as experimenters. In the words of Davy, 'After reading a few books, I was seized with the desire to *narrate* ... I gradually began to invent, and form stories of my own. Perhaps this passion has produced all my originality. I never loved to imitate, but always to invent: this has been the case in all the sciences I have studied.'[7]

Wordsworth's and Davy's friend Samuel Taylor Coleridge thought science, 'being necessarily performed with *the passion of Hope* ... was poetical' and wrote in 1802 that 'I attended Davy's lectures to enlarge my stock of metaphors ... Every subject in Davy's mind has the principle of Vitality. Living thoughts spring up like Turf under his feet.'[8] In the Preface to *Lyrical Ballads* (1802) Wordsworth and Coleridge could state confidently (and again competitively),

> If the labours of Men of science should ever create any material revolution, direct or indirect, in our condition, and in the impressions which we habitually receive, the Poet will sleep then no more than at present; he will be ready to follow the steps of the Man of science, not only in those general indirect effects, but he will be at his side, *carrying sensation into the midst of the objects of the science itself.*

In the same year, the philosopher Friedrich Schelling professed to his students, 'at the present time, everything in science and art seems to be tending toward unity, when matters that long seemed remote from each other are now recognized to be quite close, and a new more universal vision, encompassing almost all disciplines, is taking shape'.[9] For Mary Shelley, appreciating and synthesising early scientific principles of voltaic electricity, vitalism and the terminology of the laboratory allowed her to make *Frankenstein* (1818).

For the Romantic natural philosopher or poet, nature was a landscape of senses and emotions. It is still impossible to trek the landscapes of Cumbria without holding a Wordsworthian Claude Glass. Charles Darwin's descriptions of tropical worlds observed on his *Beagle* voyage in 1831–6 reflected his ardent admiration of the writings of the naturalist and Romantic Wilhelm von Humboldt, commenting in his journal how 'he like another sun illumines everything I behold' yet at the same time holding to scientific inductive method: 'I worked on true Baconian principles, and without any theory collected facts.' Darwin later repudiated his more imaginative or emotive turns of phrase. Humboldt also subsequently argued that written science should not proceed in his previously favoured form of 'historical narrative' and that it 'is scarcely possible to connect so many different materials with the narration of events; and that which we may call dramatic gives way to dissertations merely descriptive'.[10]

Systematic scientific writing – what we might call the mapping of knowledge – usurped Davy's storytelling. In a process of knowledge expansion, akin to natural selection, science found its voice in precise expository description and the passive tense: the overthrow of the 'I'. 'Art is I; science is we' claimed the nineteenth-century French psychologist Claude Bernard who also advised, 'Put off your imagination as you put off your overcoat, when you enter the laboratory. Put it on again, as you put on your overcoat, when you leave.' Victorian polymath William Whewell fingered the divide: 'The object of science is knowledge; the objects of art are works. In art, truth is the means to an end; in science, it is the only end. Hence the practical arts are not to be classed among the sciences.'[11]

Julius and Augustus Hare argued in 1865 it was necessary to invent a dead, antipoetic language because 'it is well for the vocabulary of Science [to] be common to all nations . . . Of all words however the least vivacious are those coined by Science . . . It is Poetry, the Imagination, in one or other of its forms [creative writing], that produces what has life in it.'[12] At a stroke Poetry (by which we mean creative writing) became the Dodo for written information however much vigour might linger in the *corpus*. As the physicist Paul Dirac said, 'In science, you want to say something nobody knows before, in words everyone can understand. In poetry, you are bound to say something that everybody knows already in words that nobody can understand.'[13] Again: for 'poetry', read 'creative writing'.

In the twentieth century, the shift of cultural confidence in science and arts was powered by the perception of their contribution to accepted western concepts of progress and action – in medicine, industry, commerce and warfare. As W.H. Auden wrote in the 1960s, 'The true men of action in our time, those who transform the world, are . . . the scientists . . . When I find myself in the company of scientists, I feel like a shabby curate who has strayed by mistake into a drawing room full of dukes.'[14] The poet's very British discomfiture was sharpened no doubt by the debate over C.P. Snow's 1959 lecture on 'The Two Cultures and the Scientific Revolution'.

The novelist Snow observed a class-war between scientists and literary intellectuals: scientists experienced difficulty reading the novels of Dickens, while humanities professors felt themselves and their subjects on a higher plane to utitilitarian, practical science. Snow believed the education system fostered cultural snobbery, forcing children to specialise in subjects with the highest-grade minds being directed to 'traditional culture' and the professions, while science and industry were viewed with disdain. Commenting on the legacy of the Two Cultures debate, Roger Kimball has written: 'The phrase has lived on as a vague popular shorthand for the rift – a matter of incomprehension tinged with hostility – that has grown up between scientists and literary intellectuals in the modern world.'[15]

This cultural snobbery could now be said to have switched sides in our universities and schools. A new shame game calibrates subjects (and implicitly their students and teachers) by their impact in social and economic terms. Serious investment tends to go to the fields of science, medicine and new technologies while the arts get on with whatever scraps are left. In addition, many commentators believed – rightly – that creativity was no longer the sole reserve of the artist. As the historian of microbiology Horace Freeland Judson claimed, 'Science is our century's art.'[16] What this brief history goes to show is that the cultural relationship between 'science' and 'creative writing' is a cultural double helix that was first combined, then untwined and is now occasionally recombined – more for the sake of greater public understanding of science and occasionally for the making of literature.

Science as subject and stimulus

Science did not just become 'our century's art': the twentieth century saw science adopt literature as a medium. There were scientists who were also distinguished creative writers such as the Italian novelist and chemist Primo Levi and Czech poet and immunologist Miroslav Holub. There were popular science books beautifully written by scientists such as Margaret Boden, Stephen Jay Gould, Max Perutz, Steven Rose, Carl Sagan, Ian Stewart, E. O. Wilson, Steven Pinker and Richard Dawkins, all of whom can be regarded in this way as substantial creative essay writers. The curtains may have drawn on the 'drama of discovery' in the mid nineteenth century, but the practice revived through works of popular science and scientists' desire to speak about their work on television and electronic media. The danger of popular science writing, as one commentator claimed, was 'Saganisation', the delusion that the science writer believed they were automatically interesting to the reader because of their subject rather than their literary style. Another problem was an unease about scientists writing popular science outside their field; and that a gentle book of essays was the only form by which to reach readers.

Since Mary Shelley, many creative writers have adopted concepts and terminology from science to create new worlds through fiction. Some of these are recognisable worlds but some writers make use of the strangeness and open-endedness of science to unfold a fictional continuum in which scientific plausibility and possibility are bent and reconstructed to make a strong and inevitable narrative. What we call science fiction is really just another act of fiction which writers such as China Miéville prefer to call 'weird fiction': a tradition that extends from Mary Shelley to *The Time Machine* by H. G. Wells (1895), *At the Mountains of Madness* by H. P. Lovecraft (1931) and *I, Robot* by Isaac Asimov (1955). Fiction writers have created stories and novels that investigate the nature of the universe and world at a slant to the business of narrative and character. Scientific concepts are not *the* story but part of the canvas of setting and the language of science is used quite naturally. Concepts have included: relativity in Ian McEwan's *The Child in Time* (1987); physics in Rebecca Goldstein's *Properties of Light* (2001) and Ursula Le Guin's *The Dispossessed* (1974); geology in Susan M. Gaines's *Carbon Dreams* (2001); biology in Andrea Barrett's *Ship Fever* (1996) and Anthony Doerr's *The Shell Collector* (2001); molecular biology in Richard Powers's *Gold Bug Variations* (1992); nanotechnology in Linda Nagata's *The Bohr Maker* (1995); and alternative universes in China Miéville's *The City and The City* (2009). Playwrights explored science for character, dramatic effect and concept and these interventions although rare have achieved a fine effect. As the introduction to the anthology *The Shape of Content: Creative Writing in Mathematics and Science* (2008) states,

> Creative writing about the content of mathematics and science is rare, and creative writing about the activity of mathematical and scientific creation is even rarer. And yet, when it occurs, it can be extremely popular, as well-known plays like *Proof* and *Copenhagen* and biographies like *A Beautiful Mind* and

> *The Man Who Loved Only Numbers* attest ... Mathematics and science are part of world culture, part of the human spirit, fit subjects for art of all kinds.[17]

There are also numerous and numinous examples in contemporary poetry. The poet Jan Zwicky was one of the editors of *The Shape of Content* anthology. In her poem 'The Geology of Norway' from *Songs for Relinquishing the Earth* she creates a word-drama of the young Ludwig Wittgenstein in a poem that encompasses plate tectonics, erosion and extinction written in a 'language / that could bend light'.[18] Many other poets made elegant and precise use of scientific concepts including: bioacoustics and ethology in Les Murray's *Translations from the Natural World* (1993);[19] physics in Jorie Graham's *The Dream of a Unified Field* (1996) and Kim Maltman's *Technologies/Installations* (1990); radioactivity in Mario Petrucci's *Heavy Water* (2004); ecology in John Kinsella's *The New Arcadia* (2005); and biology, geology, mathematics, chemistry, physics and engineering in the spry poems of Marianne Moore, a poet who in William Logan's words 'found the poetry lying asleep within prose, in manuals and monographs ...'.[20] None of these poets was attempting to recreate the instructive, scientific verse of Erasmus Darwin; they were curious and open about science, its language and perceptions. As the physicist-poet Mario Petrucci observed, 'I believe science and poetry can successfully co-exist ... The science has to be fully absorbed into the creative writing process, so that the poems achieve a negotiated co-habitation.'[21]

There have been events in which creative writing and science converge all their Baconian 'wires and veins' and make something greater and stranger than their parts: a synthesis releasing a fresh form of writing. One twentieth-century example is the Russian poet Osip Mandelstam's *Journey to Armenia* written in 1933. Precision of observation and elliptical expression are mapped in a language both personal and impersonal. The literary structure proceeds by a combination of narrative, collage and epiphany. Writing is continually and illuminatingly compared to music. Biology, geography, geology, history and anthropology are seen as fit subjects and their vocabulary is alert and gravid: 'And on the table there is an elegant syntax – of confused, hetero-alphabet, grammatically wrong wildflowers, as though all the preschool forms of vegetative nature were coalescing into a pleophonic anthology poem.'[22] Mandelstam's work is alive to possibility: 'I only want to remind my reader that a naturalist is a professional teller of tales, a public demonstrator of new and interesting species', he writes, and 'I have signed an armistice with Darwin and placed him on my imaginary bookstand next to Dickens.'[23]

By invoking naturalists such as Darwin and Lamarck, Mandelstam created a strange internalised travelogue. The journey from Moscow to Armenia is a psychological journey from death to life; and the life-affirming destination is – biology! The narrative deals obliquely with the realities of Soviet collectivisation even though the aim for its sponsors was propaganda disguised as travel writing. The physical attention of Mandelstam's writing in *Journey to Armenia* is also a tensioned field study in a literary style similar to Marianne Moore's: 'Gothic pinecones and hypocritical acorns in their monastic caps pleased me more than mushrooms. I would stroke the pinecones. They would bristle. They were trying to convince me of something. In their shelled tenderness, in their geometrical gaping, I sensed the rudiments of architecture, the demon of which has accompanied me throughout my life.'[24] It is as if Osip Mandelstam were saying we can gain consolation from natural precision; that not all knowledge is loaded against us so long as we pay attention to its life and to its own language.

One of the most illuminating explorers in the literary-scientific field was the novelist J. G. Ballard who, in his introduction to Barry Atkins, *More Than a Game: The Computer Game as a Fictional Form*,[25] wrote interestingly: 'I feel that, in a sense, the writer knows nothing any longer . . . His role is that of a scientist, whether on safari or in his laboratory, faced with an unknown terrain or subject. All he can do is to devise various hypotheses and test them against the facts.' Such fictions and poems may look and feel like literary genres but at best they defy categorisation. Strangeness and mystery are at the heart of them, but also precision and emotion. As Einstein once said, 'The most beautiful experience we can have is the mysterious – the fundamental emotion which stands at the cradle of true art and true science.'[26] Attention, precision and imagination provide the means to unlock the science of the natural world in our writing without forcing the effect, without merely burgling the worlds of science and natural history for our own literary ends. As in Osip Mandelstam, Marianne Moore or Les Murray, when language is both mathematical and metaphorical it is still, above every other consideration, entirely natural. Such writing depends very much on the quality of attention, and that quality of attention to fact and to language has found its place in contemporary environmental writing.

Environmental writing

Without wishing to exploit the mineral deposit of metaphor, we live in a silver age of environmental writing. Environmental nonfiction is usually written from a personal point of view but is never less than informed in science. I have written elsewhere how creative nonfiction shares the perceptual and philosophical possibilities of poetry and fiction but it reaches out further to readers: it teaches us about the real world; yet *it treats imagination as part of the natural world*.[27] Environmental nonfiction is an elastic, generous genre. In an imitation of evolution, it possesses an apparent freedom of form while also authoring hybrid forms when the weather of narrative demands a fresh tone or voice.

Writers such as Mark Cocker, Roger Deakin, Annie Dillard, Barry Lopez, Robert MacFarlane, Richard Mabey and Rebecca Solnit – among many others – have taken bearing and inspiration from John Muir, Henry David Thoreau and T.H. White whose work defied simple categories. In *The Environmental Imagination* Lawrence Buell wrote of Thoreau's *Walden*: 'nothing is more striking than its variegated character . . .. it can be read as a poem, a novel, an autobiography, a travel narrative, a sermon, a treatise. Sometimes the text positively flaunts its diversity, fragmenting into multi-generic collage.'[28] In blending and blurring the categories of science and art, storytelling and fact, environmental nonfiction at its best creates new syntheses in form, and also becomes an inspired force in the re-engagement of creative writing and science as in Mandelstam's *Journey to Armenia* and Jan Zwicky's 'The Geology of Norway'.

For Barry Lopez, imagination is a part of the landscape – an interior landscape – one in which we can all participate given discipline, craft and a clear sense of the world around and within us. In 'Landscape and Narrative' he writes,

> I think of two landscapes – one outside the self, the other within. The external landscape is the one we see – not only the line and color of the land and its shading at different times of the day, but also its plants and animals in season, its weather, its geology, the record of its climate and evolution . . . The second landscape I think of is an interior one, a kind of projection within a person of a part of the exterior landscape.[29]

Lopez uses narration and the storyteller's arts to create a synthesis 'between the two landscapes' by drawing on relationships in the exterior landscape and projecting them on to the interior landscape.

What's important here isn't that Lopez can write wonderful sentences and draw on systematic knowledge and local colour; it is that he has developed a fully formed and generous poetics for his writing. To rephrase an earlier quotation by Humphrey Davy, philosophy, as well as the reason, is also necessary to perfection in the imaginative mind. The language of science moved away from the language of literature by overthrowing the 'I'. So writerly self-regard is an uneasy point of view from which to write about the damage we as a species inflict on our world. Lopez offers us a scale of humility and a sense of adventure along with a wider – and wilder – recognition that nature, like art, releases the medicine – not the morphine – of imagination. As he says, 'We will always be rewarded if we give the land credit for more than we imagine, and if we imagine it as being more complex even than language.'[30] Lopez never writes with a palpable design on the reader because his poetics allow his own personality to disappear into style.

The notion of 'palpable design' was a literary quality derided by John Keats whose ecological metaphor for poetic composition was that it should 'come as easily as leaves to a tree' (Keats could have no knowledge of spatial competition for light). Like Lopez, Australian poet John Kinsella is a scientifically literate environmental activist. He argues that 'the metonymic connection between the trees we exploit for paper, and our writing, is just cause for investigation of source and culpability on behalf of the writer . . . What we write with and on are part of the responsibility.' Computers are seen as part of that responsibility and Kinsella has given them up for good. Kinsella doesn't perceive 'activist writing' as palpable design. He views it as part of the process of creative writing, inasmuch as our writing is an extension of ourselves, and therefore a wholly natural procedure. He claims, 'A poem is an extension of the body: of self, of community, of body politic. When I write an "activist" poem, it is not a matter of getting on a soapbox, but of my placing my body in the line of discussion.'[31]

If environmental pressure groups have taught us anything it is that idealism and activism are most effective when they are informed, pragmatic and engaging of communities who might not normally associate themselves with the cause. It also comes down to how we choose to write. Some genres gain greater attention: Rachel Carson's *Silent Spring* (1962) still provides tangible pressure many years after publication. Awareness of our range is important; and of our sense of scale. Finding the means to expand readership is vital but that needs to be done with the clear-sighted knowledge that many readers are also writers and that creative writing, like creative reading, is a complex engagement. In an interview Barry Lopez has said that too many writers are over-concerned with the 'interiors of the writer's mind. There is an utter disregard for the reader's imagination. Wherever our society is going, it will require an expansion of imagination.'[32] In effect, he is saying the cost of writerly narcissism may well be the planet itself. In order for our bodies of writing to be 'in the line of discussion' they must be recognised by the metaphorical loggers buzz-sawing their path towards them.

Discerning pattern

To increase the scale for writing, and to reach beyond communities not normally associated with creative writing, some creative writers collaborate across disciplines. A number of projects have seen poets writing in response to scientists and the scientists responding to this scrutiny with their own prose.[33] Creative writers have taken part in workshops in which they responded to concepts in mathematics – and to mathematicians – by creating remarkable poems, short stories and plays. 'Discerning pattern: that's what writers, mathematicians and scientists do' concluded the editors of *The Shape of Content: Creative Writing in Mathematics and Science*.[34]

John Dee believed that 'Many arts there are which beautify the mind of man; of all other none do more garnish and beautify it than those arts which are called mathematical.'[35] The members of the Oulipo would agree. Mathematicians, creative writers and academics founded the Oulipo or Ouvroir de littérature potentielle (Workshop for Potential Literature) in 1960. Their purpose was to explore how abstract restrictions might produce imaginative writing. Some of the mathematical restrictions collide delightfully with how we usually construct a narration or a poem including 'N + 7' or 'NOUN + 7' in which one takes a creative work, usually one of one's own, and reads through the piece noting the position of all nouns. One looks up these nouns in a dictionary and, counting forwards in the dictionary by seven nouns (not seven words), one replaces each noun with the seventh. Various permutations are possible of course and results are provocative and funny.

The 'results' of the experiment often make more artistic sense than the original: such mathematical games can release strange juxtapositions of language that yield surprise and delight. Here mathematicians and writers are seeking to expand the diversity of what literature might do, rather than say what it cannot do or should do, and their work is displayed to advantage in the *Oulipo Compendium* edited by Harry Matthews and Alastair Brotchie.[36] Writers have also created poems and stories based on the order of Fibonacci numbers: sequences of numbers found naturally in the botanic patterns, for example in the branching of bushes and trees or in the arrangements of tines on a pine cone. Thus have Voltaire's 'thorns of mathematics' yielded the flowers of poetry as well as the scent of equations.

Realms for writing

What the Oulipo parade with such mock-solemn merriment is 'serious play', a notion that reaches back to Erasmus and which was the maxim of the immunologist and poet Miroslav Holub, who wrote, 'The emotional, aesthetic and existential value is the same . . . when looking into a microscope . . . and when looking into the nascent organism of the poem.'[37] Holub's clinical research was into that most unstable of viruses, the common cold; his poetry was mythic, vivid, rebarbative. His honesty about the importance of poetry to science is characteristically forthright: 'The best one can get from poetry in a scientific career is some kind of vivid imagination which must stay at all times under the strict control of available knowledge. Science is the art of the soluble, said Peter Medawar: poetry is the art of the possible.'[38]

In conversation with Holub about specialisation in schools and universities, he mischievously suggested to me that the solution to any problems was to create a totalitarian state that simply didn't allow chemists *not* to read poetry or look at paintings, nor artists to dodge the empirical sciences. Holub described how, as a science student in the former Soviet Republic, he had been 'required' to attend lectures in philosophy, history and literature. This requirement had not been resented by the keener students who regarded the acquisition of knowledge beyond science as part of what it meant to be a whole person. Arts students were also required to attend lectures of chemistry, mathematics and anatomy but their discomfort often led to bohemian truancy.

This conversation informed a less than totalitarian decision by me and my colleagues at our university to introduce curricular flexibility into our undergraduate degree in English and Creative Writing. Arts students could, if they chose, take modules in science and technology, while students from science could equally take modules in creative writing. Some adventurous students took up the opportunity with impressive results. The surprise wasn't that students performed well once the wall between disciplines was breached. Whereas the arts students found a welcome in science departments, the presence of scientists on humanities courses wasn't always appreciated by fellow students or their tutors.

In the passage above, Miroslav Holub goes on to quote George Steiner:

> I remain unrepentant in my hunch that intellectual energies, imaginative boldness and sheer fun are currently more abundant in the sciences than they are in the humanities. Courteous inquiries by colleagues in the sciences render more embarrassing the casuistic jargon, the pretentious triviality which now dominate so much of literary theory and humanistic studies.[39]

In a post-theoretical age one can hope such receptions and perceptions have moved on from the time of the Two Cultures.

I have come to accept that the cultural relationship between science and creative writing is unequal. Science pays back any former historical allegiance to the arts with technology and medicine, while continuing to extend its imaginative franchise on mystery and wonder. The examples of Elizabeth Bishop, Miroslav Holub, John Kinsella, Barry Lopez, Osip Mandelstam, Marianne Moore and Les Murray suggest that a polymath's approach to subject and language provides the most elegant, precise and respectful means for creative writers to engage with scientific materials. Their works also possess a natural energy of expression that derives authority and playfulness from science and their voices bring light to scientific matters. William Blake said 'energy is eternal delight' and eternal delight is the mc^2 of a living literature even when we are delighting in a mass of difficulty. The hope and wish for the arts might be that, in Holub's words, they enlarge the imaginative scope to science – 'under the strict control of available knowledge'. However, I suggest creative writing could also open up an interdisciplinary relationship with the sciences. The craft of science and the craft of writing require technique, perception and imagination. We can remake parts of our curriculum to reflect the acquirement of such crafts.

In 1992, Barry Lopez and E. O. Wilson, the Harvard biologist, designed a new undergraduate major for Texas Tech University's Honors College: the BA in Natural History & the Humanities. Students learn from a variety of disciplines including science, philosophy, literature and the arts. Though it is focused on the natural world and our place in it, the degree can be customised to fit a student's future academic and occupational goals, such as nature or environmental writing, the study of law, natural history interpretation and photography. Such an approach recalls Leonardo da Vinci's Principles for the Development of a Complete Mind: 'Study the science of art. Study the art of science. Develop your senses – especially learn how to see. Realize that everything connects to everything else.'[40]

To repeat the point made by Barry Lopez, 'Wherever our society is going, it will require an expansion of imagination.' Auden claimed, 'Both science and art are primarily spiritual activities, whatever practical applications may be derived from their results. Disorder, lack of meaning, are spiritual not physical discomforts, order and sense spiritual not physical satisfactions.'[41] Einstein wrote in 1932, 'When the world ceases to be the scene of our personal hopes and wishes, where we face it as free beings admiring, asking and observing, there we enter the realm of art and science.'[42] Writing games are like thought experiments in language. The exercises offered below are attempts – like the poem that opened this chapter – to help you enter the realms of science and arts simultaneously.

It is not about what creative writing can offer to science, nor what science can offer to creative writing. It is about values and experiences we have in common. All writing, at its best, is creative writing.

Writing exercises

'Translations from the Natural World': using Les Murray's poetry from the volume of this name as a stimulus, take a field trip to observe the sounds and movements of specific animals (e.g. birdsong and flight pattern), recording your perceptions precisely and verbally. Write a prose account or poem from the point of view of a species using rhythms and syntax that imitate your recordings as vividly as possible.

'The World in a Grain of Sand': take a magnifying glass or microscope and study for two hours a small surface area (e.g. a stone covered with algae or lichen) or object (e.g. a bird's feather), making notes on it using precise description as well as extended metaphor. Your notes provide the setting for your poem, drama or short story about something entirely different from the observed area or object.

'Natural Magic': write a poem or story based on the order of Fibonacci numbers: sequences of numbers found in the patterns of leaves, grasses and flowers; in the branching of bushes and trees; or in the arrangements of tines on a pine cone. This exercise can also be used to create calligrammes or 'shape poems' based on natural designs and/or chemical structures.

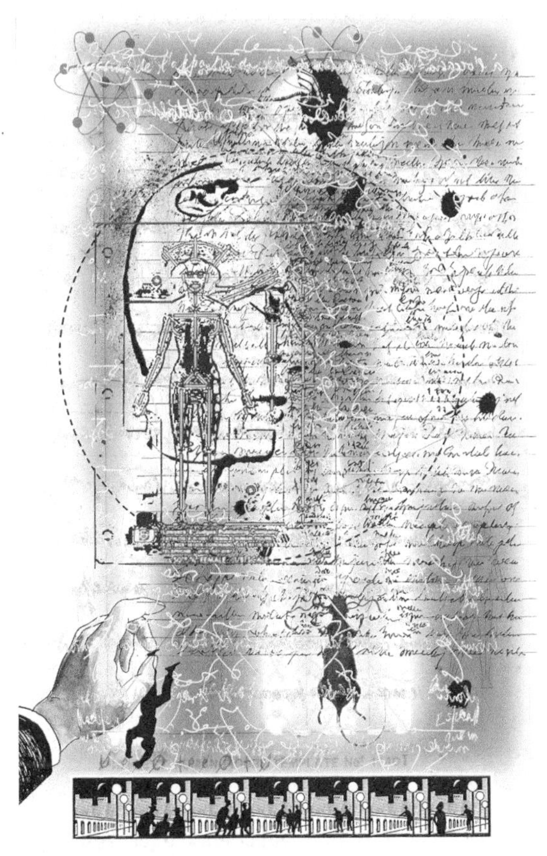

4. 'Template Man' by Peter Blegvad, copyright Peter Blegvad

'Discerning Pattern': look closely at the visual elements that make up Peter Blegvad's 'Template Man' and take a photocopy. Allow enough time to take in the complex visual effects of the piece. This composition draws on images from chemistry, geometry and biology. It plays with perception; it plays on expectation. It is 'weird fiction' in visual form. You will notice text ghosting across the composition. Write a flash fiction of 500 words that brings together the narrative of the cartoon strip and the patterns and images of the composition. Write this short story across the text of your photocopy.

'Finding Language Asleep in Science': field guides to natural history, star systems, clouds and oceans are full of fascinating, exact and vivid language as well as facts and ideas. Read through these guides for ideas for your own writing but also try to 'find poems' in the language of science and in the traditional names for animals, trees and flowers. This exercise also enhances your understanding of precision in language and style and can be complemented by reading poems about natural history by precisionist poets such as Marianne Moore and Elizabeth Bishop and prose stylists such as Barry Lopez and Osip Mandelstam.

'Interviews with Nature': using the form of a prose poem or a dramatic monologue, take a natural phenomenon and interview it at length, e.g. one of the four seasons, one of the laws of thermodynamics, one of the elements from the Periodic Table. Find out everything you can about this phenomenon from science, literature and history so that the voice of the phenomenon is self-informed, but playful and completely authentic.

'Fieldwork': enroll in a course at a residential field study centre; take full part in all laboratory activities and fieldwork. Respond to your experience with poetry, flash fiction and dramatic monologues.

NOTES

1. Barry Lopez, 'Landscape and Narrative', in *Crossing Open Ground* (New York: Vintage, 1988), p. 64.
2. Richard Holmes, *The Age of Wonder: How the Romantic Generation Discovered the Beauty and Terror of Science* (London: Harper Press, 2008), p. 276.
3. Max Perutz, *I Wish I'd Made You Angry Earlier* (New York: Cold Spring Harbor Laboratory Press, 2003), p. 204.
4. John Keats, 'Letters', *The Norton Anthology of English Literature*, 7th edition, vol. 2, general editors M.H. Abrams and Stephen Greenblatt (New York: Norton, 2000), p. 889.
5. Ted Hughes, *Winter Pollen* (London: Faber and Faber, 1994), p. 31.
6. Mark Kipperman, 'Coleridge, Shelley, Davy, and Science's Millennium', *Criticism: A Quarterly for Literature and the Arts*, 40 (2) (Summer 1998), available online at

www.findarticles.com/p/articles/mi_m2220/is_n3_v40/ai_21182131, accessed 30 July 2010.
7. Quoted in Holmes, *The Age of Wonder*, p. 239.
8. Quoted in ibid., p. 288.
9. Schelling quoted in Kipperman, 'Coleridge, Shelley, Davy, and Science's Millennium'.
10. James Paradis and Thomas Postlewaite, *Victorian Science and Victorian Values* (New Brunswick: Rutgers University Press, 1985), p. 101.
11. Samuel Austin Allibone, *Prose Quotations from Socrates to Macaulay* (Philadelphia, 1875), p. 45.
12. Hare quoted in Paradis and Postlewaite, *Victorian Science and Victorian Values*, p. 66.
13. Paul Dirac, quoted in David Spooner, *The Insect-Populated Mind* (Oxford: Hamilton Books, 2005), p. 24.
14. W.H. Auden, *The Dyer's Hand and Other Essays* (London: Faber and Faber, 1965), p. 81.
15. Roger Kimball, '"The Two Cultures" Today: On the C.P. Snow–F.R. Leavis Controversy', *The New Criterion*, 12 (February 1994), available online at www.newcriterion.com/articles.cfm/-The-Two-Cultures–today-4882, accessed 18 July 2010.
16. Horace Freeland Judson, *The Search for Solutions* (New York: Holt, Rinehart & Winston, 1980), p. 10.
17. Chandler Davis, Marjorie Senechal and Jan Zwicky (eds.), *The Shape of Content: Creative Writing in Mathematics and Science* (Wellesley: A.K. Peters, 2008), p. ix.
18. Jan Zwicky, *Songs for Relinquishing the Earth* (London and Ontario: Brick Books, 1998), p. 33.
19. Les A. Murray, *Translations from the Natural World* (Manchester: Carcanet Press, 1993).
20. William Logan, *The Undiscovered Country* (New York: Columbia University Press, 2005), p. 89.
21. Mario Petrucci, 'Pheromones and Poems', Liverpool University Centre for Poetry and Science (2008), available online at www.liv.ac.uk/poetryandscience/poems/plutonium.htm, accessed 31 July 2010.
22. Osip Mandelstam, *Journey to Armenia*, in *The Noise of Time: Selected Prose* (Evanston: Northwestern University Press, 2000), p. 203.
23. Ibid.
24. Ibid.
25. Barry Atkins, *More Than a Game: The Computer Game as a Fictional Form* (Manchester University Press, 2003).
26. Albert Einstein quoted by Eoin Lettice in 'The Cradle of True Art and True Science', *Communicate Science* (2010), available online at www.communicatescience.eu/2010/06/cradle-culture-and-science.html, accessed 31 July 2010.
27. David Morley, *The Cambridge Introduction to Creative Writing* (Cambridge University Press, 2007), p. 178.
28. Lawrence Buell, *The Environmental Imagination*, 2nd edn (Harvard University Press, 1996), p. 397.
29. Lopez, 'Landscape and Narrative', pp. 64–5.

30. Barry Lopez, *Rediscovery of North America* (New York: Random House, 1990), p. 37.
31. John Kinsella, 'Lyric and Razo: Activism and the Poet', *Poetry Review*, 97 (1) (2007), pp. 66–79, p. 77.
32. Barry Lopez in an interview with Paul Pintarich of the *Portland Oregonian*, 20 October 1994.
33. Robert Crawford, *Contemporary Poetry and Contemporary Science* (Oxford University Press, 2006); David Morley, *Dove Release: New Flights and Voices* (Tonbridge: Worple Press, 2010).
34. Davis, Senechal and Zwicky (eds.), *The Shape of Content*, p. xii.
35. John Dee, 'The Mathematical Preface' to Henry Billingsley's English translation of Euclid's *Elements* (London: John Daye, 1570).
36. Harry Matthews and Alastair Brotchie (eds.), *Oulipo Compendium* (London: Atlas, 1998).
37. Miroslav Holub, *The Dimension of the Present Moment* (London: Faber and Faber, 1990), p. 143.
38. Holub quoted in Crawford, *Contemporary Poetry and Contemporary Science*, p. 12.
39. Holub quoted in ibid., p. 14.
40. Quoted in Tony and Barry Buzan, *The Mind Map Book* (London: BBC Books, 1993), p. 288.
41. Auden, *The Dyer's Hand and Other Essays*, p. 66.
42. Albert Einstein quoted in David Morley, *Scientific Papers* (Manchester: Carcanet, 2002), p. 83.

12

RICHARD BEARD

Outside the academy

University Creative Writing Course seeks published writer.

It starts, like many modern dilemmas, with a line from a specialist website. You are a writer of prose fiction or nonfiction, or possibly a playwright or a poet, and you subscribe to jobs.ac.uk or the *Higher Education Chronicle* or www.unijobs.com.au. You too are desperately seeking something. You want to make ends meet, and answering this ad may be the structural breakthrough your life as a writer needs, the beginning that leads to the middle and the happily-ever-after.

There is, however, a snag. This is not a transaction without complications. You set out, perhaps some time ago, ambitious to be a writer. You're now about to apply for a job as a teacher.

Me. I am. I want to describe my thinking when I applied for a University Creative Writing post at the end of 2008. I'd published four novels and three books of nonfiction, all with mainstream houses, but was yet to be distracted by extravagant sales or the glittering prizes. My books, which in the dread phrase of Iain Sinclair seemed pre-forgotten, turned out to have a secondary value as the job-specific 'proven track record of publication'.

Academic institutions offer writers another chance. The writer–teacher John Gardner, in his essential *The Art of Fiction*, argues that 'every true apprentice writer has, however he may try to keep it secret even from himself, only one major goal: glory'.[1] Gardner knows this because he was once a writer himself, and he hasn't lost the habit of honesty. For many of us, the most simplistic rewards of glory – critical and financial success – can sometimes prove elusive. Happily, there's a fall-back position while we keep on working at the craft. We can enter a decently paid profession from the side, somewhere middling on the pay-scale, our books our stand-out credentials. I have no doctorate and no teaching qualification but my books, here at least, have a concrete exchangeable value.

I can't say I've convinced myself. I distrust my motives, doubting whether teaching should ever be a safety-net beneath the high-wire thrills of real writers writing.

Read on, I thought, what else do they want?

Most universities will ask writers for 'evidence of a strong commitment to teaching'. This is right and proper. The side-door is unlocked, but not unmanned. As a freelancer I'm a veteran of short-form teaching engagements for organisations like Arvon (UK) and workshops at literary festivals. I've taught one-off semesters as a visiting lecturer. These experiences have been fun and rewarding (mostly), and for the purposes of an interview I can lay hands on appropriate testimonials and references. My teaching experience might almost look like a commitment.

But think, be honest: am I *strongly* committed, at the age of seven full-length books, applying for my first permanent teaching job? I have yards of evidence confirming a strong commitment to writing. My books, primarily, followed by a catalogue of domestic grievances and a nuanced understanding of the rental housing market.

For me, this becomes the decisive question. Can any writer honestly, or satisfactorily, live with these two strong commitments, an invitation to professional bigamy? I'm anxious in advance. If Creative Writing and writing are incompatible, then one or the other must suffer.

First, the writing. Faced with a full-time teacher's obligations to reading, reports, admin, institutional crises, budgets, departmental politics, as a writer I might be forgiven (might I?) for reminding myself, and perhaps occasionally my colleagues, that the university asked for a practising writer, and in every tight spot I may (perhaps should) shirk my paid responsibilities to concentrate on writing (to which I also have a responsibility, and in which my identity is invested, and for which I was in the absence of qualifications employed). Obviously, for a teacher, this is not a great attitude to have. If I discover I think like this, I will thank myself for coming and show myself the door.

I am, however, supposed to continue writing – this may even be a condition of my employment. It would be unprofessional (would it?) to demonstrate a commitment to teaching at the expense of the very facility that made me eligible for the role in the first place.

Otherwise, if I take my new commitment to teaching seriously, the result may be equally corrosive in the other direction.

When exactly am I planning to keep up with the writing? In snatched moments at home and in the long vacation. Faced with the writer's obligations to the desk, concentration, truth, beauty, originality, endurance, as a teacher I might be forgiven (might I?) for reminding myself that I am, after all, a professional university lecturer. That's what I'm paid for and what puts the bacon on the butter on the bread.

For a writer, this evasion is the beginning of the end. Or maybe the end of the beginning, a timely injection of realism. How will I know unless I try it?

Hesitation is the essence of wisdom, I tell myself. It makes sense to prepare for moments of ambivalence. But again, be honest. I'm not faced with a free choice, a clean fork in the path. I need the money, and my dependence on a secondary income is unlikely to change anytime soon.

The standard contracts favoured by publishing houses assume that writers must also be earning elsewhere. Mid-list books can then make acceptable returns for the publisher which are not shared by the author. The longer a writer stays mid-list (my next book is *always* a bestseller) the more the financial risk (and emotional investment) is shouldered by the writer alone. This situation has partly been allowed to develop because of the flourishing Creative Writing industry. Educational institutions make up the financial shortfall.

In our era, this is the model of the writing life. Other eras had different models: in the age of patronage, writers made concessions for wealthy individuals. The printing press then allowed a Grub Street contribution to a writer's lifestyle and income. Writers have always fed themselves as best they can, although some refuse to compromise. Modernist authors popularised a template of rejected genius followed by irresistible late acclaim, which itself was a throwback to the Romantic requirement for writers to go to the edge and look over the side. Every single day.

Today's default option is less dramatic. Leaving aside instant notoriety and unabashed stardom, writers teaching Creative Writing is the most accessible contemporary template for a literary career. There are many fine writers squaring the circle in universities throughout the English-speaking world (though not, intriguingly, in significant numbers anywhere else). These writers teach and also sustain a prolific creative output. They take full advantage of the way writing works at this time.

So there's the money. It would be dishonest to pretend otherwise. Writing books is a full-time job that doesn't pay – join in and don't be precious. Get your feet beneath a faculty desk. My feet. Cold feet.

I recognise a nonfiction world where instead of writing people *work*, doing something they don't always want to do, but for money. Put on a brave face, like Nobel Prize winner J. M. Coetzee, who spent many years at the University of Cape Town. This experience may have influenced the attitude of the narrator in his novel *Diary of a Bad Year*: 'I would cheer myself up by telling myself that at heart I was not a teacher but a novelist.'[2]

There it is again; one or the other. Teaching is not writing. The self-justification begins.

Temperamentally, although it isn't writing, teaching Creative Writing is recognisably in the rightish area. I know that I can find the experience of teaching rewarding, and going full-time seems less of a backward step than becoming a full-time postman. Not that writers can afford to be selective. Investment banking? Law enforcement? Let's face it: writing books, or having written books, is not a qualification that opens every door.

It feels reasonable to be attracted by the model of a modern writing life, and perhaps also by the promise of salvation. The attitude of latecomers to regular university work is nicely expressed by John Irving in *The World According to Garp*. 'It was for his writing, in the beginning, that he had never taken the idea of a job seriously. Now it was for his writing that he was thinking he needed a job. I am running out of people I can imagine, he thought.'[3]

The list of positives is growing: the money, the spirit of the times, the raw material. Colleagues, meetings, coffee in plastic cups. Gossip and misunderstandings, the brain-food of human contact. In the best possible light, I'll be dividing my time between wise professors and curious students, enthused by one and all. This is a tempting prospect. After seven books and a diminished fund of experience, I can feel weakness when confronted by temptation.

I'm a creative writer, the kind the university wants to employ, so I let my imagination construct a perfect collegiate environment for Creative Writing. This vision is not dissimilar to Professor Malcolm Bradbury's one-time ideal for his pioneering MA course at the University of East Anglia. In the preface to *Class Work*, an anthology of twenty-five years of writing produced by his students, Bradbury formulates a retrospective manifesto for what he hopes his years in teaching have achieved. He wants his courses to have created 'a significant climate around writing, in which talented and promising authors are taken through the problems, general and specific, universal and personal, of their form and ambitions, shown the options and possibilities, challenged, edited, pressured, hastened, treated as members of a serious profession'.[4]

In the profession itself – publishers, agents, booksellers, critics – a sense of significance around serious writing is sometimes hard to identify. Literary fiction, in particular, is barely a serious profession. If it was, it would be rewarded as such. It may be that university courses, independent of market forces and editorial chair-hopping, are now the *only* place where Bradbury's significant climate for creative writing reliably exists. This may explain why teachers as well as students can find universities creatively inspiring.

I've almost talked myself into it: a significant climate, financial security, the zeitgeist, company, social and professional validation – that's quite a package. Until now I've survived on the hunter–gatherer model of freelance activity, but the search for piecework can fray the nerves: the approach, the kill, the endless beginning again. I feel like a throwback to the era BCW, Before Creative Writing. If I carry on like this, I feel doomed to extinction.

I need this job. Talented and right-thinking writers apply in impressive numbers for similar jobs all the time. They accept their appointments with gratitude. I should do the same myself. That's exactly what I did.

I made it to the safe side of the college gates, a sanctuary out of the weather. By this time I had a polished idea of why I needed the university. It wasn't long before I was wondering why the university needed me.

At this point it's worth saying that I believe Creative Writing can be taught. For me, good writing is unlikely to appear by the postal muse at three in the morning, by candlelight, overseen by angels. In that sense, dissecting writing into its component parts is not anathema to my own way of working. I do believe there are communicable techniques that ease the writer's task.

I also believe that some of the disciplines and skills of writing are transferable, and understand that undergraduate students, in particular, are not being trained to earn a living as writers. Those who go on to write professionally, and there will always be some, benefit from a comprehensive tour of the basics, while later adding the finishing and more important touches themselves (perhaps by candlelight, at three in the morning overseen by angels – there are no wrong answers).

I'm therefore not in denial about the educational value of Creative Writing as an academic option. Techniques can be taught and writing assessed. Learning outcomes can be displayed in spreadsheets, and transferable skills presented as bullet-points, just as they are in the UK NAWE's Creative Writing Subject Benchmark Statement.[5] In paragraph 2.7 of this recent creed, the National Association of Writers in Education (to give the full mouthful) claims that Creative Writing can develop, among ten other transferable benefits, 'skills in team working' and 'an appreciation of diversity'.[6]

If the argument about teaching Creative Writing has been won, and the subject by itself can develop skills other than writing, I wonder why it needs to be taught by me? Why should I, or any other practising writer, be invited to enter this established academic discipline from the side, half-way up the pay scale? What makes a writer as a teacher so special?

Never mind the qualifications, feel the passion. No one can doubt my commitment to writing (if not teaching). To make sense of my appointment, I intend to communicate my knowledge with energy and urgency, in the belief that students appreciate my active connection to the practice and business of writing. Students may even decide that only publishing writers have 'the necessary intimate connection with language, the necessary urgency and depth of engagement with the problems of making writing, the commitment to the possibilities of the form and the life of the imagination'[7] required to produce texts of conviction and marketable potential.

However true this may be, Creative Writing as an academic subject has matured. Courses have their templates, their indicative content and study modes, their intended learning outcomes and approved modular structures. Creative Writing, like any other subject, will tend towards a syllabus, especially as increased course fees mean that students want to know what they can rightfully expect. Plot, characterisation, POV, dialogue, all will be included. To ensure that the stated learning outcomes are achieved, it is safer to teach such a curriculum as a set of established procedures. These will combine, over a sufficient number of modules, into a coherent programme of study leading to a certified educational qualification.

Anyone with an aptitude for teaching, and preferably a teaching qualification, could deliver just such a programme of precepts and drills. There are legions of employable Creative Writing graduates who themselves have come through this system. They may not have a proven track record of publication, but then neither will they dither and deliberate as I did. Their studies will, presumably, have brought them skills in team working and an appreciation of diversity. They are proven academic professionals who specialise in Creative Writing: they're available and competent to take their subject forward.

If Creative Writing is destined to evolve along these lines, then why bother with writers on the staff? It can't be for our divided commitment or the lure of the empty page. Originally, when Creative Writing was first offered as a graduate course of study, writers conferred authority on an uncertain discipline. In the days before the institutional reassurance of modular approaches and external quality audits, the writer could at least say: this is how I did it.

In universities today, the 'how I did it' approach sits uneasily with the more objective process of Creative Writing in its mature systematic form. This is just as well. My commitment to writing has informed techniques and strategies that work for me in the context of my published books. I can't honestly say that these techniques will work more generally for other writers on their particular projects. Once I'm in the classroom, how I write is less important than how I teach.

Any classroom authority that accrues to me, simply because I've published books, seems insecure and probably irrelevant. Creative Writing academics can read the same growing body of 'How To' literature that I also have read. We may both be following the same modular syllabus honed by others who came before us. We have a carefully calibrated marking structure to ensure that technical proficiency is rewarded. We make our equal contribution to a fair and moderated system.

If Creative Writing becomes a subject like any other (which is the battle writers in universities have chosen to fight) then these courses may soon outgrow the need for writers as permanent members of staff. Teaching methodologies are harmonising and the analytical literature about the subject area is deepening. Before long, I and my books will have very little of consequence to add.

It seems strange, then, that universities should still be seeking writers with 'a proven track record of publication'. Unless, of course, this betrays an uncertainty about where Creative Writing is going. The practising writers on the faculty act as a reminder of where it came from.

In the early days of the subject, the practising writer provided legitimacy. Learn what this writer has learned (if you like this writer) with the suggestion that the course could guarantee nothing more transferable or durable. Now that learning outcomes must be formulated and approved in advance, and Creative Writing is a fact of academic life, the captive writer looks like a relic of arguments resolved.

I don't expect universities to run a writer subsidy scheme at the expense of their students, and having written books is in itself no reliable indicator of added value. There is no mystical genius for teaching that inherently attaches to published writers. However. If a writer in some way *does* offer more than a qualified university lecturer, then that needs to be adequately recognised and valued within the system. This requires an adjustment – sometimes the advocates of Creative Writing at universities can be worst enemies to writers who love teaching but want to make a virtue of their difference.

I can turn up on time and go through a repeatable set of established and assessable procedures, but that's not what I want to do. I want to turn up on time and communicate the enthusiasm that comes from my engagement with my own writing, and I want to promise to deliver that level of energy year after year. After year.

Part-time contracts are a part-time solution. They can lead to a clock-watching attitude (by either writers or employers) that is unhelpful. There is scope to be more innovative. One intriguing suggestion is to employ writers in pairs on a four-year cycle. Working two years on and two years off, the writer would have to renew, periodically, a commitment to succeeding or failing as a writer (by finding from writing the money to make up the biannual financial shortfall). The students would also benefit from hearing a range of voices and approaches.

By becoming more adaptable, educational employers can recognise that a writer is not exactly, or not always, a teacher. This kind of innovation would also make sense of the small print. Universities want a writer with a proven track record who may be required 'to co-ordinate the design and implementation' of various courses, and (to continue quoting from a random advert) 'participate in relevant university administrative procedures'. Not to mention the teaching. They'd also like their resident writers 'to continue to develop a personal writing profile'. This means keep writing, keep publishing.

If universities are sincere about this part of the exchange, and sincerely believe that practising writers bring added value, then more thought could be given to creating space to write within the university system. In Australian and UK universities, a creative work qualifies officially as a 'creative practice research publication' (most writers will still think of it as a book). This can bring direct funding benefits, although some departments take a short-term view of this hard-won concession. They employ writers with books in the publishers' forthcoming catalogues, when these books may only exist because the writer has resisted the constraints of the academy until now.

Am I asking for special treatment? I think I am, because I'm contributing something the university can't provide without me. If it could, why advertise for writers?

It would appear that the argument for Creative Writing hasn't been won. The universities don't have complete confidence in their systems and outcomes, and their courses still need validating with magic. In these competitive times, it is ultimately the students who make this decision. Writers bring interest, energy, creativity, something different. The students may even be drawn by the mystic touch of the published, because they don't wholly believe in the academic logic of Creative Writing. The learning outcomes from official benchmark protocols are not what they had in mind.

I have to say, in all honesty, that in fifteen years of teaching I've never met a student who enrolls on a writing course in search of the transferable skills. I see all students as aspiring writers, as I believe they see themselves. They are eager to improve their work to a publishable level, and this ambition is implicitly encouraged by departments of Creative Writing with their employment of 'practising writers'. Never mind the mature syllabus, feel the occult power of the published word.

In this way, writers risk becoming complicit in a deception. The published status of the teachers suggests a professional outcome that not every university is equipped to provide. At the most basic level, universities run accredited courses that award university degrees. They are not obliged to develop privileged access to commercial publication gateways. Some courses have excellent links to the industry, but not all. There are too many courses, not enough publishers.

If writers had nowhere else to go for their secondary income, none of this would matter. Universities could act as if these contradictions didn't exist, and writers would continue to apply for the jobs they need. However, thanks to the success of the *idea* of Creative Writing, the model of the writing life may be about to change. The faculty suddenly has competitors, because if Creative Writing can be taught, there's a growing awareness that it doesn't have to be taught in college.

In the UK there has been a noticeable rush on mentoring services, editorial agencies and start-up writing academies. These private initiatives (although some in the UK are aided by the Arts Council[8]) are providing services that aspiring writers must have decided they can't with certainty find in the university sector. Usually, these services will include bespoke individual feedback, close attention to specific projects, and detailed critical editing of manuscripts. These are precisely the skills I've accumulated from my experience of writing and publishing books. I know more about coaxing a book to completion, on its own terms, than I do about generic guides to constructing character.

These new agencies, in my opinion, offer creative writing work that is more immediately suited to the skill-set developed by the practice of writing. They do not require a knowledge of modular parameters or transferable outcomes, but a concentration on the work for its own sake.

On a practical level, these new outfits can offer equally rewarding but less constrained employment. Meetings can be paced to suit the unpredictable rhythms of writing, rather than the academic year's intermittent momentum towards mandatory assessments and awards. Practising writers are better able to drop in and out of employment depending on their writing commitments.

Unless universities start to make comparable allowances, this more flexible option may provide a new model for the writing life. We can already catch a glimpse of the beginning of the era ACW, After Creative Writing. Writers will continue to make a contribution to university courses, but as extracurricular visitors not permanent members of staff. In this capacity I can be an expert on what I know best – writing techniques that have worked (or otherwise) for me, even if they contradict the precepts of the syllabus, as they often will.

Students will have a choice. Those starting out, or with only a casual interest, may decide that the measured and modular approach of a timetabled university course is the most effective way to learn how to write. They will be taught by qualified teachers, and universities have many years' experience of creating favourable environments for writing. Creative Writing academics will continue to be properly competent at organising, supervising and examining successive generations of students.

Some of these graduates will follow the career path of their teachers, and run the university Creative Writing courses of tomorrow. They will develop their own academic vocabulary and practices, and negotiate the necessary internal and external challenges to maintain Creative Writing as a valid strand of the humanities curriculum.

Elsewhere, writers should feel confident about the future of outside opportunities. The rising cost of university provision means that small-scale, writer-conceived enterprises can be competitive in the expanding spaces outside the academy. Courses can be organised exclusively for the benefit of writers, both teachers and learners. And without large bureaucracies to subsidise, writers who work on these schemes can be properly remunerated for creating a serious climate for writing in a way that a curriculum alone does not.

Writers too can then start to revise the vocabulary of what they do. No more students, only emerging writers at different stages of development. No semesters and assignments, but an ongoing commitment to the habit of production and improvement. Teamwork is laudable, as is a sincere appreciation of diversity, but writers may also need a single-mindedness that is antisocial and blinkered. There is less need, outside the academy, to hide the hard edges of a hard-edged pursuit.

If a sufficient number of aspiring writers are left unmoved by the promise of university awards and transferable skills, as I suspect they are, then the model of the writing life will change. Practising writers will resist the small-ad appeal of Creative Writing programmes. They will find opportunities outside the academy that make more relevant use of their time, experience and skills.

NOTES

1. John Gardner, *The Art of Fiction* (New York: Knopf, 1983), p. 200.
2. J. M. Coetzee, *Diary of a Bad Year* (London: Harvill Secker, 2007).
3. John Irving, *The World According to Garp* (London: Black Swan, 1986).
4. Malcolm Bradbury, *Class Work: The Best of Contemporary Short Fiction* (London: Hodder and Stoughton, 1995).
5. National Association of Writers in Education: NAWE, *Research: Background* (2010), available online at www.nawe.co.uk/writing-in-education/writing-at-university/research.html, accessed 21 March 2011.
6. Bradbury, *Class Work*, p. 5.
7. Andrew Cowan, 'Questions, Questions: Can the Creative Survive in Proximity to the Critical?', *Writing in Education*, 41 (Spring 2007), pp. 56–61.
8. See as an example: Arts Council England, *Adventures in Fiction: Mentoring and Manuscript Appraisal* [n.d.], available online at www.adventuresinfiction.co.uk/index.html, accessed 21 March 2011.

13

CHRIS HAMILTON-EMERY

Contemporary publishing

The background to literary publishing

What is the trade?

The world of contemporary literary publishing is astonishingly diverse, complex and entering a period of substantial, indeed pivotal, change. Before we look at some of the key features of this evolving industry, it might be useful to set out some terms of reference. Literary publishing is not a monolithic, clearly identifiable strand of the publishing world; it is fragmented, with widely varying economies of scale and trajectory, both in business terms and in terms of the wider culture industry. One way we could assess this landscape is through the prism of trade publishing – that is publishing which sells through distributors to wholesalers and retailers and on to consumers through bricks-and-mortar shops and, increasingly, through online retailers and supermarkets. Another may be direct sales, bypassing shops and much of the supply chain to deal directly with consumers, with readers. Another may be the powerful effects of the World Wide Web and where, when and how we now read in a networked society that transgresses national boundaries.

The book trade has traditionally united several discrete industries: printing, publishing, logistics and bookselling. However, as we'll examine in this chapter, the entire nature of the book trade is under considerable pressure and those traditional relationships are in flux. Logistics may look odd in that list above and yet this component of the trade, in many respects, has come to influence and drive all other players in the field.

First, let's look at *some* of the people who work inside a publishing business.

Who works inside a publishing business?

Traditionally, any publishing business comprises a range of staff with highly specialised skills; this will include (in no particular order and not exhaustively):

- Publishers: those who control a wide range of staff and structure the broad publishing aims of the business and its financial targets, shape lists and construct the personality of a given brand within a company.
- Acquisitions editors or commissioning editors: those who make decisions about which titles a business should consider betting money on. They often have clearly defined financial targets to meet. They are the core revenue-generating staff.
- Desk editors or project editors: staff who may work on a text to improve it or oversee all aspects of the publishing lifecycle to bring a book to market.
- Production editors or production controllers: those who purchase services in the collation, correction, assembly and manufacturing of a given work. Production staff are the hub of most publishing businesses, with most publishing operations touching upon them or directly controlled by them.
- Publishing assistants: staff who may work with a group of editors and production staff to help administer a project and deal with correspondence and necessary bureaucracy.
- Marketing controllers: staff who in some instances may define the areas of reader interest for commissioning editors to find books for. In many instances this sense of audience is formed in a relationship between editor and marketer, and beyond this, the sales team. Marketing controllers may well have control over book information, too, the bibliographic data that the entire industry relies on.
- Marketing assistants: those individuals who have a special responsibility for motivating and coordinating those in the supply chain who can stimulate sales. This is often a pragmatic role in controlling systems and procedures which spread information about a book to key stakeholders in the supply chain. Marketing often involves working with partners inside the book trade.
- Publicists: the driving force of much modern publishing. Where a marketer spends money on advertising and print, information systems and tangible systems in the book trade, the publicist works with the *media* – all media, TV, radio, print and online – to create free advertising for a work. They may also talk to festivals, bookstores and libraries to create reading and performance opportunities. They may help develop events. They create or construct choices for consumers. You could argue that publicists create consumer desire.
- Sales managers: those who are responsible for developing, in house, channels to market, managing accounts, taking books to buyers in key accounts in the trade and convincing them of a work's value (as in the cash it can generate through profitable book sales). There are often sales conferences within publishing businesses where editors and marketers formally present

books, series and sets to senior sales staff (who may be divided into international and domestic sales teams, regional teams, special sales and so on) to provide them with the information to sell products more effectively, and sometimes to win support for products. Some businesses will centre operations on sales managers, and sales managers will *pull* certain forms of publishing into the business. Other companies will *push* works towards their sales staff, hoping to convince them of their decisions.

- Sales representatives: those people at the coal face selling individual products to buyers in bookstores, the head offices of national chains, to library suppliers, wholesalers, overseas agents and everyone capable of purchasing a book from the publishing company. Feedback from such staff is vital in planning future publishing strategy.
- Rights sales: those staff who sell subsidiary rights, as territorial publishing rights, foreign language rights, broadcast and performance rights, permissions for a primary work's quotation and use in third-party content. Such rights may be the difference between a title's overall profitability and beyond this to a company's overall success.
- Book designers: those staff with highly specialised skills and knowledge around constructing a text for manufacturing. Their concerns are aesthetic as well as ensuring product quality (as in its effectiveness in any given market). This may include sophisticated product design, and on occasion, an author may rewrite to fit a design model. They often work with other 'creatives' in the industry, for example, picture researchers, illustrators, typesetters, even programmers, to complete a project.
- Financial controllers and accountants: staff who may work closely with publishing teams to create, agree and monitor budgets for products and product lines. They can provide guidance and expertise on forecasting profit and loss and even assess the commercial context of publishing decisions. In most businesses, a layer of financial modelling is central to commissioning strategy where product lines as opposed to titles are financially defined and aggregated into broader financial objectives.
- Distribution or logistics managers: those charged with getting products from A to B, and for holding the right level of stocks to ensure no business runs out of goods to sell. In most publishing businesses, so much money is tied up in stocks, this role is of central importance in maintaining a healthy cash profile. And in publishing, nothing is more important than cash.

This is by no means a complete list. But a publishing company will almost certainly draw together teams of people listed above into imprints and sub-imprints of a business. It is a feature and a legacy of the industrialisation of publishing. Some businesses may be so fragmented that individuals with their own skills and experience may have entire careers within their own profession. However, some publishing staff have to have sufficient overview of all these skills to coordinate them, to balance them, and to direct them to achieve the overall goals of the business. At this end a tier of middle and senior management will represent the specialisations of core staff, and together plan the operations of the business. No specialisation can be effectively ignored, some may be contracted out. In smaller presses, the specialisations are identical, but you may find one person performing a wide range of these.

Who else works in publishing?

The publishing world, with its long history of practices and precedents, has surrounding it an economic structure of agents, marketers, publicists, book information services, researchers, literary magazines, broadsheets, trade magazines, printers, typesetters, text and cover designers, picture researchers, copy-editors, proofreaders, indexers, illustrators, typographers and font designers, software companies, computer companies, sales representatives, reviewers, bloggers, book clubs, lawyers, financiers, foundations, colonies, retreats, radio and television shows, festivals, libraries, competitions, literary prizes, writers' groups, reading groups, and beyond this, institutional economic dependencies in the wide range of courses, degrees, higher degrees, indeed a whole industry of educational services to feed every single aspect of it. It is an ecosystem built on a high degree of specialisation and cultural expectations, skills and, indeed, beliefs – beliefs which all help to construct value, choice and purchasing imperatives for each consumer when choosing a book to read.

Creating choices and influencing readers

No reader is isolated from these forces, and a characteristic of the major changes in the industry today is a war of mediation. One way to consider trade publishing is that it is an industry built around constructing choices for you. Of course, constructing choices is an issue of competitive advantage and sometimes of ideology, and any choice, by definition, excludes part of the vast range of new and existing publications. In fact one might argue that trade publishing is determined upon a kind of consumer myopia. The stakes were never higher, and so more and more money is expended in building choices and excluding the competition. No party is immune from this. It is a high-risk strategy.

At the outermost extent of this complex system lie readers. If a publishing business is selling through the trade to reach consumers, a very great deal of attention is focused on all members of the supply chain, and it could be argued that, until very recently, not very much attention was paid to having direct relationships with consumers who, beyond their statistical segmentation, were largely an anonymous if entirely dependent aspect of the publishing economy.

The economics all come down to individual books

For a moment, consider the abbreviated list of people above and how they impact on literary publishing. Consider how such a structure can resist change, can be so innately confined and determined by its dependencies. Consider the stakeholders and why all those involved would seek to preserve the economic balance and beyond this the control of what choices you, personally, are afforded and how those numerous skills and the combined effort of tens of thousands of individuals are purely intended to make you pick up a $14.95 or £7.99 paperback. This is the trade.

Because of the incredible number of intermediaries involved directly and indirectly in publishing, the money afforded to each, and derived from that cover price on that single copy of a book, is rather small. Because it is small it will be fiercely defended. It is also built from an aggregation of many sales and so trade publishing is constantly under pressure to increase unit sales, to make selections which have a track record of success, to reduce risk and to be ever watchful for shifts in consumer taste. In fact, trade publishing is, for all of this infrastructure and mutual shared dependencies, a remarkably fickle thing. As you might also imagine, it is hegemonic in nature. As trend spotters assess the competition, approaches to acquisitions, to sales expectations, to branding, list development, all tend to shift towards the centre ground and to a diminishment of diversity in the actual content on offer.

In recent years, we have seen new market pressures pushing trade publishers to even greater dependencies on bestsellers – we'll examine some features of this below. As publishers seek to find the key titles that can deliver the revenue growth and profits needed, so agents and authors have subdivided the rights in a work to sell, in order to maximise the income for the author and in many cases creating bidding wars for titles, pushing up the value of advances and royalties. An advance is a speculative investment made by a publisher in an author and their content and its likely earnings in a given market. It is almost a futures market, gambling on a likely return on the publishers' money. Unearned advances are written off, and this economic model is one of the biggest threats to modern publishing. When a book fails, the publisher has sunk money into an author and a title, drawn into play its full resources and by extension the resources of the wider publishing industry into an enormous gamble. It is shocking how few of these gambles pay off and how rarely advances are earned back for a publisher. The role of an acquisitions editor is to find titles that work in the market, that will make money; and as advocates of a title they must convince their colleagues that it is a sound investment worth the gamble that can make or break a list. No editor is right in all their selections and the difference between a good editor and a bad one can be the difference of a few percentage points. Every editor is as good as their last book.

Consolidation and competition in trade publishing

Before we leave this introductory overview of trade literary publishing it is also interesting to consider scale. Over the past century there has been an increasing tendency for mergers and acquisitions to take place within literary publishing. Publishing has increasingly become a tale of a few very significant players in a global market. Scale matters, market share matters; and as publishing is driven in part by meaningful aggregations of content, well-branded, clearly identifiable imprints can help consumers discover the writers, the subjects, the books they wish to attend to. In this heady period of consolidation, once famous imprints have all been subsumed into vast conglomerates. This is not to say that books, like fast food, have almost become a commodity, for each imprint may have a fiercely loyal team working almost in isolation from the larger corporate structure, but the federal approach of most large publishing houses does effectively yield better returns for investors. Profits are often so slim, that building larger and larger structures has seemed the only way to gain power over parts of the industry – offering an ability to dictate terms and adjust the balance of power in favour of the publisher and thereby to improve profits.

Many factors have contributed to this change in the publishing landscape, but one we should pause to consider is the collapse of the net book agreement (NBA), an agreement that preserved, some would say protected, pricing and discounts to allow all aspects of the trade to coalesce with a degree of financial stability. In the wake of its collapse, a free market has led to considerable changes in the balance of power, and a substantial shift towards distributors and logistics businesses in the supply chain. The pressure on price and discount has been unprecedented, and led to several new entrants into the book trade not seen before. At the same time, changes in technology have brought about new models for delivering goods to consumers, especially in the unstoppable force of the World Wide Web.

Let's look at an example of these changes. Publishers working through the trade are dependent on booksellers to reach their consumers, and as a feature of this pressure there has been considerable consolidation among booksellers, where national bookstore chains have gained substantial market share and through scaling up their operations have engineered a position where they can influence pricing and discounts from publishers to improve their own profitability. This has had a detrimental impact on independent bookstores, who cannot compete in terms of price and range, and in the UK, cannot negotiate discounts as robustly as the chains can. As rent and rates have risen on the high street, the pressure on profits has become ever more problematic. Booksellers and publishers are increasingly tied to concentrating on those titles and genres which yield the biggest rewards.

Now let's consider the growth of Amazon and other online retailers, which has had a considerable impact on bookstores. Amazon can offer infinite range without the costs of rent and rates tied to expensive property. They can reach consumers worldwide and more consumers are available to them each day as the world moves online. Amazon represent a war on range and diversity for bricks-and-mortar chains and independent bookstores. They also represent a major pressure on price, as they have *disintermediated* part of the supply chain – taking links out of the chain and their associated costs – and are able to offer substantially discounted products direct to consumers. Amazon are a logistics business and as their success has grown, their market share has grown, so they have expanded the range of their catalogue. They are now one of the world's largest online department stores.

Thirdly, let's consider supermarkets, which have rapidly become one of the powerhouses of new book sales. In the war to attract customers and to expand their percentage of our weekly spend, supermarkets have constantly increased their range of goods and services. In the wake of the collapse of the NBA, they have turned their attention to books, not in terms of range and diversity but cherry-picking high-volume mass-market titles that they can entice customers with, drawing them into the store with targeted promotions. Who won in the Harry Potter sales wars? The supermarkets won.

Where does this leave traditional bookstores with their limitations of space, their inability to infinitely extend their range and their dependency on fast-moving titles to maintain cash flow and profitability? It has left us with a fiercely, indeed, savagely, aggressive war on price and a tendency to commodify some titles. This has all been good news for consumers: books are cheaper, more widely available and easier to procure. But range and diversity in terms of content have become normalised and the entire infrastructure has only served to reinforce this hegemonic new trading landscape. Bookstores are being squeezed into an ever smaller, more expensive space. Publishers are being left with fewer routes to market and less power in maintaining a profitable strategy to publish.

However, it is arguable that this has spiralled out of control and new participants in the book trade do not necessarily have an interest in books as books but as stock-keeping units of a certain price offering a certain value to consumers. Publishers and traditional booksellers are rapidly becoming the losers in this new world. Margins are being squeezed and even as market share may increase, the profits are in some cases shrinking and often collapsing. Is this new world sustainable? Well, whether it is or not pales into insignificance when we consider the massive changes in the patterns of how, where and with what we read.

So perverse is this new landscape that supermarkets sell books below cost (making their profits on other consumables in your weekly shopping) and bookstores treat Amazon as a wholesaler from whom they buy their stocks.

Direct-to-consumer publishing and non-traditional markets

We have considered how important scale is for publishers in terms of building market share, maintaining power over costs and maintaining a position of power vis-à-vis other players in the supply chain. Let us now consider how publishers bypass the trade entirely in dealing with consumers directly. This pattern of publishing is often more immediately profitable for smaller, medium-sized businesses and is a model widely adopted by independent publishers who often operate, exhaustively, in a well-defined niche market.

As the large conglomerates and their partners and competitors in the supply chain have coalesced around fashionable areas of publishing mass-market products, this has left a vacuum in which independent publishers and booksellers can occupy a (marginally) profitable space. Part of this model is dependent on publishers having an intense and on occasion dominant understanding of a specific subject or genre.

For many, the problem of bypassing the trade has been one of cost and scalability. How do you reach consumers? What will it cost to engage with them? Where can you find them? What will trigger them to make a purchase? In some cases a highly specific interest can define its own audience, though this very specificity may also make the market fundamentally unprofitable or make it hard to engineer an economically viable publishing model. For some this may be solved by forms of grants, subsidy or alternative income – and this is indeed a model for a great deal of not-for-profit publishing, whose primary income is not derived from product sales, but from other government and non-government agencies. Can one have a genuine literature based on an absence of readerships or where the choices and judgements involved in publication are in effect a by-product of a funded culture industry? Some may fully support the idea of state intervention as necessary to the lifeblood of the nation (whichever nation one lives in), others may argue that the very culture of the nation is being distorted and is fundamentally inauthentic. In this way, much of the nature of independent literary publishing is politicised and ideological.

Of course, not all direct-to-consumer publishing is funded or subsidised. Traditionally, this form of selling has been dependent on cataloguing, leafleting, inserting, and attending conferences and trade fairs, to name just a handful of techniques. Direct marketing which, in the past two decades, has become a highly controversial aspect of modern life and the modern postal services (which are often dependent on the profits from the practice), is an extremely expensive way to reach book customers. Renting mailing lists, targeting consumers, printing high-quality marketing materials certainly form a feature of many literary publishers' operations.

The most far-reaching change in managing direct sales has been the emergence of the World Wide Web and the enormous changes in reaching targeted groups of consumers. Interest groups commonly have websites, as do professional societies, and in the past five years the astonishing explosion of social networking has changed our sense of the world forever. Individuals are no longer united by national boundaries, national concerns, local economies or local concerns but have been exposed to vast numbers of other people who may share their concerns, beliefs and hopes. We shan't debate the way social media have affected human behaviour here, which is outside the scope of this chapter, but we can assess how small-press publishing is categorised by its links to the Web, to social media and community.

Independent and small-press literary publishing

What are the differences between independent and conglomerate?

Independent publishing is not constitutionally any different from larger corporate publishing. The maths involved, the human relationships involved, the suppliers and customers are all the same. Aside from size, what makes independent publishing different?

Let's get the content question out of the way first. Some may argue that the literary publishing that truly matters is largely a product of the small-press world. It is important to unpack these assertions for yourself. Despite the nature and magnitude of corporate publishing – driven by profits and following the money to where customers and their taste coalesce – it is clearly not without its merits and does have a major part to play in discovering and nurturing exceptional literary talent as well as sustaining a broader economic framework in which independent publishers of all sizes can carve out their niches. It's also important to consider whether it is consumers, as in readers, who create an important work of literature, or an author and her publisher. Clearly there would not be a publishing world without the conglomerates, and the people working within them are no less passionate or dedicated to their authors. The size of a business has little bearing on the quality and value of its books. Independence is no guarantee of quality or value. So what might be the benefits of the independent sector?

Characteristics of independence

Let's make an assumption, that for a press to be independent it simply needs to be privately owned, and not form a subdivision of some larger company structure. Some independent presses are state assisted, some regularly, some periodically – but despite being dependent on state funding, they may consider themselves as independent for they are not formally state-owned businesses. Independent presses need not be small; in fact, it is a serious impediment to success to persevere in being small for its own sake. Some independent presses are hobbies and do not provide their owners with a living. Just as there are no virtues in constraining size, the blind pursuit of growth may also be a foolish strategy (and often starves a business of cash). Aside from the constitutional nature of an independent business, there are no clear differences at all to those of larger corporations. Ultimately, they need to make money by selling books. So what makes an independent press different? There is a different answer for every business, but a few characteristics we might examine are: (a) a predisposition to literary debuts in tough genres, (b) the publication of non-mainstream or marginally profitable or unprofitable literatures and (c) taking risks not solely defined by profits but by other forms of value. Let's add to that (d) the sheer intense focus an independent publisher may have on a single subject or genre. Most independent presses have a narrow range of interests, not because their owners have narrow interests, but because they have to compete against huge conglomerates. They must be focused to survive.

Routes to market

Another characteristic, which may provide some further differentiation, is that very many independent presses do not sell, primarily, through the trade. They may not seek to reach their customers through bookselling chains and independent bookstores, nor even through online retailers, still less through supermarkets, newsagents and airside and rail stationery franchises. Many independents reach their customers through what might be described as non-traditional routes to market. That can include direct mail, relationships with institutions or professional markets, relationships with communities of interest (defined by almost any subject from autism to trainspotting), through newsletters, bulletin boards, members' societies, museums, art galleries, stately homes and so on.

The skills that independents have developed over the years have found an entirely new channel in the age of the World Wide Web and especially since the explosion of social media. We could characterise this further by saying that independent publishing is often determined by communities. It is community publishing. Rather than being folksy, this notion is of extreme importance at this juncture, for community is central to the future of the industry. We'll examine this in the final section.

The independent sector is not comprised solely of small presses (which we might define as businesses with less than £1 million turnovers); it contains a wide range of privately owned businesses whose turnovers exceed £1 million. Some may read this thinking that some of our literary presses have turnovers of less than £100,000, and we might further break down small presses into micro-presses. With the development of new routes to market, we can now further subdivide the publishing ecology into self-publishers, too, where the author is the publisher and there are *no* intermediaries, with the exception of the distributor/retailer.

There is perhaps one further model of independence, the final extreme, where the author sells directly and not through any form of physical or digital distribution. A very great deal of this happens at readings, and this, too, is a form of community publishing, driven by audiences and interpersonal relationships. If profits are not the key driver in independent literary publishing, what makes people risk their livelihoods to do it?

Conviction publishing

One thing we can be sure of is that the communities that surround independent literary publishing are highly informed, specialised social groupings, with deeply held convictions and values. A press comes to symbolise a set of communal concerns and mediates this sense of shared values so that the group can cohere; of course, there may be more than one group an individual wishes to belong to. By extension, for a book to succeed (though one should examine what constitutes its success) it may have to extend beyond one group into the realms of many others. Independent publishing is all about traversing such groupings and uniting them through a range of marketing and publicity techniques. The most powerful marketing tool lies in our beliefs and shared sense of values; publishing *into* those values, fulfilling the expectations of the social group, is an important feature of what we might call 'conviction publishing'.

An independent literary press's offer may be of product quality, political assertion or aesthetic conviction; it may be tied to a range of specific literary practices; it may even stretch to a range of lifestyle choices and personal hopes and ambitions. For some customers it may validate their sense of themselves and what matters in their lives. It may represent choice, diversity, opportunity, validation, religious and political conviction, even ideas of beauty and truth. The ethical and moral framework of a press may even be more compelling than its ultimate economic viability and this is both fascinating and problematic. No independent press, no matter how large or small, is free from the larger-scale forces affecting its larger compatriots in corporate life. They are intimately bound together in the publishing ecology of a country. What affects the conglomerates will affect the independent sector. The customers for both sectors are the same. What they share is a market. The same pressures come to bear: an independent publisher has to construct a choice for its customers (or stakeholders) and has to convince its 'polity' of the offers being made. This is becoming a key feature of new social publishing. The process of selection, validation and acceptance is being driven more by consumers than by artisan judges in the supply chain. Put more simply, the reader is becoming the editor.

Breeding grounds and killing fields

Independent literary publishers are often seen as breeding grounds and stepping stones to build a writing career, and there are certainly many examples where an author has migrated from one press to another, moving to larger and ever larger presses, before finding a home in one of the conglomerates or the largest independents. This kind of literary progression can become a kind of marker for literary success. Can this also be a function of the independent sector? Well, the independent sector does have a lot of success in talent spotting and risk taking, and it is arguable that the commercial imperatives of the conglomerates may make them more averse to taking chances on unknown writers and difficult genres. There is a tendency for all successful presses large or small to move towards the centre, and the centre has become a very crowded place. This has led many to wonder if the independent sector should further fragment and take more risks on new writing, exploiting new markets that may emerge or can be created around developing talents. How such a breeding ground can be financed and sustained is heavily tied in with the very rapid changes we are seeing in literary publishing, its economics, its lifecycles; the entire basis of the industry is in flux.

For some this signals the end of conventional publishing, akin to the demise of major music labels and much of the infrastructure of the music industry. If the independent sector is a breeding ground, it is also becoming a war zone as powerful commercial forces affect where and how readers read, what they buy, how it is delivered to them and by whom. We are in an age where the distributor has become the retailer and the publisher, where the author has become exposed to millions of competitors increasingly making their content available and often for free, where publishers can no longer make profits outside a syntax of bestsellers, prizes and publicity, where celebrity has become a new publishing commodity, where books themselves are commodified by information giants. It is a world where the forces acting upon publishers are no longer those of the book trade itself, but of IT manufacturers, Web services, information businesses who have no regard for books and publishers, for booksellers or anyone working in the trade. Even the nature of the book as an integral consistent singular work is being challenged. In the final section of this chapter, we'll look at some features of this explosive new landscape.

The future is now

I'm going to end this chapter with some assertions, assumptions and speculations made in the context of our current publishing world, a world which is undergoing a significant transformation. No one can feel secure in their assessment of these changes for the nature of the problem and the solutions on offer are changing with lightning speed. Publishers are closing. Genres are dying. Booksellers are disappearing from our high streets. Physical books are being created as electronic ones. What might these changes bring?

Self-publishing is perhaps the fastest growing sector of the new publishing landscape; this will only be exacerbated by online retailers allowing authors to publish content for free or for a small fee. Some authors are likely to capitalise on this, especially those debuting, and those at the pinnacle of their careers (the former to bypass barriers, the latter to increase their share of revenues). Author services business, which developed in tandem with print-on-demand services in the 1990s (manufacturing books to order, one at a time), will be replaced by retailer-owned self-publishing products – within a decade, everyone will be a media publisher in one form or another.

The power of online retailers will make the 'selection infrastructure' of publishing largely redundant – why risk getting it wrong when you can let the writers take the risk on whether their book is worth anything to consumers and then reward them, once in pole position, more robustly on their proven sales potential? Books will succeed through powerful referral engines, and human intervention will not be needed – you can see this on sites like authonomy.com. Publishers (who may well be retailers and search engines) will use mulching sites to monetise the slush pile and increasingly let readers determine what will be formally published and supported. Editorial speculation will be replaced with user feedback. Consumers will determine how writers move a story forward.

The most popular content will rise to the top. Ideas of value and price will permanently shift to the reader. Critical assessment, scholarly evaluation will undergo a radical reappraisal, centred less on the conjecture of abstract authorial evaluation (based on those academic schemas of assessment) and shift towards understanding why readers value what they do and how they select and become stakeholders in a text, transforming it into literature. Judgement will be increasingly democratised and large-scale evidence-based reader response will become central to our understanding of a text. All books will become 'societies of meaning'.

Electronic publishing will replace much conventional print publishing within a decade; we will read books on a wide range of devices, but most significantly on pocket-sized devices which will also serve as phones, navigation tools, personal computers, as well as control handsets for operating other technical services in the home and on the move. Reading will thread through the content of our lives and not necessarily be a solitary activity. Reading will become a participative, fugitive and fragmented experience. Books will explode into vast corpora of interrelated texts, as well as performances, audio and video experiences.

Many bookshops as we know them will cease to exist, though one exception will be specialised genre shops. The large online retailers will be threatened by white-labelled, genre-specific or subject-specific specialists, centred upon online communities.

What readers get may be increasingly determined by 'desire engines' – systems which clearly identify the kinds of experiences readers want from writers, and writers will increasingly service the topographies of desire, laid bare by powerful analytical tools based on real-time reading experiences. Writers will have access to fully annotated editions of their works, with thousands of comments and assessments. Writers will have direct contact with reading groups, and provide online surgeries to explain their latest writing, testing out chapters as they are written, rewriting based on user feedback.

The industry will massively contract and fragment. Social media will become the central tool of doing business. Books will themselves become a form of social media, with readers 'occupying' the text throughout its inception, writing and final construction. Works may extend indefinitely into continual texts, and the concept of the work as an integrated singular stoppage in the writer's life may just become an episode in the creative text stream. Readers will subscribe to writers, gaining access to texts as they are being produced.

Traditional skills within publishing may well be replaced by digital expertise, drawn from the gaming industry as much as from today's publishing degrees.

14

JEWELL PARKER RHODES

Imaginative crossings: trans-global and trans-cultural narratives

When I was a young writer, writing teachers and books all said to 'write what you know'. That is, your writing is best if it is 'authentic', if it reflects the people you have met and the places you have been. To that end, as an American writer, I have often been advised only to write about black characters. My instinct as a student was always to rail against such advice. I sought joyfully to write what I could imagine – about people I'd never met and places and times I'd never been.

Decades and many published novels later, some editors were still subtly advancing the workshop admonition – 'write what you know', by suggesting that I delete from my novel *Douglass' Women* Ottilie Assing, a character based upon a nineteenth-century German woman with a Jewish and Christian heritage. The assertion was that as a woman of colour, I didn't 'know' such history, such people, and my readers – all black, of course! – could not have cared less about the white mistress of abolitionist, Frederick Douglass. The novel, *Douglass' Women*, ultimately (and gratefully) published by Atria Books, became an award-winning and critical success.

Of course, a writer should write about whomever and whatsoever they please, whether it be unknowable aliens, or ethnic and racial groups from far afield. If race, itself an artificial construct, prevents us from 'knowing' and writing about one another, then we are suggesting that people are not a common family. Equally dangerous is the notion that readers, too, only want to read what reflects their cultural reality. Letters from readers – within and without America's borders – of diverse cultural and religious backgrounds, have long disabused me of this silly notion.

Is it not the point of art, both the production and the experience of it, to transcend your own reality, your own autobiography? I have always told my students to write what they can imagine instead of simply what they know. Because it is in the imagining that more knowledge is found, about yourself as well as about others. The adventure of entering the mind of a character a thousand miles away from yourself challenges you to untangle the differences between you. You discover more about yourself than you would ever have known by challenging yourself to step outside the Ego, the 'I', the narcissist.

For the past six years, I have been teaching Sichuan University faculty in Chengdu, China, creative writing and creative writing pedagogy. At our first meeting, I introduced the faculty to *Joe Turner's Come and Gone*, from August Wilson's 'Century Cycle', his plays based upon American racial struggles during each decade of the twentieth century. For the play cycle, Wilson imagined himself into the hearts and minds of countless people divided by history. Maybe that is why his writing so touched the readers in Chengdu. Wilson refused to write about himself, but, instead, spent his career travelling into the mythic and symbolic realms that connect the slave to the abolitionist to the free man. Most particularly, Wilson, in *Joe Turner's Come and Gone*, writes about the 'bones people', ghosts of ancestors who died during the slave trade. These ghosts resonated deeply with the Chinese who have their own rich legacy of spirits wandering real and imaginary halls.

Next, I introduced the Chinese student writers to Dominican writer Jean Rhys's story 'We Don't Live Here Anymore', in which two twentieth-century children climactically realise that they are invisible and dead. Creatively, the Chinese students were inspired by the symbolic connections, the cross-cultural reference points of ancestors, spirits and ghosts, and by writers that wrote about what they didn't tangibly 'know' but imagined. As they began writing about their own 'bones people' and ghosts, the Chinese writers reaffirmed their cultural differences as well as their commonality with global writers. Within a year, they were writing about diverse characters in diverse settings – proving to themselves that with imaginative effort and, at times, with needed historical and cultural research, they could write the world. In their bones, sinews and spirit, the world was already written within them.

In my view, to 'write what you know' fosters provincialism. Beginning writers especially can become entangled in the narrow confines of what I ate, what I saw, what I felt and what I know. The 'I' viewpoint dominates and a creative selfishness often results. Their own worlds are worth so much that they need not step outside them to imagine another's. Encouraging such creative selfishness at a time when beginning writers should be exploring, empathising with others does more, in my view, to hamper their efforts to learn the craft at a most critical juncture. Indeed, exercises in writing about minor and secondary characters in a story can often lead to better fiction. The homeless woman who is a detail in one story begins to tell her own through a writer's expanded imagination. Add in differing cultural contexts (Anglo, Korean, Mexican, etc.), a different time and different place, and humanistic resonances abound. My students, I hope, are empowered not to write to the limits of their understanding but seemingly beyond it. They become even more creative as they discover the connective tissue of human spirit, mind and heart that transcends a singular time, place and character.

Many creative writing texts encourage students to keep a journal, reporting on their daily thoughts, conversations, actions and interactions. Reporting is the dull cousin to imagination. *Stretching* one's imagination is the skill requiring cultivation. Daydreaming and night dreaming have always been more paramount to me. Museums, of all sorts, are a fertile ground. Landscape paintings, abstracts, portraits, all encourage 'what if?' dreaming, the bulwark for creating plots and for exploring such questions of who, what, where and why rooted in alternative, made-up realities. There are infinite possible stories in Georges Seurat's pointillist painting *Sunday Afternoon on the Island of La Grande Jatte*. Likewise, just as secondary and minor characters need to be promoted to main characters in stories, I encourage students to dream a story about the secondary and tertiary focus of a painting. Goya's *Witches' Sabbath* with the standing, crowned bull as the prime focus stirs images of religious and pagan Sabbaths. But among the multitude of petitioners, two children are being offered – one, a round, pink-fleshed child, the other, skeletal, olive-toned. Focusing imaginatively on these two characters might encourage an epic novel of two lives. What came before, what comes after the 'offering'? Is the world a medieval Spanish community? Or a future dystopia?

Writing more imaginatively (than less so) also provides beginning writers with lessons in editorial distance. The made-up world has to become more particular, more detailed to make it 'knowable' to readers. Likewise, writing outside one's cultural and ethnic boundaries, the writer has to become even more skilled at using specificity and concrete images to make their characters credible and persuasive. Science fiction writing takes the 'trans-global, trans-cultural' narrative to extremes – mixing varied animate and inanimate life forms in extrapolated worlds. Yet, few still doubt the power of this literature to speak across nations and to our present time.

My admonition is to write what you can dream ... write what you wish to discover ... write what you need to know about human nature. Stories, for me, have always been a wish fulfilment – an opportunity to make my life larger by stimulating my intellect, deepening my empathy, and connecting rather than distancing my self from others. What would it be like to live in 2050 in Antarctica? Or to be a young soldier, part of the British expedition to Tibet in 1903? My personal dream is to write a story about the decline of the samurai class during Japanese industrialisation. Why not? I'm human and, therefore, I have the power to cross imaginatively gender, social and historical boundaries. Of course, cultural study and research will be required to stimulate and root my imagination. But I don't doubt (and I don't want my students to doubt) that even as I delve into the unknown, what *is* known is my universal humanity. It is this that gives me authority to write.

Suggestions for the beginning writer

1. *Be brave, bold and original*
   Stimulate, stretch, your imagination by playing 'what if?' with visual arts in a museum, or 'who held this?' with a tool or pottery from a folk arts museum, or ask 'why, who lives there?' on a star spotlighted in a planetarium. Generating back stories, histories for persons written about in magazines and newspapers, can also invigorate one's imagination, as does travel, and meeting new people with different interests than yours. Connect with dreams.
2. *Remember: character drives plot*
   When starting a new story, focus on what connects us all – namely, interior emotions. What do your characters want – need – fear – dream about? This interior life is what expands and motivates your characters. Some desires may overlap but without any desire, your characters will be still-born.
3. *Characters act – react – think – speak*
   They become flesh and move through the space of your created world. Action allows you to tailor your characters; and it is action, I believe, more than a pronouncement of skin colour or ethnic identification, that gives characters their distinctive personalities. An urban Pakistani acts, reacts, thinks and speaks differently from a rural Italian farmer. Resources such as history books, art work, and travel can assist in delineating speech patterns, providing knowledge about social rhythms, as well as culturally appropriate and inappropriate actions and reactions. But never underestimate, after all your study and research, the enormous power of sitting before a computer and simply imagining, asking oneself: 'What would it have felt like to be this character, and to live in such a time and place?' Such questions, imaginings can unlock essential and universal human yearnings. Like the method actor transforming into a character, so, too, the writer needs to make the dramatic imaginative leap to truly 'know' their characters.

   Always, however, guard against writing stereotypes. Cultural assimilation and acculturation as well as the opposite, cultural tension and rifts, can produce, at times, one-dimensional impressions of people and culture. The writer's responsibility is to create multidimensional characters that are not types but unique, complex beings. 'Love all your characters', I tell my students. Even antagonists need to be understood, and portrayed with empathy.

4. *Consider: who owns the story?*
   Don't let writing in the first person be your automatic point of view. Consider whether a default use of 'I' is hampering your imaginative growth. Is the first-person narrator really you and, possibly, a narcissistic indulgence? Consider whether a different narrator and different point of view might make the story more interesting, more imaginative. *Rashomon and Other Stories*, by Rynuosuke Akutagawa, and the Akira Kurosawa film adaptation, *Rashomon*, explore brilliantly the subjectivity of perception. As a writer, don't be afraid to explore this terrain and to potentially optimise your story by experimenting with point of view. You may have multiple narrators with differing backgrounds or a single narrator like Nick in F. Scott Fitzgerald's *The Great Gatsby*, who tells the tale better, more humanely, yet off-centre from the perspectives of the main characters.
5. *Don't underestimate the supporting role of time and place*
   World building is essential to fiction. Whether your setting is a futuristic, alien world, Kuala Lumpur, or New York, concrete details of time and place can enhance your story's 'authenticity'. Don't be afraid of letting time and place soar and be reconfigured by your imagination. Kuala Lumpur, in your fictional reality, may be reconfigured as a paradise for Christians and Muslims. New York may become, in your specific detailing and retelling, a world paralleling Dante's world and his descent towards Hell.

   Futuristic and alien settings allow for the most imaginative range, but the details of such worlds, too, must be rendered with such precision as to appear emotionally, if not factually, authentic. Fiction writers 'tell lies' – and sometimes, reimagining, tweaking what is, and what was once real in the world, can create a far more satisfying and emotionally truthful story about the human condition.

Don't just 'write what you know'. Do better.

Write, firmly believing that imagination is the quintessential self/the quintessential way of 'knowing' the world. This imaginative knowing has the potential to dispel barriers that isolate individuals and communities. Exercising imaginative 'knowing' allows, always, for a potentially transcendent narrative, that is trans-global, trans-cultural and speaks to our common humanity.

15

A. L. KENNEDY

Does that make sense?

Approaches to the creative writing workshop

I am in a stuffy room in a poorly maintained building which is, like so many poorly maintained buildings, intended to be a community resource. I am sitting in a rectangle of shabby desks and seats with a group of visually impaired young people – they are making a video about being visually impaired. Their choice. The filming has been completed, we are at the end of another very long day, full of unexpected technical challenges and small triumphs – we are now all tired, hot, and battering at the long prose poem which will make up our narration. It isn't quite right. It needs one more word which – if we're being technical – has to be an amphibrach. We aren't being technical. We're writing. We are spending a good deal of time saying *du-DA-du* – which feels right. It could be built out of one, or two, or three words, we don't know and we wouldn't mind which – the rhythm is the thing. The sense and the rhythm – we need them both. We have the rest of the sentence, the rest of the piece ... we tap the rhythm. We repeat the rhythm. We think the rhythm. We sit. We continue to be tired and hot. And then, here comes the word. We can almost feel it – there is a sense, in fact, of it falling, beautifully and effectively, into the head of a dark-haired young man – who, as it happens, hasn't been too committed to the wordy side of the project – and then emerges, as we might say, wearing his voice. It is confident and his and itself and ours and the perfect word, the one that sits well in the sentence and in our spines – *regardless*.

Regardless opens and echoes and is impressive – as if it had walked out of paradise and spoken its name for the first time, only to us – that level of impressive. One word with a kick which increases our respect for a whole language and for ourselves. It is both important and – apologies in advance – *fucking beautiful*. We have just made something *fucking beautiful* – the writer who found it, the rest of the writers who found the rest of the words, all of us, we have made beauty. And soon we will give it to other people, this very fine thing which is of us, but not us, like some magnificent bird we have coaxed inside to fly on our behalf. We are silent for a while and then very overexcited.

When a workshop works, you remember. When a workshop works, you learn. When a workshop works, you leave it with faith in the efficacy of your craft and yourself as its practitioner, in its ability to transcend itself, in humanity's ability to transcend itself.

But how often do workshops really work?

I have spent the last thirty years giving writing workshops. That is to say, I have spent three decades trying to use a communal, public instrument to help people perfect what is an individual and private, sometimes very private, craft. I have studied the form, attended workshops, heard about others, read about still more. My own workshops have taken place in settings from the oppressively tranquil to the moderately unwise with participants ranging from highly experienced authors to tentative newcomers, participants including university students, non-literate groups, people with special needs, people with degenerative illnesses, prison inmates, the visually impaired, children, residents in elderly care and psychiatric facilities, adults in community groups and passers-by at arts events. In short, I have worked with a relatively wide spectrum of those who, for whatever reason, have chosen to spend time examining their own and others' voices, who have an interest in developing their expressions of themselves and their worlds and in finding new ways of seeing and being. I have worked with those who wish, or hope, or intend to be heard. I remain uneasy with the workshop as a tool – it can undoubtedly be useful, but in its most widely accepted form it is almost completely unfit for its stated purpose and in any form it can invite laziness, calcified thinking and emotional abuse. In a climate which makes the 'teaching' of creative writing a low-cost source of revenue for a variety of organisations and institutions, I am increasingly concerned that bad workshop practice and bad workshops are becoming the cornerstone of an industry which takes aspiring writers' money while rendering them less able to be writers, or to enjoy the benefits of what we might call a writer's mentality.

If we are writers, workshops are expected of us – often by people who are not writers and who do not understand what we do and how we do it. Worse still, we may be set mildly or wildly inappropriate tasks by those who think they do understand what we do and who will never take the trouble to find out they are wrong. But we may also not understand how best to use workshops, perhaps because we are busy and/or tired and/or scared and/or fundamentally interested in our own work rather than that of others, and perhaps because we may have stopped trying to explore and expand what we do, or because it may never have occurred to us that we should. We may simply be earning money by delivering something which is, after all, expected of us, which fills timetables and makes libraries and community centres look slightly dynamic, something which is believed to be useful so strongly that whether it serves much purpose at all, whether it is in actuality destructive, has become irrelevant. This situation seems less than ideal.

What follows will mainly consist of questions which I hope will help us examine ourselves, our craft and the workshop as a medium in a constructive manner. I believe that if I have as clear a grasp as possible of my relationship with writing and myself as a writer and if I understand my aims and as much as I can about my workshop participants, then I have a chance of giving workshops which work. I believe a process of long-term interrogation can help us be better writers and give better workshops.

I will not be suggesting exercises. Exercises in general, games, snappy mnemonics, PowerPoint presentations, flipchart-bothering and the whole battery of workshop and masterclass strategies and gimmicks will only ever be as effective as the intentions and intelligence behind them – so I would rather spend this time looking at what's behind them. I believe this will represent the best use of our time. This is no more than my opinion – but for what it's worth, it is very firmly held.

What do you believe writing is?

I know, this is a ludicrously huge question, but we can't avoid answering it – even our ignoring it will be a kind of answer. Regularly asking this question means that, in the preparation of any workshop, we can learn more about our relationship with our craft, how our emphases are altering, if we really know as much as we think and enough to allow us to distil our knowledge in ways that others can grasp. Do we seek to disguise our ignorance and bluff our way, to coast along with what we know already, or to push our understanding? I would suggest the latter.

I currently believe that writing is a way of life, that it is a massively demanding discipline, that it is an almost irresistible source of enrichment, expression and change. I think it is possible and useful to use the workshop to show how writing can inform all other activities – including the workshop – and how all other activities can feed the writing. This means that I will often tend to deconstruct the workshop process as it progresses.

I believe writing is personal – personal to you and personal to me. This belief, like all my beliefs, affects how I run workshops – they can't just be about an end product, or simply examining the utility and qualities of voices, tenses, constructions. My understanding would be that writing touches writers – professional and amateur – so deeply that, for example, issues of safety and intimacy need to be addressed from the outset – for the sake of the workshop and as a note for future writing. I think it's legitimate and sensible to discuss workshop practice within the workshop, to ask people to be aware of whether they feel unsettled, manipulated, confused. I hope to allow participants to be both comfortable and happy to report anything which seems amiss, to warn them of bad practice they may encounter in the future – either from their own poor self-employment, or from others, including myself. I feel that creating a place of safety from which to write is hugely useful for any writer – this means that I will discuss issues of confidence, doubt, fear – and means that the workshop must be manifestly safe. Threats and negative intrusions can't come from me or from others, or must be swiftly dealt with if they do.

To choose a small example, I make a point of asking 'Does that make sense?' when I have explained something to a group and I need to know if they have understood it. This seems to be the least threatening way of checking if we can all go forward. The wording of every question and comment directed to the group is important. I have witnessed more than enough encounters during which care assistants gatecrash sessions to bellow at participants, 'What's your address?' – when writing is often and most interestingly about the questions only the writer can answer, our privileged knowledge, the certainty and creativity of ourselves. Writing isn't about those questions with which others bully you, although it may sometimes be a response to them. I have bitten my lip while tutors have fired off, 'Do you understand?' at students so often and so violently that their communal IQ has withered and the session has simply clotted into an exercise in self-defence. Just as ungenerous writing tends to be less effective, ungenerous workshops tend to communicate information poorly.

Any workshop leader can only bring groups to levels of intimacy with which they are comfortable, but I have certainly run and observed workshops where participants have wept, where depths of experience have been shared – just as much as rooms have become helpless with laughter, or have pottered amicably. If emotional release is necessary, then I feel a tutor has to find a way of welcoming it, rather than locking it down – with always the emphasis on safety. This takes a degree of watchfulness, confidence and concentration, but is worthwhile.

What kind of person are you?

Without plunging off into chasms of analysis, I would hope I can assume that – if you are a writer – you have some level of self-awareness.

(If you are not writer, I would rather you didn't give writing workshops. If you fully commit yourself to the process of your workshops, you become a writer ... Allow me to assume that you are.)

As a writer, like any person behaving creatively, you will draw upon yourself to produce work. Again, it's realistic to acknowledge this in others when we offer workshops. The fact that our work comes from ourselves (whether it is in any way autobiographical or not) is part of why revealing it to others can be so nerve-wracking and why it is so deeply pleasant and positive if we can build something beautiful and realise it is appreciated beyond ourselves. We have to bear this in mind when we construct our workshops and help participants to engage without feeling over-exposed. Safe opportunities for sharing work, safe opportunities for creating work in real time and succeeding are to be maximised.

More prosaically, we do have to consider if we ourselves are shy, funny, anxious with crowds, likely to forget things, if we work better with a flipchart, or with notes, if we enjoy improvising. Perhaps ask an honest friend what your social manner is generally like. Consider how best you explain things, your presentational weaknesses and strengths. Taking a mixed bag of exercises out of books and then presenting them in a manner alien to our natures is possible but more targeted preparation might mean everyone can actually be comfortable together. And, of course, do find out if you're generally audible and specifically audible for any given venue or participant. There's no reason for you to turn into a game show host, but if you are at ease and confident with the material you are presenting, then your writers will have the opportunity to relax and take part rather than being unconvinced by your content and worrying if you're going to drop something, or faint. High percentages of your writers will need you to have faith in them before they can – you won't be able to give them this, if you give every appearance of having no faith in yourself. If you are incurably rattled by groups you may want to find one-to-one work, to act as a mentor, or to team up with another writer. Workshops are a huge source of income, but if they're unbearable for you, then they won't do you – or the people who attend them – much good.

If you are the kind of person who wants to make cash by rolling out the boilerplate workshop – *everyone reads their work out and comments while you occasionally throw in something that sounds definitive, or better yet, make no effort at all and simply bounce back something like 'and what do you think about that?' thus making no actual effort at all* – then I'm very surprised that you're still reading this and I dislike you. Sorry, but I do. Everyone deserves better – always. Even you.

What is your attitude to your participating writers?

If we honestly ask ourselves this question the results can be interesting. It's very easy – particularly after we are established in workshopping – to find that our initial response might wear down to something along the lines of – *I think they are narcissistic, untalented people who stand between me and my own writing. There is no helping them and therefore I need not particularly try to help them. They make me tired.* Although it may seem counter-intuitive, the best remedy for tiredness, staleness and misanthropic revulsion within workshops is increased effort and increased knowledge of your participants. If you can feel that your workshop is somewhere you can go to in order to explore and expand your work, while others journey with you, then – no matter how desperately you want time to write – it won't feel like a waste of your energies. If you take an interest in your group, your group will duly become interesting. If you can bring, in a reasonable and practical manner, your own doubts, troubles and vulnerabilities as a writer, to the workshop this not only encourages others to share and address their own, it also allows you to look at the nature of character. What interests us in people? We identify with emotions, past experiences, weaknesses and quirks. We have our own, our characters should have theirs. This area alone can produce a month's worth of discussions, study of pieces, objects, music, film segments and exercises.

If you approach a group with a convincingly magisterial air, intent upon setting them tasks which will burn up their allotted session time and keep them quiet, they may never complain. If you assume they will have roughly the same problems as most writers at their stage of development, you may not be entirely wrong. If you give them the same old notes on page layout, application of grammar, dialogue, how to use the *Writer's and Artist's Yearbook*, they may not storm your desk and hit you. If you mainly kick back and offer them literary anecdotes and name-dropping, they may not throw up in your face. Equally, they may not come back, they may not tell their friends they've had a great workshop, they may not fill in the feedback forms with enthusiasm, they may not help you to get more gigs and earn more money, they may not offer you the pleasure of seeing them discover themselves as writers or their company as you grow and learn together. Behaving altruistically is, very quickly, its own reward – spending an hour in a room with twenty happy people is infinitely nicer than sixty minutes spent trapped with some strangers you're conning, or scared of, or who are clearly tolerating you but largely dismayed.

There are, naturally, grotesque and tedious people in the world and occasionally some of them are moved to take writing workshops, and you will have to deal with them – but they will be relatively rare and usually surrounded by the kind of slightly nervous and almost unreasonably pleasant and patient people who are more commonly workshop participants. Treating people with respect allows them to respect you, themselves and what they are doing. If you are a writer, it is probably good practice to respect writers.

And, in all seriousness, in every workshop – as in every short story, every poem, every novel – you have an opportunity to change your participants' lives. Your workshops can change how they write and who they are. This isn't me being grandiose – I'm stating a not unreasonable aim which can inspire us. We may rarely succeed spectacularly or on a massive scale, but it is relatively easy to help someone become positively different, more themselves, more articulate, more fulfilled by adjusting their interior and exterior voices. Why wouldn't it be? Our voices are hugely important to our identities, deeply embedded in our personalities and our bodies – so when we make our voices stronger, more flexible and more articulate, we can set up a cascade of positive effects. (Just as when we fail in a workshop, or behave badly, we can do actual and unpleasantly intimate harm.) At this level, the writing workshop isn't about being published – given the current state of publishing it would be an agonising activity, if it was – it is about being more deeply alive. And that goes for the tutor, too. There are few things more wonderful that seeing someone come into focus, surprise themselves, sing out who they are, through writing. All writers get wearied at times, get stale – seeing writing at work in others reminds us of why we love it, reconfirms its power.

Under certain circumstances, having an attitude of respect for your participants may mean you have to withdraw from a workshop or an institution if forces beyond your control mean that participants or their work are poorly treated, that their privacy can't be guaranteed, that the expectations and enthusiasms you raise will actually open them to abuse or disappointment. Although I would always want writers' work to be confidential if they wish it to be, working within prisons and psychiatric hospitals may mean that their material must be open to others – all we can do is point out this lack of privacy, or choose to avoid working in these contexts.

Do you know the abilities, wants and needs of your participants?

Sometimes you won't. In fact, very often you won't.

It might be great to read work in advance, to vet participants in advance, to read potted biographies – but this will almost never be arranged and, if it is, the additional work involved will probably be unpaid. Sometimes you will build up knowledge of a group organically over a number of weeks, months, even years. Sometimes, you will enter into an existing community of writers and have to bear in mind that you are both an invited expert and a guest. But, on many occasions, you will walk in cold to an unsuitably arranged room filled with mysteries and this one hour, or two hours, or day will be all you have. Which is where time management, good planning and a depth of understanding of what writers might require – of what support you yourself might have wanted a various stages – will help you.

In some contexts – usually where you are working with the most vulnerable participants possible: children, those with special needs – you will usually have very little prior information and may be dealing with staff who cannot answer your advance enquiries helpfully. You may not even know how many people you will have in your group. This is where your self-knowledge, your wider interrogation of what you believe writing to be and how best to examine it and a small amount of practical consideration will help you.

I'll deal with the practical points first. If you are going to work with the young and vulnerable you will, of course, get a CRB check and if you are working with the public at all – even apparently sane and healthy adults – you will have as much Public Liability Insurance as you can afford. This is sensible and easy to obtain and the Society of Authors will help you with it.

If you are working with people who have health or mental difficulties, or both, you need to know what these difficulties are and you need enough people with you to deal with any problems. If you are working in a prison or a secure mental hospital, you need someone from the institution with you at all times and you need to know where the panic button is. It is impossible to overestimate how easily and quickly you will, in fact, find yourself alone in a room where almost anything might happen. You may be surrounded by people, all of whom may have potentially fatal fits at any time, or who may be experiencing a radically different reality to yours. Should your workshop have proved successful last week, or should you simply have failed to kill anyone on your last visit, you may find your space packed with all manner of participants, abilities and potential risks – in a way, this is a vote of confidence, it is also something to avoid. People who work with the vulnerable or potentially unpredictable can become blasé – we shouldn't. Be safe and be safe and be safe and also always ensure that you and your writers are going to be safe. Apart from anything else, we shouldn't reinforce the Hollywood/*Dead Poets Society* model for artistic endeavour – every group does not require a death, or even a minor injury. What we do is about life and if some of us insist on suffering for our pleasures then writing is quite hard enough work to satisfy without additional impositions.

In what might be seen as a more conventional workshop context it is still worthwhile trying to ensure that the room you are placed in will be fit for the purpose, that any equipment you aren't bringing with you will actually be provided and will work and that you won't be disturbed. This may mean your initial interactions with your employer can seem fussy, anal-retentive or irritating – but remember that you want your workshop to have the best chance of success and, as you respect yourself and will respect your participants, you probably need others to have some respect, too. Be diplomatic and understanding, but also firm. Of course, something will usually go wrong despite all manner of good intentions – mechanisms will break, fire alarms will go off, animals will intrude, latecomers will come late ... It is perhaps best to always arrive knowing that, should you be left with nothing to work with beyond yourself, you could still deliver a useful and meaningful workshop.

What is your workshop?

The answer to this question will partly be a product of what you have learned from the preceding questions. Your idea of writing, its qualities and strengths, your understanding of yourself as a writer and your relationship with your own writing, your attitude towards and knowledge of the writers in your workshop will all interact to produce pathways and responses.

My understanding would be that the best possible use I can make of time with a writer would be to read their work in advance and to give them fastidiously detailed notes – I use a numbered key so that as many notes can be packed into the text as possible with the minimum negative emotional impact. The numbers in the key not only identify problems, they also give general notes about possible sources of problems and therefore show a way forward. The key is revised on a yearly basis. The aim with any writer I see over several sessions would be for their work to transcend the key, to become so individual (and articulate) that there are no quibbles, or that the points queried need to be individually described. These notes – or anything else the writer wishes – are then discussed in individual sessions of about an hour.

This is the most effective way that writers can learn, in depth, from their own writing, how they are to progress as writers.

This is how a writer learns to write.

This is how I remember how I am learning to write.

This is the service I am most rarely asked to provide.

Outside some university programmes and Arvon courses truly effective help for writers is thin on the ground. Worse still, truly ineffective help appears to be epidemic.

Which brings me to the classic writer's workshop format – the one that is expected of us – writers present their work in progress in a group, the group discusses, everyone goes home. It is almost impossible to describe how many things are wrong with this. But I will try.

The work is being presented at too early a stage – exactly when the individual writer should be taking control of the piece, it is being opened to a barrage of opinions. These opinions are very often simply statements of what other writers would have done if they were writing the piece and are therefore useless. These opinions are very often as bewildered and bewildering as any you might expect from people who don't yet know how to do something effectively and yet who are being forced to discuss it. Unless the tutor exercises such iron control that the group is no longer really operating as a group – Richard Ford is notoriously good at maintaining purity of workshop focus – then this workshop format will consist of the metaphorically blind leading the metaphorically deaf up a very unpleasant creek.

Those who are socially dominant prosper in groups – even if their writing is appalling – because groups are about groups, not about writing. Those whose work is already individual, which falls at either end of the possible bell curve, and is most likely to be of quality, will often feel that they are unusual within the group – because they are – and are as likely to have their confidence destroyed by a workshop as they are to find their egos inappropriately distorted by premature praise.

Writing consists of a multitude of individual decisions, massive and complex control of language in depth and considerable personal responsibility – the classic workshop can accustom writers to avoiding decisions, or averaging out solutions to possibly irrelevant problems with texts which they should be learning how to master. And in a scrum of opinion, play and risk become silenced or stunted. Meanwhile, workshop exercises which set subjects remove a huge part of the writer's responsibility – subject choice – and remove opportunities for writers to learn what their inspirations feel like, how they develop, how they can be encouraged. The workshop process can infantilise writers – having abandoned responsibility for subject and craft, the writer cannot progress without the workshop. An art which is supremely independent, adaptable and low-cost has been rendered feeble and expensive.

A good and authoritative tutor can offset some or all of the workshop's failings to some extent and a good group of writers can police itself and be intelligently supportive without a tutor, but still we are faced with the unalterable fact that no text can ever be examined closely enough using this medium – it might do for a spot of light 'Have you read and understood?' – which could be of use to undergraduates taking an English degree, but it does not adequately address writers' requirements. Writers need *other people* to read and understand – the difference may seem small, but it is vast enough to hold the work of a lifetime. Unless we are willing to extend sessions over periods of days and can rely on immense patience from all concerned in examining others' work and immense tolerance when their own is subjected to scrutiny, we simply cannot use the standard workshop to look at texts in anything other than a cursory way. Beloved of higher education institutions and English departments, it is a time-filling farce and we should not indulge it.

What do we put in its place ?

Everything else.

That sounds flippant, but I mean it quite literally and writers given half a chance already do break away from the form as often and imaginatively as they can. If we accept that the aim of the writing workshop is simply and purely to help writers to write better then every possible source of inspiration and stimulation is opened to us. Yes, there are times when there will be a flip-chart and when we may look at passages of text. But it may often be infinitely more effective, for example, to stimulate voice by working literally with voice, to take one potential positive aspect of the standard workshop – the act of reading our work aloud to an audience – and to develop writers' ability to present their work, while releasing and exploring their voices. If a group is tentative, perhaps it might benefit from looking at relaxation techniques, guided visualisations, ways of maintaining comfortable mental states. If we want to look at character, surely we should look at drama, we may talk to actors and directors, we may wish to perform ourselves, or to interact with our characters and their development in a variety of situations. If they go on to be anything like full-time writers, the people who attend our workshops are going to be savagely self-employed; surely, then, the writing workshop should address methods of sustaining personal enthusiasm and inspiration? This might take the form of field trips, interacting with animals, with articulate professionals in other fields, with as many manifestations of beauty as we can encounter. Any workshop will have limitations – and in a recession there may be many – but we needn't insist that everyone (including the tutor) would benefit from a three-week trip to Buenos Aires – part of the joy of writing is the ability it gives writers to inhabit the moment in whatever circumstances. It may be that our workshop helps the infirm elderly to look out of their windows and see more, feel more, express the complexity and dignity of their experience. A group might simply eat together, go to a concert, take a walk, or be offered texts, films, music, images, that they may not have encountered – or that they have not encountered as that group. It may be that a group occasionally writes as a group in real time, works full tilt on the challenges of a sentence in the relative safety of communal effort, but with a chance of examining the detailed choices and issues within the writing process. Just as writers may relax and really enjoy reading other authors' work aloud, it can be exhilarating to enjoy the act of writing as a group – it can offer a strangely intimate appreciation of language as an entity outwith any individual author.

Used imaginatively, the workshop can address both vaguely tedious but necessary points – how to compose a covering letter, how to find an agent – but can also engage with the kind of powerful metaphors that can alter and permanently strengthen someone's craft. I fully intend to run a workshop using horses at some point. Horses are powerful, beautiful, frightening animals which magnify the rider's emotional state, yet which respond readily to moderate discipline and carry the rider where they wish to. They are useful as a metaphor for writers who also know about horses, why not make them available to other writers?

The workshop can create the icons, the good luck charms, the positive habits, the strength to carry writers through. The workshop can help writers to appreciate that inspiration and support are ubiquitous, it can challenge and nourish both tutors and participants and make mature, independent and confident voices ready to move beyond it. The workshop should aim to make itself redundant, not to render writers dependent.

And all of this does take effort, it is more difficult and does take more planning and negotiation than doling out photocopies of work and sitting in a circle not quite addressing our work or each other as we grow older but not wiser. I would argue that any effort expended tends to be more than repaid. A positive and open approach to group work allows the energy of the group to be released and harnessed, rather than ignored or wasted.

Have you addressed all the necessary technical issues?

This is the tedious bit – but it does reflect another layer of respect for yourself, your participants and the people who are paying your wages. I feel that the buck stops with us – we may not be in our own building, the disasters playing out before our horrified writers may have nothing to do with us and everything to do with the chemical plant across the road, but we should try our utmost to control those elements we can for everyone's convenience and comfort.

It will take a while to get the feel of how long it takes you to deal with the points you wish to address in any session – and groups vary massively in their ability to grasp concepts and move on. It may be fine to spend two hours in a small area, it may mean you have lost control and not provided the session as advertised. Try not to overrun massively – even if people are enjoying themselves, they have lives and buses to catch and want to feel their experience has come to a proper conclusion, rather than ended with treats they couldn't share because they were running for a train.

And I take this opportunity to say that I am prone to overrun.

It is now possible to give groups satisfying and impressive multimedia experiences – this probably does mean that you have to familiarise yourself with a variety of technologies and the ideal would probably be to travel with your own equipment. Even this will not save you from inadequate power supplies, lack of tables, poor sightlines, inadequate blackouts, lost batteries and the unforeseen. Try to foresee the unforeseen.

Do try to establish realistically what the context will be for your workshop. If you are working in one place for any length of time it's best to come in with something amounting to a contract, or bullet points giving people an idea of what you will provide, possible pitfalls and support that you will need. I feel that the group should always be protected. If they write a musical, it should be possible for it to be produced, not just put on a shelf – if they express opinions, it should be possible for them to be received and taken seriously – if they produce work, it should be possible for it to be shared and celebrated – if they can be published at some level, or helped towards editors and agents, then this shouldn't be (although it usually will be) dealt with as a series of scrambled favours out of hours. Generally, if you have misgivings about individuals and institutions it's best to walk away, rather than betray your group and/or yourself later.

Are you genuinely achieving your aims?

Any writer should be able to look at their work and offer it the benefit of serious criticism – the same should apply to our workshops. Writers attending workshops can be kind and may be unfamiliar with how much they could get out of a workshop – their comments may not be accurate. It is best if we check regularly to see if we are continuing to develop our ideas or if we are stagnating. Perhaps in some areas, we have found pretty much the best way we can deal with this or that set of points, but maybe with a different type of group we might come in differently, maybe there are still improvements to make, maybe our opinions have changed slightly and we are not reflecting that fact. When was the last time we tried an entirely new workshop? What have we learned from the last year of workshops that we can use and take forward? Are we improving or are we complacent? Are we working within institutions and organisations that stimulate our work, or that encourage despair? The despair may not be our fault, but shouldn't we try – if we can – to move somewhere that can mean we have joy in our work again? As our writing progresses, has our use of workshops kept pace? Are we serving our own needs effectively when we workshop? These questions shouldn't be accusatory, they are merely a way of ensuring a level of professional contentment for ourselves and as good a workshop experience as possible for others.

In closing, I would like to thank the students of the 2009/10 MA in Creative Writing at Warwick University who asked me for a workshop on workshops, from which much of the material for this essay came.

And I will offer one last question – *When is the last time you gave a workshop and knew something special had happened, that you would never forget it, that a life had been changed?* We may always fail a little, sometimes more than a little, but I believe that if we commit ourselves to the pursuit of writing's qualities and their transmission, to the care of our craft, then we will do no harm and may do a great deal of good.

When a workshop works, you remember. When a workshop works, you learn. When a workshop works, you leave it with faith in the efficacy of your craft and yourself as its practitioner, in its ability to transcend itself, in humanity's ability to transcend itself.

It's something to aim for.

FURTHER READING

Abbott, H. Porter, *The Cambridge Introduction to Narrative*, Cambridge University Press, 2002; 2nd edn 2008.

Anderson, Linda (ed.), *Creative Writing: A Workbook with Readings*, London: Routledge, 2006.

Atwood, Margaret, *Negotiating with the Dead: A Writer on Writing*, Cambridge University Press, 2002.

Austin, J. L., Urmson, J. O. and Sbisà, Marina (eds.), *How to Do Things with Words*, 2nd edn, Harvard University Press and Oxford: Clarendon Press, 1975.

Barry, Elaine (ed.), *Robert Frost on Writing*, New Brunswick: Rutgers University Press, 1973.

Behn, Robin and Twichell, Chase (eds.), *The Practice of Poetry: Writing Exercises from Poets who Teach*, New York: HarperResource, 2001.

Bell, Julia and Magrs, Paul (eds.), *The Creative Writing Coursebook*, London: Macmillan, 2001.

Bernays, Anne and Painter, Pamela, *What If? Writing Exercises for Fiction Writers*, New York: Quill, 1991.

Besant, Walter and James, Henry, *The Art of Fiction*, Chapel Hill, NC: Algonquin Press, 1900.

Bishop, Wendy and Ostrom, Hans (eds.), *Colors of a Different Horse: Rethinking Creative Writing Theory and Pedagogy*, Urbana: NCTE, 1994.

Bishop, Wendy and Starkey, David, *Keywords in Creative Writing*, Logan: Utah State University Press, 2007.

Bly, Carol, *Beyond the Writers' Workshop*, New York: Anchor, 2001.

Boden, Margaret A., *The Creative Mind: Myths and Mechanisms*, London: Routledge, 2004.

Bourdieu, Pierre, *The Field of Cultural Production: Essays on Art and Literature*, ed. Randal Johnson, Cambridge: Polity, 1993.

Brande, Dorothea, *Becoming a Writer*, New York: Harcourt and Brace, 1934; reprint New York: Tarcher Penguin, 1981.

Bulman, Colin, *Creative Writing: A Guide and Glossary to Fiction Writing*, Cambridge and Malden, MA: Polity, 2007.

Burroway, Janet, *Imaginative Writing* (2nd edn), New York: Longman, 2006.

Carlson, Ron, *Ron Carlson Writes a Story*, Minneapolis: Graywolf Press, 2007.

Cox, Ailsa, *Writing Short Stories*, London: Routledge, 2005.

Dawson, Paul, *Creative Writing and the New Humanities*, London: Routledge, 2005.

Dillard, Annie, *The Writing Life*, New York: HarperCollins, 1989.
Dobyns, Stephen, *Next Word, Better Word: The Craft of Writing Poetry*, New York and Basingstoke: Palgrave Macmillan, 2011.
Earnshaw, Steven (ed.), *The Handbook of Creative Writing*, University of Edinburgh Press, 2007.
Fish, Stanley, *How to Write a Sentence: And How to Read One*, New York: HarperCollins, 2011.
Freed, Lynn, 'Doing Time: My Years in the Creative Writing Gulag', *Harper's Magazine*, July 2005, pp. 65–72.
Gardner, John, *The Art of Fiction*, New York: Knopf, 1983.
On Becoming a Novelist, New York: HarperPerennial, 1985.
Goldberg, Natalie, *Writing Down the Bones: Freeing the Writer Within*, Boston: Shambhala Publications, new edition, 2005.
Gutkind, Lee, *The Art of Creative Nonfiction*, New York: John Wiley, 1997.
Haake, Katharine, *What Our Speech Disrupts: Feminism and Creative Writing Studies*, Urbana: NCTE, 2000.
Harper, Graeme and Kroll, Jeri (eds.), *Creative Writing Studies: Practice, Research and Pedagogy*, Clevedon: Multilingual Matters, 2007.
Haslam, Sara and Neale, Derek, *Life Writing*, London: Routledge, 2009.
Herbert, W. N. and Hollis, Matthew (eds.), *Strong Words*, Newcastle upon Tyne: Bloodaxe Books, 2000.
Hirsch, Edward, *How to Read a Poem: And Fall in Love with Poetry*, Boston: Mariner Books, 2000.
Holroyd, Michael, *Works on Paper: The Craft of Biography and Autobiography*, London: Little, Brown & Co., 2002.
Hughes, Ted, *Poetry in the Making*, London: Faber and Faber, 1967.
Hugo, Richard, *The Triggering Town: Lectures and Essays on Poetry and Writing*, New York: W. W. Norton, 1979.
Hunt, Celia and Sampson, Fiona, *Writing: Self and Reflexivity*, New York and Basingstoke: Palgrave Macmillan, 2006.
King, Stephen, *On Writing*, London: Hodder, 2000.
Kinzie, Mary, *A Poet's Guide to Writing Poetry*, Chicago University Press, 1999.
Lamott, Annie, *Bird by Bird*, New York: Anchor Books, 1995.
La Plante, Alice, *The Making of a Story: A Norton Guide to Creative Writing*, New York: W. W. Norton, 2010.
Le Guin, Ursula, *Steering the Craft*, Portland: The Eighth Mountain Press, 1998.
Leahy, Anna (ed.), *Power and Identity in the Creative Writing Classroom*, Clevedon: Multilingual Matters, 2005.
Lennard, John, *The Poetry Handbook*, Oxford University Press, 1996.
Lodge, David, *The Practice of Writing*, London: Penguin, 1997.
McGurl, Mark, *The Program Era: Postwar Fiction and the Rise of Creative Writing*, Harvard University Press, 2009.
McKee, Robert, *Story*, London: Methuen, 1999.
Matthews, Harry and Brotchie, Alastair, *Oulipo Compendium*, London: Atlas, 1998.
May, Adrian, *Myth and Creative Writing: The Self-Renewing Song*, Harlow: Longman, 2010.
May, Steve, *Doing Creative Writing*, Abingdon: Routledge, 2007.

Mayers, Tim, *(Re)writing Craft: Composition, Creative Writing, and the Future of English Studies*, University of Pittsburgh Press, new edition, 2007.
Mills, Paul, *The Routledge Creative Writing Coursebook*, Abingdon: Routledge, 2006.
Morley, David, *The Cambridge Introduction to Creative Writing*, Cambridge University Press, 2007.
Moxley, Joseph M. (ed.), *Creative Writing in America: Theory and Pedagogy*, Urbana: NCTE, 1989.
Myers, David Gershom, *The Elephants Teach: Creative Writing Since 1880*, Upper Saddle River, NJ: Prentice Hall, 1996.
Neilsen, Philip and Murphy, Ffion, 'Recuperating Writers and Writing: The Potential of Writing Therapy', *Text*, 12 (1) (2008), available online at www.textjournal.com.au/april08/murphy_neilsen.htm
Novakovich, Josip, *Fiction Writer's Workshop*, Cincinnati: Story Press, 1995.
O'Rourke, Rebecca, *Creative Writing: Education, Culture and Community*, Leicester: National Institute of Adult Continuing Education, 2005.
Olsen, Tillie, *Silences*, New York: The Feminist Press, 2003.
Ostrom, Hans, Bishop, Wendy and Haake, Katharine, *Metro: Journeys in Writing Creatively*, New York: Addison-Wesley, 2001.
Poe, Edgar Allan, 'The Philosophy of Composition', in David H. Richter (ed.), *The Critical Tradition: Classic Texts and Contemporary Trends*, New York: St Martin's Press, 1989, pp. 371–8.
Pound, Ezra, *The ABC of Reading*, New York: New Directions, 1934; reissued 1960.
Prose, Francine, *Reading Like a Writer*, London: HarperPerennial, 2007.
Ritter, Kelly and Vanderslice, Stephanie (eds.), *Can It Really be Taught? Resisting Lore in Creative Writing Pedagogy*, Portsmouth: Boynton/Cook, 2007.
Sampson, Fiona, *On Listening*, Cambridge: Salt Publishing, 2007.
Schaefer, Candace and Diamond, Rick, *The Creative Writing Guide*, New York: Addison-Wesley, 1998.
Shapiro, Nancy and Padgett, Ron, *The Point: Where Teaching and Writing Intersect*, New York: Teachers and Writers Collaborative, 1983.
Smith, Hazel, *The Writing Experiment: Strategies for Innovative Creative Writing*, Sydney: Allen & Unwin, 2005.
Strand, Mark and Boland, Eavan, *The Making of a Poem: A Norton Anthology of Poetic Forms*, New York: W. W. Norton, 2000.
Strunk, William and White, E. B., *The Elements of Style*, Needham Heights, MA: Allyn & Bacon, 2000.
Turner, Frederick and Pöppel, Ernst, 'The Neural Lyre: Poetic Meter, the Brain, and Time', *Poetry*, 142(5) (August 1983), pp. 277–307.
Turner, Mark, *The Literary Mind*, Oxford University Press, 1996.
Venuti, Lawrence (ed.), *The Translation Studies Reader*, London: Routledge, 2000.
Wandor, Michelene, *The Art of Writing Drama*, London: Methuen, 2008.
The Author Is Not Dead, Merely Somewhere Else: Creative Writing Reconceived, Basingstoke: Palgrave Macmillan, 2008.
Wardrip-Fruin, Noah and Harrigan, Pat (eds.), *First Person: New Media as Story, Performance, and Game*, Cambridge, MA: MIT Press, 2004.
Wilbers, Stephen, *The Iowa Writer's Workshop: Origins, Emergence and Growth*, Iowa City: Iowa University Press, 1980.
Zinsser, William, *On Writing Well*, New York: Collins, 2005.

INDEX

Cambridge Companions to . . .

AUTHORS

Edward Albee edited by Stephen J. Bottoms
Margaret Atwood edited by Coral Ann Howells
W. H. Auden edited by Stan Smith
Jane Austen edited by Edward Copeland and Juliet McMaster (second edition)
Beckett edited by John Pilling
Bede edited by Scott DeGregorio
Aphra Behn edited by Derek Hughes and Janet Todd
Walter Benjamin edited by David S. Ferris
William Blake edited by Morris Eaves
Brecht edited by Peter Thomson and Glendyr Sacks (second edition)
The Brontës edited by Heather Glen
Bunyan edited by Anne Dunan-Page
Frances Burney edited by Peter Sabor
Byron edited by Drummond Bone
Albert Camus edited by Edward J. Hughes
Willa Cather edited by Marilee Lindemann
Cervantes edited by Anthony J. Cascardi
Chaucer edited by Piero Boitani and Jill Mann (second edition)
Chekhov edited by Vera Gottlieb and Paul Allain
Kate Chopin edited by Janet Beer
Caryl Churchill edited by Elaine Aston and Elin Diamond
Coleridge edited by Lucy Newlyn
Wilkie Collins edited by Jenny Bourne Taylor
Joseph Conrad edited by J. H. Stape
H. D. edited by Nephie J. Christodoulides and Polina Mackay
Dante edited by Rachel Jacoff (second edition)
Daniel Defoe edited by John Richetti
Don DeLillo edited by John N. Duvall
Charles Dickens edited by John O. Jordan
Emily Dickinson edited by Wendy Martin
John Donne edited by Achsah Guibbory
Dostoevskii edited by W. J. Leatherbarrow
Theodore Dreiser edited by Leonard Cassuto and Claire Virginia Eby
John Dryden edited by Steven N. Zwicker
W. E. B. Du Bois edited by Shamoon Zamir
George Eliot edited by George Levine
T. S. Eliot edited by A. David Moody
Ralph Ellison edited by Ross Posnock
Ralph Waldo Emerson edited by Joel Porte and Saundra Morris
William Faulkner edited by Philip M. Weinstein
Henry Fielding edited by Claude Rawson
F. Scott Fitzgerald edited by Ruth Prigozy
Flaubert edited by Timothy Unwin
E. M. Forster edited by David Bradshaw
Benjamin Franklin edited by Carla Mulford
Brian Friel edited by Anthony Roche
Robert Frost edited by Robert Faggen
Gabriel García Márquez edited by Philip Swanson
Elizabeth Gaskell edited by Jill L. Matus
Goethe edited by Lesley Sharpe
Günter Grass edited by Stuart Taberner
Thomas Hardy edited by Dale Kramer
David Hare edited by Richard Boon
Nathaniel Hawthorne edited by Richard Millington
Seamus Heaney edited by Bernard O'Donoghue
Ernest Hemingway edited by Scott Donaldson
Homer edited by Robert Fowler
Horace edited by Stephen Harrison
Ted Hughes edited by Terry Gifford
Ibsen edited by James McFarlane
Henry James edited by Jonathan Freedman
Samuel Johnson edited by Greg Clingham
Ben Jonson edited by Richard Harp and Stanley Stewart
James Joyce edited by Derek Attridge (second edition)
Kafka edited by Julian Preece
Keats edited by Susan J. Wolfson
Rudyard Kipling edited by Howard J. Booth
Lacan edited by Jean-Michel Rabaté
D. H. Lawrence edited by Anne Fernihough
Primo Levi edited by Robert Gordon
Lucretius edited by Stuart Gillespie and Philip Hardie
Machiavelli edited by John M. Najemy
David Mamet edited by Christopher Bigsby
Thomas Mann edited by Ritchie Robertson
Christopher Marlowe edited by Patrick Cheney

Andrew Marvell edited by Derek Hirst and Steven N. Zwicker

Herman Melville edited by Robert S. Levine

Arthur Miller edited by Christopher Bigsby (second edition)

Milton edited by Dennis Danielson (second edition)

Molière edited by David Bradby and Andrew Calder

Toni Morrison edited by Justine Tally

Nabokov edited by Julian W. Connolly

Eugene O'Neill edited by Michael Manheim

George Orwell edited by John Rodden

Ovid edited by Philip Hardie

Harold Pinter edited by Peter Raby (second edition)

Sylvia Plath edited by Jo Gill

Edgar Allan Poe edited by Kevin J. Hayes

Alexander Pope edited by Pat Rogers

Ezra Pound edited by Ira B. Nadel

Proust edited by Richard Bales

Pushkin edited by Andrew Kahn

Rabelais edited by John O'Brien

Rilke edited by Karen Leeder and Robert Vilain

Philip Roth edited by Timothy Parrish

Salman Rushdie edited by Abdulrazak Gurnah

Shakespeare edited by Margareta de Grazia and Stanley Wells (second edition)

Shakespearean Comedy edited by Alexander Leggatt

Shakespeare and Popular Culture edited by Robert Shaughnessy

Shakespearean Tragedy edited by Claire McEachern

Shakespeare on Film edited by Russell Jackson (second edition)

Shakespeare on Stage edited by Stanley Wells and Sarah Stanton

Shakespeare's History Plays edited by Michael Hattaway

Shakespeare's Last Plays edited by Catherine M. S. Alexander

Shakespeare's Poetry edited by Patrick Cheney

George Bernard Shaw edited by Christopher Innes

Shelley edited by Timothy Morton

Mary Shelley edited by Esther Schor

Sam Shepard edited by Matthew C. Roudané

Spenser edited by Andrew Hadfield

Laurence Sterne edited by Thomas Keymer

Wallace Stevens edited by John N. Serio

Tom Stoppard edited by Katherine E. Kelly

Harriet Beecher Stowe edited by Cindy Weinstein

August Strindberg edited by Michael Robinson

Jonathan Swift edited by Christopher Fox

J. M. Synge edited by P. J. Mathews

Tacitus edited by A. J. Woodman

Henry David Thoreau edited by Joel Myerson

Tolstoy edited by Donna Tussing Orwin

Anthony Trollope edited by Carolyn Dever and Lisa Niles

Mark Twain edited by Forrest G. Robinson

John Updike edited by Stacey Olster

Virgil edited by Charles Martindale

Voltaire edited by Nicholas Cronk

Edith Wharton edited by Millicent Bell

Walt Whitman edited by Ezra Greenspan

Oscar Wilde edited by Peter Raby

Tennessee Williams edited by Matthew C. Roudané

August Wilson edited by Christopher Bigsby

Mary Wollstonecraft edited by Claudia L. Johnson

Virginia Woolf edited by Susan Sellers (second edition)

Wordsworth edited by Stephen Gill

W. B. Yeats edited by Marjorie Howes and John Kelly

Zola edited by Brian Nelson

TOPICS

The Actress edited by Maggie B. Gale and John Stokes

The African American Novel edited by Maryemma Graham

The African American Slave Narrative edited by Audrey A. Fisch

Allegory edited by Rita Copeland and Peter Struck

American Crime Fiction edited by Catherine Ross Nickerson

American Modernism edited by Walter Kalaidjian

American Realism and Naturalism edited by Donald Pizer

American Travel Writing edited by Alfred Bendixen and Judith Hamera

American Women Playwrights edited by Brenda Murphy

Ancient Rhetoric edited by Erik Gunderson

Arthurian Legend edited by Elizabeth Archibald and Ad Putter

Australian Literature edited by Elizabeth Webby

British Literature of the French Revolution edited by Pamela Clemit

British Romanticism edited by Stuart Curran (second edition)

British Romantic Poetry edited by James Chandler and Maureen N. McLane

British Theatre, 1730–1830 edited by Jane Moody and Daniel O'Quinn

Canadian Literature edited by Eva-Marie Kröller

Children's Literature edited by M. O. Grenby and Andrea Immel

The Classic Russian Novel edited by Malcolm V. Jones and Robin Feuer Miller

Contemporary Irish Poetry edited by Matthew Campbell

Creative Writing edited by David Morley and Philip Neilsen

Crime Fiction edited by Martin Priestman

Early Modern Women's Writing edited by Laura Lunger Knoppers

The Eighteenth-Century Novel edited by John Richetti

Eighteenth-Century Poetry edited by John Sitter

English Literature, 1500–1600 edited by Arthur F. Kinney

English Literature, 1650–1740 edited by Steven N. Zwicker

English Literature, 1740–1830 edited by Thomas Keymer and Jon Mee

English Literature, 1830–1914 edited by Joanne Shattock

English Novelists edited by Adrian Poole

English Poetry, Donne to Marvell edited by Thomas N. Corns

English Poets edited by Claude Rawson

English Renaissance Drama, second edition edited by A. R. Braunmuller and Michael Hattaway

English Renaissance Tragedy edited by Emma Smith and Garrett A. Sullivan Jr.

English Restoration Theatre edited by Deborah C. Payne Fisk

The Epic edited by Catherine Bates

European Modernism edited by Pericles Lewis

Fantasy Literature edited by Edward James and Farah Mendlesohn

Feminist Literary Theory edited by Ellen Rooney

Fiction in the Romantic Period edited by Richard Maxwell and Katie Trumpener

The Fin de Siècle edited by Gail Marshall

The French Novel: from 1800 to the Present edited by Timothy Unwin

Gay and Lesbian Writing edited by Hugh Stevens

German Romanticism edited by Nicholas Saul

Gothic Fiction edited by Jerrold E. Hogle

The Greek and Roman Novel edited by Tim Whitmarsh

Greek and Roman Theatre edited by Marianne McDonald and J. Michael Walton

Greek Lyric edited by Felix Budelmann

Greek Mythology edited by Roger D. Woodard

Greek Tragedy edited by P. E. Easterling

The Harlem Renaissance edited by George Hutchinson

The Irish Novel edited by John Wilson Foster

The Italian Novel edited by Peter Bondanella and Andrea Ciccarelli

Jewish American Literature edited by Hana Wirth-Nesher and Michael P. Kramer

The Latin American Novel edited by Efraín Kristal

The Literature of London edited by Lawrence Manley

The Literature of Los Angeles edited by Kevin R. McNamara

The Literature of New York edited by Cyrus Patell and Bryan Waterman

The Literature of the First World War edited by Vincent Sherry

The Literature of World War II edited by Marina MacKay

Literature on Screen edited by Deborah Cartmell and Imelda Whelehan

Medieval English Culture edited by Andrew Galloway

Medieval English Literature edited by Larry Scanlon

Medieval English Mysticism edited by Samuel Fanous and Vincent Gillespie

Medieval English Theatre edited by Richard Beadle and Alan J. Fletcher (second edition)

Medieval French Literature edited by Simon Gaunt and Sarah Kay

Medieval Romance edited by Roberta L. Krueger

Medieval Women's Writing edited by Carolyn Dinshaw and David Wallace

Modern American Culture edited by Christopher Bigsby

Modern British Women Playwrights edited by Elaine Aston and Janelle Reinelt

Modern French Culture edited by Nicholas Hewitt

Modern German Culture edited by Eva Kolinsky and Wilfried van der Will

The Modern German Novel edited by Graham Bartram

Modern Irish Culture edited by Joe Cleary and Claire Connolly

Modern Italian Culture edited by Zygmunt G. Baranski and Rebecca J. West

Modern Latin American Culture edited by John King

Modern Russian Culture edited by Nicholas Rzhevsky

Modern Spanish Culture edited by David T. Gies

Modernism edited by Michael Levenson (second edition)

The Modernist Novel edited by Morag Shiach

Modernist Poetry edited by Alex Davis and Lee M. Jenkins

Modernist Women Writers edited by Maren Tova Linett

Narrative edited by David Herman

Native American Literature edited by Joy Porter and Kenneth M. Roemer

Nineteenth-Century American Women's Writing edited by Dale M. Bauer and Philip Gould

Old English Literature edited by Malcolm Godden and Michael Lapidge

Performance Studies edited by Tracy C. Davis

Postcolonial Literary Studies edited by Neil Lazarus

Postmodernism edited by Steven Connor

Renaissance Humanism edited by Jill Kraye

The Roman Historians edited by Andrew Feldherr

Roman Satire edited by Kirk Freudenburg

Science Fiction edited by Edward James and Farah Mendlesohn

The Sonnet edited by A. D. Cousins and Peter Howarth

The Spanish Novel: from 1600 to the Present edited by Harriet Turner and Adelaida López de Martínez

Travel Writing edited by Peter Hulme and Tim Youngs

Twentieth-Century British and Irish Women's Poetry edited by Jane Dowson

The Twentieth-Century English Novel edited by Robert L. Caserio

Twentieth-Century English Poetry edited by Neil Corcoran

Twentieth-Century Irish Drama edited by Shaun Richards

Twentieth-Century Russian Literature edited by Marina Balina and Evgeny Dobrenko

Utopian Literature edited by Gregory Claeys

Victorian and Edwardian Theatre edited by Kerry Powell

The Victorian Novel edited by Deirdre David

Victorian Poetry edited by Joseph Bristow

War Writing edited by Kate McLoughlin

Writing of the English Revolution edited by N. H. Keeble